Pidgin 32

Spring 2024

Contents

4	Editors' Note	
8	**Office Landscape: Landscape Office**	
	William Dolin	
20	**American Dream 2**	
	Steven Sculco	
30	**A Discontinuous Border: Between India and Bangladesh**	
	Samarth Vachhrajani	
46	**Contortions**	
	Dhruv Mehta	
56	**Four Acts: Some Concepts for Queer Histories and Pedagogies of Architecture**	
	S.E. Eisterer	
74	الطريق لبيت العيلة	
	The Route to Beit Al-Eileh	
	Maysam Abdeljaber	
90	**Terrafictions: On Representation in Landscape Architecture**	
	Tekena Koko	
104	**Scanning Theory: Observations of a Traveling Photogrammeter**	
	Jonathan Russell	
122	**Subtractive Nature**	
	Andy Kim	
136	**The Poiesis of Miesian Corners**	
	Pavan Vadgama	

160	**Forget LEED: Dollar General to Save the Planet**	
	SALK	
	Sarah Aziz and Lindsey Krug	
178	**Media on Media: Returning to Jean-François Lyotard's *Les Immatériaux***	
	Ariane Fong	
190	**Ten Reasons to Abstract Reflective Ceiling Plans**	
	Ryan Tyler Martinez	
204	**Chinese *Xiaoqu*: From Utopia to Dystopia**	
	Zee Ruizi Zeng	
224	**Reimagining Cultural Narratives: Sumayya Vally on Architecture, Biennales, and the Global South's Voice**	
	Guillermo S. Arsuaga and Shivani Shedde	
248	**Say Hello, Wave Goodbye: The Concrete Aspirations of the Pearl Bank Apartments in Singapore**	
	Joshua Tan	
266	**References**	
278	**Image Credits**	
284	**Contributors**	

Editors' Note

Without stable ground, building a foundation is pointless. But with too much stability, the ground calcifies ideas. When the ground beneath our feet shifts, its instability begs questioning. The contributors of this issue are on such ground, describing situated conditions of precarity.

It's this view from the ground—this rejection of distance—that gathers many of the pieces in this issue. Moving on foot[1] or by boat,[2] looking in between[3] or around a corner,[4] staring at ceilings[5] or across landscapes[6] (or both[7]), this issue's contributors try to make sense of their worlds and how they came to be. Their interest in experience is not only phenomenological, but something more intimate, more affective, and more self-conscious. Proximity renders neutrality meaningless, and positionality emerges from our connections. Interweaving first-hand observations and speculative imaginings, the issue describes personal revelations while engaging with current debates in the field.

The unstable grounds and imbalances explored here are often intimate despite the vast networks they implicate. As Donna Haraway reminds us,[8] our

1 Abdeljar, *The Route to Beit Al-Eileh*, 74-89.
2 Vachhrajani, *A Discontinuous Border*, 30-45.
3 Kim, *Subtractive Nature*, 122-135.
4 Vadgama, *The Poiesis of Miesian Corners*, 136-159.
5 Martinez, *Ten Reasons to Abstract Reflective Ceiling Plans*, 190-203.
6 Koko, *Terrafictions*, 90-103.
7 Dolin, *Office Landscape*, 9-19.
8 Quoted in Eisterer, *Four Acts*, 69.

views are never objective. They are always a view from somewhere: situated perspectives made of past experiences, histories we know, and those we do not that have nonetheless brought us to a particular vantage point. Digging where we stand reveals the inequalities hidden by quantified variables as it cuts across the database itself. This disorienting assemblage echoes the daily strangeness of our hybrid digital and physical existences.

The world requires us to rethink the disciplinary, discursive, and epistemic conditions in which our tools have been developed and deployed, and reflect on all kinds of historical contingencies of the production of architectural knowledge. Our contributors encourage us to relate to our work in a more authentic and politically conscious way. They demonstrate through the second-person[9] and three-dimensional scans,[10] revealing everyday hyperobjects,[11] a contorted quasi-object,[12] and the immaterial.[13]

9 Sculco, *American Dream 2*, 20-29.
10 Russell, *Scanning Theory*, 104-121.
11 SALK, *Forget LEED*, 160-177.
12 Mehta, *Contortions*, 46-55.
13 Fong, *Media on Media*, 178-189.

6

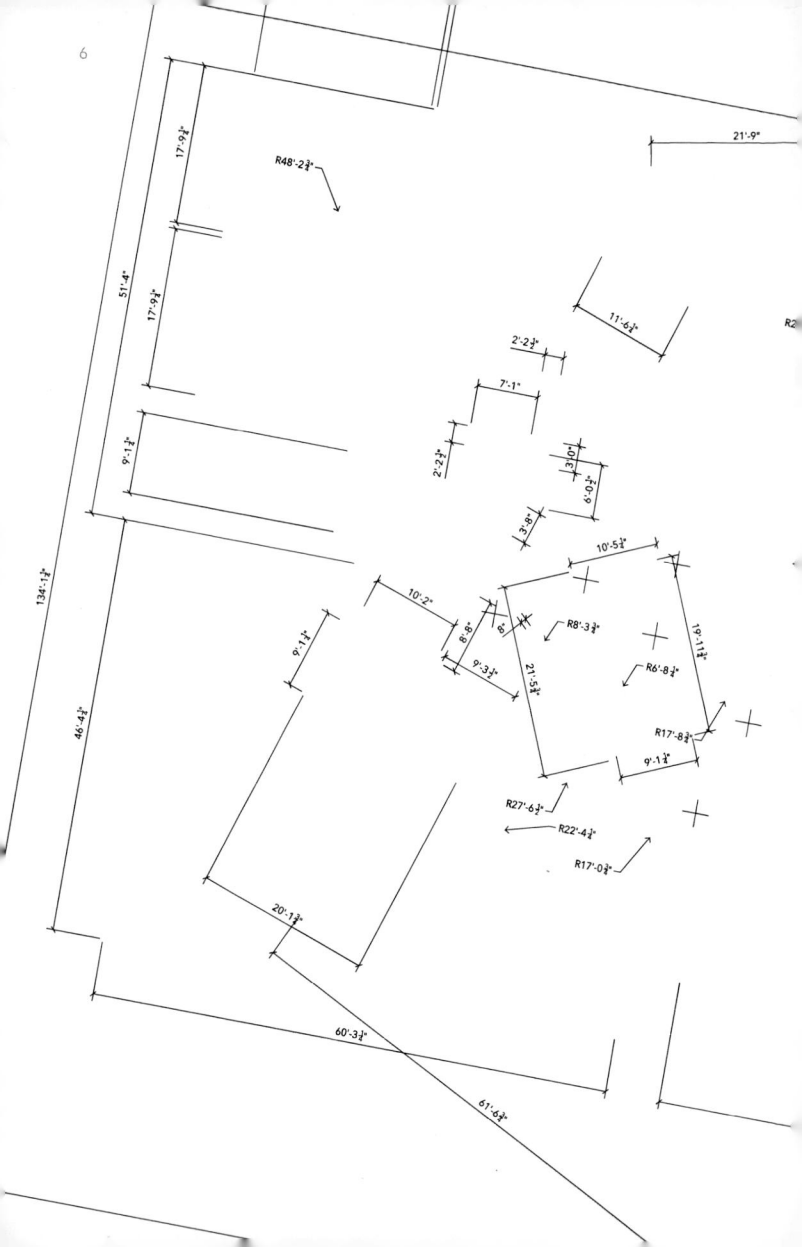

21'-9"

R48'-2¾"

17'-9¾"

51'-4"

17'-9¾"

9'-1¾"

11'-6¼"

R2

2'-2¾"

7'-1"

2'-2¾"

3'-0¼"

6'-0¼"

4'-3"

134'-1¾"

10'-5¾"

10'-2"

8'-9"

6"

R8'-3¾"

19'-11¾"

46'-4¾"

9'-1¾"

9'-3¼"

21'-5¼"

R6'-8¼"

R17'-8¾"

9'-1¼"

R27'-6¾"

R22'-4¼"

R17'-0¾"

20'-1¾"

60'-3¾"

61'-6¾"

7

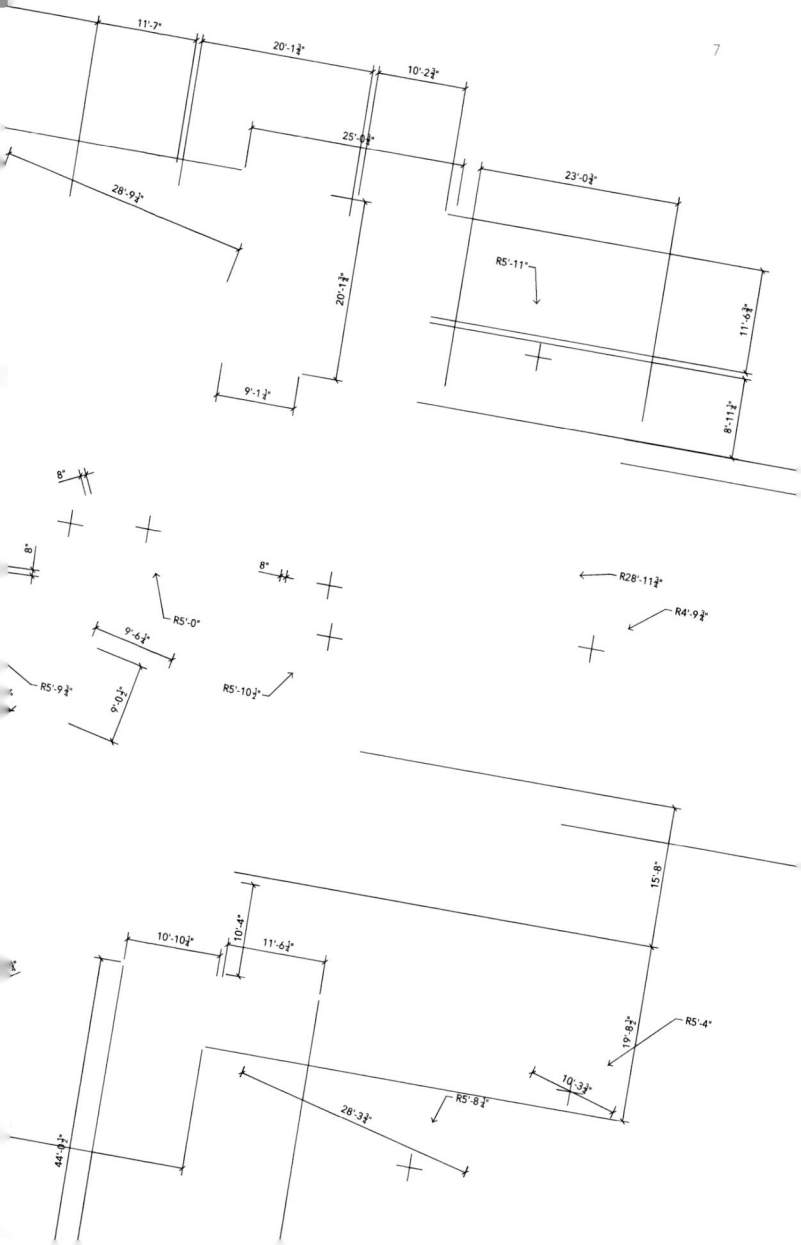

Office Landscape:
Landscape Office

William Dolin

Weyerhaeuser Corporation's 1971 annual report is uncertain: simultaneously basking in the completion of its new monumental corporate headquarters while warning shareholders about existential legislative threats looming over the forestry industry. A nighttime photograph of the building's quarter-mile long north façade adorns the front cover: brightly lit ribbon windows are reflected perfectly in the still water of the abutting artificial pond, and dimly lit edges of the colossal structure seamlessly merge with the adjoining hillsides at the edge of the frame. The result is a dramatic, somewhat ominous picture when read in conjunction with the clear sounding of alarm from

Figure 1.
Weyerhaeuser Corporate Headquarters Exterior./
Photograph by
Ezra Stoller

CEO George Weyerhaeuser. In his opening presidential message, he writes:

> Corporations are creatures of the society in which they exist, and are increasingly affected by the changing priorities of that society. As a natural resource and industrial company, the social priority with the greatest implications for Weyerhaeuser Company today is environmentalism.
>
> Since we are not a substantial user of public timber, the controversy that has arisen in recent months with respect to cutting practices in our national forests (clearcutting) has no immediate impact on us. However, the long term impact on the entire U.S. forest industry, and the people it serves with its diverse products, could be disastrous.[1]

1 Weyerhaeuser, "Annual Report 1971," 3.

Two years later, the passage of the Endangered Species Act in 1973 would permit the federal government to halt forestry operations on privately held land, confirming Weyerhaeuser's fears and eventually proving disastrous for American forestry operations as a whole. To this day, Weyerhaeuser fights legal battles over critical habitat degradation across its twelve million acres of U.S. land.[2]

Reading the Weyerhaeuser headquarters against the company itself—its new horizontal corporate structure, its changing forestry techniques, and its engagement with a broader public through media—is a unique opportunity to consider the symbiotic relationship between totalizing systems of office and ecological design during the 1960s and 70s (the period which saw the burgeoning of the American environmental movement). As the 1971 annual report suggests, shifts in the legal and social landscape surrounding the forestry industry coincide with developments in pastoral corporate office typologies. More than an image of ecological harmony, the building's massive structure suggests a nuanced relationship to its ground, simultaneously nestling into a shallow valley, almost disappearing in its transparency, while substantially reshaping, reorienting, and managing its immediate ecosystem. The complexity of this relationship speaks to the high sensitivity with which the Weyerhaeuser Corporation constructed its forests, company, and image.

This image of the Weyerhaeuser Corporation, as embodied by its architecture, would not only circulate

[2] The term habitat remains relatively undefined from a legislative perspective. McCabe writes that as recently as 2022, "the Supreme Court decided in Weyerhaeuser that 'critical habitat' must also qualify as 'habitat,' but it failed to articulate any guidelines for determining what 'habitat' actually is." See McCabe, "Defining 'Habitat' Post-Weyerhaeuser," *American University Law Review*, 2465.

on the cover of financial reports but would also be distributed through popular magazines and journals. Writing in his March 1972 article, "A Building that Makes its Own Landscape," architectural critic Roger Montgomery remarked that the notable achievement of the recently completed Weyerhaeuser corporate headquarters was a dual integration of architecture and landscape: on the one hand, the timberland company's new offices appeared literally embedded within the earth, and on the other, the implementation of *Bürolandschaft* (a German term meaning office landscape popular in the 1970s) reified the corporation's ecological perspective through the ordered open plan environment of red oak partitions and potted plants.[3]

This dual environmental integration reflected and housed an organizational complex devoted to the perpetual consumption and distribution of natural resources. Weyerhaeuser's business was predicated on avaricious managerial strategies that transformed land into lumber—an increasingly scrutinized business, as what was once thought to be an endless supply of natural resources began to run out. Through images circulating in annual reports and architectural journals, Weyerhaeuser's corporate headquarters helped sell an appearance of environmental integration that appeased both anxious shareholders and an environmentally scrupulous public. Within this milieu, the production and circulation of such images need to be considered equally, if not ahead of the revised corporate hierarchy the architecture itself accommodated.

[3] Montgomery, "A Building That Makes Its Own Landscape," *Architectural Forum*, 20.

Skidmore, Owings & Merrill managed the project. Initially assigned to their New York team headed by Gordon Bunshaft, the project quickly moved west to the San Francisco office to be led by Edward Charles "Chuck" Bassett at the request of Weyerhaeuser's executives. The concrete structure forms a long, narrow bar between two gently sloping hills. Appearing as an excessively stretched ziggurat emerging from the landscape, the silhouette suggests an excavated ruin whose temporality is unclear (fig. 1). This produces a certain visual ambiguity as the building follows the landscape from certain perspectives while appearing more monumental from others. It's not indifferent or contextual. Inside, the rotated column grid creates a continuous field of open space on each floor, staging the death of the executive corner office and, in its place, a more egalitarian working environment.[4] The unbroken ribbon windows enclosing each level reflect the interior and exterior, superimposing the two at twilight—a phenomenological counterpart to the formal biomimicry of the furniture arrangements. This visual collapse between nature and culture artfully produces a form of corporate camouflage: the architecture refracted Weyerhaeuser's dealings away from public concern and governmental oversight through the illegibility of its corporeal presence.

These images of responsible land stewardship were products of a design culture extensively invested in research and programming. As landscape architect Peter Walker suggested upon completion of the project, his work was best described as "forest management" as opposed to landscape architecture.[5]

4 Kaufmann-Buhler, "Progressive Partitions," *Design and Culture*, 217.
5 Montgomery, 20.

Figure 2. Weyerhaeuser Corporate Headquarters Interior./ Photograph by Ezra Stoller

Indeed, *management* was required as the corporation exhaustively reshaped the building's site outside Tacoma, including extensive tree removal to clear the view from two abutting highways and significant terraforming to make the structure appear embedded in the earth.[6] As landscape architect and historian Louise Mozingo explains, "after Earth Day and the rise of the contemporary environmental movement, many corporate estates explicitly used their landscape spaces to orchestrate an environmentally positive image of their businesses."[7] For Weyerhaeuser, this image emerging through the cleared meadows abutting either highway and passing through the open floor plates, was not of a passive naturalism but a highly fabricated stewardship.

6 SOM, "What Ever Happened to the 'Original Green Building'?" *Medium*.
7 Mozingo, *Pastoral Capitalism*, 140.

This systematized landscape persisted within the interior of the project by integrating the architecture of SOM, custom furniture design by Knoll, space planning by Sydney Rogers, and an internal office design manager employed permanently by Weyerhaeuser to continually rearrange furniture per changes in the corporate structure.[8] Historian Jenifer Kaufman-Buhler describes the design labor of Weyerhaeuser and other landscape office plans of the 1960s and 1970s as cartographic, suggesting the designers "[mapped] the corporation (its structure, hierarchy, relationships, and communication networks) through intensive research."[9] This geographic analogy connects the interior and exterior of the project not just formally, as the name "office landscape" might suggest, but through shared systems of management, organization, and design research (fig. 2).

Diverging from the abstract art that filled many corporate estates of the 1950s and 1960s, Weyerhaeuser favored a more straightforward realism—commissioning art that melded with the interior and exterior environment, as to almost disappear.[10] Helena Hernmak's work *Rainforest* best exemplifies this; it was a tapestry based on a photograph of a forest floor that hung in the executive waiting area (fig. 3). Hernmak's tapestry quietly completes a harmonious scene framed by potted plants and beige carpeting. From far away, it can appear as a window to the outside. The authorship of the individual artist, like many of the collaborators on the project, is tampered down in service of a highly unified and cohesive whole. These interior views, like the exterior's

Figure 3. *Rainforest*, Helena Hernmarck. Wool, linen, cotton, 110 x 165 in, 1971. / Photograph by Ezra Stoller

8 Canty, "Evaluation of an Open Office Landscape: Weyerhaeuser Co," *AIA Journal*, 40.
9 Kaufmann-Buhler, 212.
10 Referencing Ada Louise Huxtable, Sullivan notes the feeling amongst certain critics at mid-century that, "art should not be concerned with harmony, but rather with providing a 'strong counterpoint' to the austere formal simplicity

of modernist architecture." Sullivan's book focuses on Bertoia, Calder, Lippold, and Noguchi as artists emblematic of achieving this juxtaposition within mid-century modernist buildings. None of these artists would be contracted to work on the Weyerhaeuser project despite being regular fixtures of many other SOM corporate office buildings. See Sullivan, *Alloys*, 14.

composition, communicate a managed naturalism through the careful integration of landscape architecture, architecture, interior design, and art.

From a media perspective, this use of the headquarters would fit into a corporate history of publicity campaigns celebrating Weyerhaeuser's fastidious occupation of land. This history of corporate advertising reveals an unwavering commitment to the message that forests require human intervention to optimally perform. Beginning in the late 1930s, the rise of scientific forestry shifted the corporation's view of the natural environment; forests were no longer merely territories to be acquired and harvested, but valuable ecosystems to be managed and optimized in perpetuity. One of the company's campaigns from 1937 introduced the slogan, "timber is a crop," which attempted to reconfigure the extractive practices of the industry as forms of care. The company also later produced a film titled *Trees and Men*, which presented the Washington landscape as pristine and untouched. The work of the Weyerhaeuser company was then shown to vitalize the local economy by utilizing a previously untapped resource.[11] The company's propaganda played into a well-worn ideology of predestined westward expansion. However consumed, the images of the 1971 corporate headquarters would continue this media legacy, framing Weyerhaeuser as benevolently paternal. Using photography and film to construct a way of seeing was critical to Weyerhaeuser's continued unfettered consumption of woodlands.

Weyerhaeuser understood its public reception to be deeply embedded within the images of its forests, often going to great lengths to scientifically study the public's reaction to images of its industrial operations through controlled focus groups. "Managing Esthetic Values," an article written by Weyerhaeuser Forest Engineer Donald Schuh in the *Journal of Forestry*, details how the company was reorienting its forestry practices in the years following the completion of the headquarters to address public concern over ecological devastation in highly public regions of the corporation's logging operations (in this case forests abutting regional highways in western Washington). The article contains a form used internally titled "Visual Sensitivity Rating

11 See *Trees and Men*, 1938. In one telling moment, the narrator describes an enormous tree that had just been felled. He states, "this tree looked pretty good standing there alongside other trees of equal size and age, but its core was rotten, and the wood remaining was not worth hauling to the mill. It should have been harvested a hundred years ago." Thus, Weyerhaeuser's forestry operations were presented as eliminating "economic waste."

System Worksheet," which includes an expansive formula factoring in a variety of data types to produce a score that would determine whether a site's logging operations should be altered based on its relative visibility. "A high score suggests a need for modification, although the form such modifications take depends on harvesting, economics, and ability to link visual objectives with other public resource protection goals, and an understanding of what particular changes might fit best with the landscape," writes Schuh.[12] Here, we understand the separation between Weyerhaeuser's forest management techniques designed through economic optimization and its management of public perception through the equally precise manipulation of images.[13] Through the scoring system, these two branches of research (the construction of a landscape and its image) are synthesized to instruct the future industrial production of the corporation. Architectural and ecological design merge here in their shared balancing of function and appearance, driven by commitments to shareholders and the conflicting political influence of the public.

This history shows how a twentieth-century media landscape compelled the restructuring of entire forests and the spaces from within which they were designed. After all, the first wave of the American environmental movement emerged largely through the nature photography of figures like John Muir.[14] Successful corporations like Weyerhaeuser owe much of their survival to adopting and reorienting such mediums as photography and film in shaping

12 Schuh, "Managing Esthetic Values," *Journal of Forestry*, 20-25.
13 Schuh, 21. The article contains a series of manipulated images showing varied levels of tree removal on a hillside off a highway in Washington. These constructed images were used to gauge public opinion in a focus group setting.
14 See Dunaway, *Natural Visions*, for an extended history of the relationship between photography and conservation in the United States.

counternarratives ferociously opposed to conservation. It seems inevitable that the corporation's architecture would continue this campaign by circulating its artfully calculated spectacle.

While the Weyerhaeuser building successfully operated for several decades, the corporation moved to downtown Seattle in 2016, leaving the modernist structure vacant. Due to Peter Walker's concerted conservation effort (he considers Weyerhaeuser to be his most important work of landscape architecture),[15] the same government that continues to threaten Weyerhaeuser forestry operations is now in talks to acquire and preserve its old headquarters as a public amenity.[16] The potential conservation of the property is a marker of the successful integration of architecture and landscape by Walker and the rest of the design team; it's impossible, or at least impractical, to conserve one without the other (fig. 4).

15 In addressing the Mayor of Seattle, Jim Ferrell, in a letter promoting the conservation of the Weyerhaeuser headquarters in 2021, Walker wrote, "from its opening in 1971, Weyerhaeuser has been a rare combination of architecture and landscape architecture. No other project in modern environmental design has achieved such a high level of integrated building and biological setting." See The Cultural Landscape Foundation, "Peter Walker Says Weyerhaeuser Is Perhaps His 'Most Important' Project."

Office Landscape

As the corporate estate (once signaling Weyerhaeuser's responsible land stewardship outside government regulation) is saved from the unsentimental processes of capitalist development by the same government it once attempted to evade, it indexes a complex history of corporate interest, public concern, and governmental regulation. The building reveals specific imaging techniques practiced by Weyerhaeuser to counter shifting perceptions of an increasingly environmentally minded public. Rather than merely suggesting an image of environmental harmony, the building went further as to naturalize a highly industrialized architecture and ecology, corporatizing a landscape and landscaping a corporation.

16 Washington Senate Democrats. "Public-Private Partnership."

Figure 4.
Weyerhaeuser Corporate Headquarters Exterior./ Photograph by Ezra Stoller

American Dream 2

Steven Sculco

You're eating a MrBeast Burger at the American Dream mall in East Rutherford, New Jersey.[1] You don't exactly know how you ended up here. Between your hands is an intoxicating "BeastStyle" burger, loaded with so much ketchup and mayo that it actually explodes with each bite. It is a double—the smallest they had—with American cheese and massive pickles. Your hands, face, and shirt are covered in sauce. With increasing levels of caution, you try taking smaller and smaller bites, but it is no use. The explosive effect, presumably by design, is simply a function of eating it. Your only option is to give in.

1 MrBeast Burger is a restaurant chain opened in 2022 by YouTube hegemon and alleged antichrist Jimmy Donaldson, a.k.a. MrBeast.

You didn't expect much from MrBeast, but now, staring up at the towering wall of TVs streaming his YouTube channel, you're entranced by a bombardment of flying cars, crashing trains, swooping helicopters, exploding dynamite, and burning buildings. The media is captivating and endless. The restaurant blasts dubstep as loud as a nightclub. MrBeast is lost at sea, floating on a makeshift raft with his posse. You feel like you're right there with them. Wouldn't that be something? You look around the restaurant: families with young children, a few teenagers. No one seems fazed by MrBeast's adventures. They focus on the food, on table conversations. They've already seen this video, a mere drop in MrBeast's ocean of optical immersion, each fifteen to twenty minute production more jacked up than the last. Picking up one of the flavor-blasted french fries on your plate, you reluctantly take a bite before looking back at the TVs. Now MrBeast is in a grassy field, blowing up increasingly expensive things. In just a single video, a multitude of unthinkable stunts, one after the next, explosion after explosion. All the TVs are synchronized and in constant motion. The video editing is brilliant with calculated escalations that keep you watching, craving more. Swift transition effects teleport you around MrBeast's vast playground complex, preventing any possibility of relief between sequences. Giant life-sized objects are miniaturized and highlighted like stickers, underscored by hyperbolic annotations to catch your eye on the YouTube homepage. Now MrBeast is back at sea, this time on a $1,000,000,000 yacht. You wonder if he'll blow that up too.

The world of MrBeast is one of constant dopamine, an unstoppable hedonic treadmill running in reverse.[2] His formula objectifies everything and everyone for their value as spectacle. It's all part of the game: landscapes are animated, houses are obliterated for a split-second thrill, cruise ships are rendered in gold, exorbitant amounts of money are enthusiastically wasted. The world's largest shredder consumes a candy-apple-colored Lambo. 84 million views in eight days. 236 million YouTube subscribers. Phrases like "Oh My God!" fill the screen. Decommissioned Cold-War era tanks fill the screen. The world's largest domino smashes an old 7-Eleven. Another Lambo—this one's blue raspberry. A rollercoaster wagon launched off an incomplete track explodes in midair. Your eyes are glued to the screen. For a brief moment, YouTube buffers, and you look down at the table. Forty minutes have passed. You could easily go on watching, but you don't think you can finish your meal, so you get up, timidly toss your plate into the industrial-sized trash compactor, and exit the restaurant.

Tauntingly, the mall feels a lot like a MrBeast video. Countless events of increasing magnitudes compete for your attention. Their audiovisual effects overlap without care for boundaries or distinctions.[3] To engage with any one thing in particular seems difficult, especially coming off your adrenaline rush of a lunch. You try taking in the scene from the edge of a three-story atrium, tracking only fragments of the enormous immersive production. Two levels down, parents and children zip around on go-karts

[2] Hedonic adaptation is the tendency to quickly return to a relatively neutral level despite major positive or negative events, reducing their affective impact. Desensitized hedonic pathways in the brain prevent persistently high levels of intense feeling.

[3] Disney's Imagineers call this feature "sensorial tingle." It is used intentionally to pass seamlessly between different countries at EPCOT.

shaped like tiny zebras and hippos. Dolls on remote-control mini quads also zip around. Someone drops their iPhone and shrieks. A promoter tries to build hype for a Jersey club performance, but only a few people seem to care. From a different location, "Party in the U.S.A." clashes with the boom of the promoter's voice. Lights shimmer on a massive brass-colored chandelier. Construction noises ricochet from behind a glittery storefront billboard. Elsewhere, large ice cream cone sculptures support soft serve topiary. Dali-inspired tumors protrude from oversized furniture. Vast expanses of glossy tiled hallway lead to *Angry Birds*–themed variations of Willy Wonka's chocolate room. Stars and bolts of graphic enthusiasm, annotated with Candy Crush victory messages, cover the walls. Zooming black and white abstract forms—imitation Zaha Hadid—pull more mall-goers into view from afar.

Foolishly, you try to pinpoint American Dream's stylistic theme. Tim Burton, crossed with Apple, crossed with Katy Perry? You're tempted to disregard your chaotic surroundings as derivative of Postmodern eclecticism, a new take on an old approach. The overlap of different images, tonalities, and activities reminds you of an architect like Charles Moore, perhaps in particular his 1967 celebration of a newfound intensity of experience in a roadside motel.[4] Your mind runs through a handful of related characters: Venturi & Scott Brown, Stanley Tigerman, Morris Lapidus, Paolo Portoghesi. Based on what you remember from Bob Stern's PoMo lectures, all these eclectic enthusiasts channeled

4 Moore, "Plug It in, Rameses, and See If It Lights up. Because We Aren't Going to Keep It Unless It Works," *Perspecta* 11.

Pop in service of their critique against Modernism, signified by the (by then) ubiquitous corporate constructions of Mies van der Rohe, SOM, and the like. You recount their handful of aims—breaking with perceived monotony and elitism, countering utopian sentiments, signifying the visual richness of history, and so on. But American Dream holds no clear statements or agendas, besides maximizing raw attention. Its elements melt together, giving rise to a result so loaded with indecipherable references that it seems impossible to interpret. Made up of anything and everything, American Dream would seem like an ideal eclectic multiplicity, an indiscriminate surface on which unlimited representations could coexist. From the inside, however, the mall operates as a perfect singularity, absorbing and reshaping every image at will, giving rise to a seemingly unbreakable, nondescript whole. Taken to this end, you discover the freedom of multiplicity paradoxically inverted; the development of an alternative viewpoint becomes hopeless.

Somehow you're not entirely overwhelmed by this disorientation. You can't make sense of it at all, but an attempt would be missing the point. You are simply connected with the flow of content as it is presented. You are the pointer finger on your iPhone, jumping from app to app. The experience is relentless but you can't afford a break. Trying to escape into the relief offered by Instagram or TikTok would only multiply your surroundings— a nonstop feed of undifferentiated media with new pop-ups at every turn. How about surfing in the wave pool at the indoor waterpark? A ride in the Nickelodeon Universe? North America's only indoor Alpine ski resort? The Van Gogh Immersive Experience? The last Toys "R" Us on earth? Unable to choose, you begin to feel like a body inside of a body. Your inner body, increasingly wanting to halt, toys with the idea of telling your outer body to quit bypassing every activity in anticipation of the next. Your outer body continues on.

An elevator opens and you enter it spellbound. Finally closing your eyes, you see strange echoes of light imprinted in your corneas moving a little faster than you can track. You hear a faint, fluttering cacophony reminiscent of Karlheinz Stockhausen, a name you haven't recalled since Intro to Music Theory freshman year. The elevator feels like it isn't moving. This mall is kind of like Stockhausen's early experiments with electronic music where musicians, instructed to "play without thinking," operated different musical instruments in separate, soundproof chambers. The sounds produced in isolation by each musician were instantaneously combined to generate an unplanned result, often to a surprisingly provocative, almost mystifying effect.

Here, you stop yourself. The fluoride in the air seems to have induced a free-associative state.[5] Is there a more relevant reference than your nephew's favorite YouTuber, Postmodern charlatans, a visionary composer? Like magic, the elevator opens to an AMC lobby. The IMAX theater is showing *Avatar: The Way of Water*. The long-anticipated

5 Free association is a state of consciousness characterized by increased subjective self-awareness and disregard for reality, together with implicit pulls for objective self-awareness and reality adherence. This facilitates the tendency to shift flexibly between otherwise loosely-connected points.

sequel—twelve years in the making—features enhanced humanoids, mystical rainforests, endless oceans, legendary whales, flying dinosaurs, diverse weapons, advanced tech, submarines, command centers, intense combat, and plenty of explosions. These elements, put to action in an interplay of countless overlapping narratives, result in a production too immense, too epic for you to gather any clear conclusion. Narratives of power, colonization, extraction, technology, hybridity, anthropocentrism, tribalism, and gender are simultaneously presented in a half-baked fashion, up for viewers to pick and choose which fragments to take home with them. In place of any definitive emotion, the production makes you feel vaguely hungover, an empty fatigue from a three-hour-long string of momentary emotional ups and downs.

Avatar 2 is over, and you're in the restroom now, rinsing your hands under a gentle stream of warm water. The sensation is grounding, a subtle reminder of life on earth. You feel a low, growing hum traveling up your torso. Suddenly a mall employee glides into the room on a *Tron*-inspired neon blue micro Zamboni, but this barely registers as a surprise. You casually dry your hands before reentering the mall. This time the mall feels a lot like *Avatar 2*: an all-encompassing high-res panoramic miracle that's irreducible to any overarching narrative or framework. You feel a mild sense of elation, but you're not sure why. It must be like this for everyone else here too. You wonder if they're also thinking about immortality, buying a yacht, a Mercedes

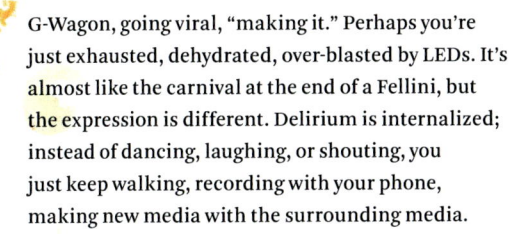

G-Wagon, going viral, "making it." Perhaps you're just exhausted, dehydrated, over-blasted by LEDs. It's almost like the carnival at the end of a Fellini, but the expression is different. Delirium is internalized; instead of dancing, laughing, or shouting, you just keep walking, recording with your phone, making new media with the surrounding media.

You try to imagine a scenario beyond this mall in which normality is an overwhelming production that feeds on dissociation, where the world inside your phone is entirely material and larger than life. A mixture of genuine awe and self-consciousness comes over you. There must be something significant about this mall, you tell yourself. It's called American Dream! You just have to keep on scrolling, strolling to find out. Suddenly, it's time to catch a bus home. You're outside. You're back in New Jersey. You're met with hot, wet rain. The mood feels strange, unenthusiastic. You remember your phone. Thirty-four notifications. The screen appears smaller and more distant than usual. Scrolling past recent likes, DMs, a new follower, and an iMessage from Mom, you land on the most recent photo in your camera roll: the Statue of Liberty made entirely of Jelly Beans. "There really must be something about this mall," you say out loud, voice cracking.

Turning your head for one last look, you catch a glimpse of a Ferris wheel protruding through the roof of a warehouse; from out here, merely thin metal elements and a few hanging buckets against a flat gray sky. Now you see the ski slope to your right; from out here, nothing more than a corrugated metal box shooting off a parking deck. Stepping inside the bus, it's dimly-lit, carpeted on all surfaces, and nearly full. You gravitate to an empty seat beside a woman in her early twenties who's wearing an oversized Fear of God hoodie with ripped jeans. Her hair is styled in two symmetrical buns with lavender highlights. Her face—a warm peach blush, silver eyeshadow, dramatic winged liner, eyebrows neatly defined—is buried in a book titled *Leave Society*. As the bus speeds onto the Jersey Turnpike, American Dream recedes into the distance.

29

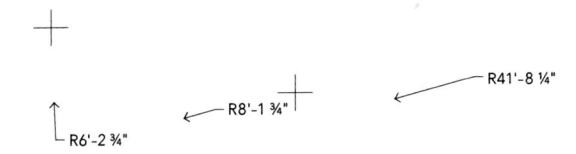

← R41'-8 ¼"

← R8'-1 ¾"

↑ R6'-2 ¾"

A Discontinuous Border: Between India and Bangladesh

Samarth Vachhrajani

Looking at a map of the India–Bangladesh border, it would appear as a set of continuous lines, stretching across the monumental Brahmaputra River, the Khasi, Garo, and Jaintia Hills of Meghalaya, and the plains of Assam and Bengal. However, at the India–Bangladesh frontier in Northeast India, I found myself on a boat along the border that behaved less like a solid line splitting apart two nations and more like a disorienting space with intentionally choreographed interplays. While a map might imprint the border as a complete line, and official state transcripts inscribe it in abstract languages, on the ground the border emerged as a complex set of interrupted fences and border apparatuses that attempted to negotiate with the region's uneven topography and unequal mobilities. Since the border's intial marking during the partition of the Indian Subcontinent in 1947, articulating the border spatially has been critical throughout the history of the region. The ethnic self-determination movements, the Bangladesh Liberation War of 1971, and attempts at territorial control by India and Bangladesh marked an urgency to fence the border.[1] While this reinforced border may ostensibly promise airtight national sovereignties, experiences along it—at the seams of global exchanges—reveal the opposite.[2] Originally intended to capture or control the movement of people, this border apparatus erodes national sovereignties and doubles as an agent for exploitative global connections.[3]

Spatial variables like the Integrated Border Checkposts (IBCs), limestone extraction projects, cement manufacturing factories, and a trans-border conveyor belt for moving stones between India and Bangladesh construct a multivalent border, undermining the logic of a continuous borderline. In addition to metal fences, these authoritative structures in the state's infrastructural milieu seek to exploit its "untapped potential" and reform the region into a critical resource frontier for profiting the national economy irrespective of existing local political issues.[4] Consequently, instead of being fixed edges for nation-states, the India–Bangladesh border has been materialized by an industrial–governance network, facilitated by spatial variables that allows multiple

[1] The 1950s saw the Naga Insurgency, followed by Mizo insurgency in the 1960s, and in the 1970s, a reconfiguration and partitioning of the northeastern states, creating the seven states of Northeast India. For more, see Baruha, *In The Name of The Nation*, 18-24; Nag, "A Gigantic Panopticon," *Kolkata*, 10; and Kikon, "The Predicament of Justice," *Contemporary South Asia*, 280.

[2] For more on 'waning sovereignty,' see Brown, *Walled States, Waning Sovereignty*, 145. See also Appadurai, *Modernity at Large*, 199.

[3] Along these lines see Krishna, "Cartographic Anxiety," *Alternatives*, 507–521. On global connections, see Tsing, *Friction*.

[4] Prime Minister Narendra Modi has been vociferous about taking India to a three-trillion-dollar economy. *The Wire*, "The Many Economic Guarantees and Promises of the Modi Government."

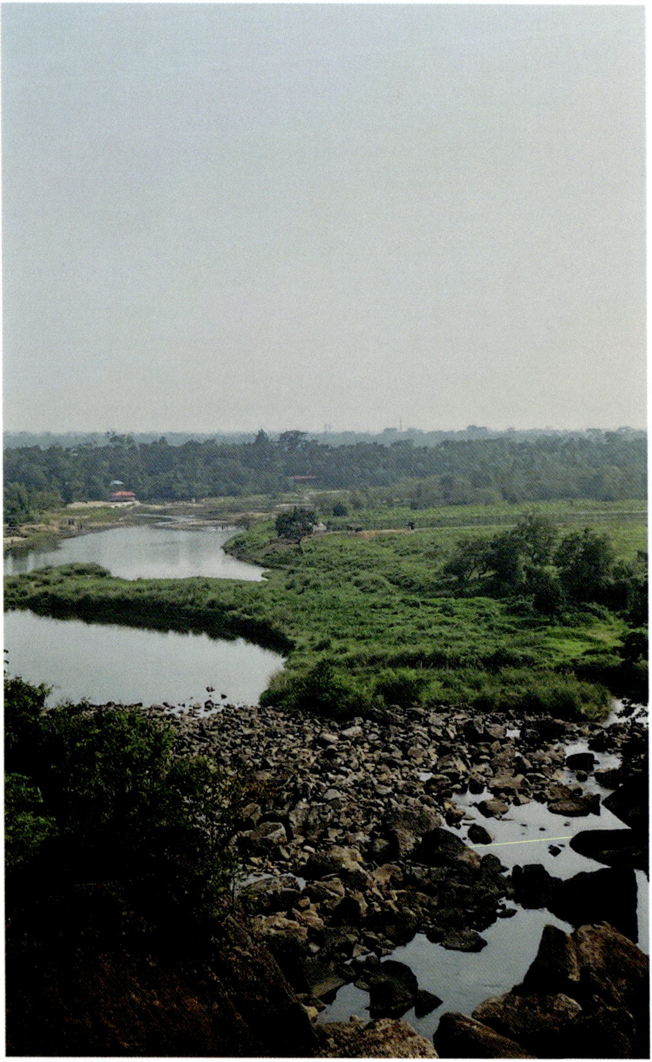

organizations and governments to construct the border politically, materially, and spatially.[5]

I traveled to the northeastern state of Meghalaya primarily to study the patchy India–Bangladesh barbed-wire border fence and the Border Security Force (BSF) policing ensemble that completes it. I wanted to understand the significance of this spatial structure—constructed by the Indian government in the 1970s and renovated, remade, and replaced over time. However, as I witnessed it on the ground, this spatialized structure and the corresponding apparatuses operate not only as an enduring security measure but also as instruments that mediate social, political, military, and economic discontinuities. The barbed wire fencing has been an unfinished project along this approximately four thousand-kilometer-long border, longer than the combined lengths of the United States–Mexico and Israel–Palestine borders. Today it is fenced more than ever, but patches of the border remain spatially unmarked. For example, standing atop a bridge overlooking a dried-up waterfall along the border, I could see a green metal fence, freshly painted and topped with barbed wire, which was interrupted as it spanned the river. Over this river, between two fence posts, a taut rope was tied to simply mark the national border.

The fence and the rope articulate the oblique relationships of the territory with the border that snakes through it. It constructs it as a space of differentiated mobilities, where people are restricted or killed for crossing the border. Meanwhile, extracted resources

5 Eyal Weizman explains how rule of law and state jurisdiction can overlap to create differentiated regimes of movement. See Weizman, *Hollow Land*, 6-7.

Figure 1.
Rope between the India-Bangladesh border. June 5, 2023. East Khasi Hills, Meghalaya./ Photo by author

like limestones from the border regions have the flexibility to be trucked between the countries.[6] According to a 2010 Human Rights Watch report, between 2001 and 2010, the Border Security Force personnel gunned down an estimated nine hundred Bangladeshis as they attempted to cross the border.[7] Out of this, the story of a fifteen-year-old girl, Felani Khatun, who was shot at the border leaving her body entangled within the sharp double-rolled barbed wire fences, became the most unnerving representation of state violence and unequal mobility.[8]

Divergent from this border violence is Dawki, a border village in Meghalaya. I first confronted the border along the Umngot River in Dawki, which

[6] See Sheller, *Mobility Justice*.
[7] Human Rights Watch, "Trigger Happy: Excessive Use of Force by Indian Troops at the Bangladesh Border."
[8] In 2013, BSF soldiers who shot Felani were acquitted. See Rajashree, "With SC Set to Hear Petition, Killings at Bangladesh Border Back in Focus," *The Wire*.

gathered fame through social media travel vlogs among Indian and Bangladeshi tourists for boating on its crystal-clear waters. India's BSF remains relatively less vigilant in Dawki due to a surge in tourists wanting to row along the glassy river and experience the thrill of being along a national border. While I was on an hour-long boat ride from the "Indian side," the sculler pointed to the opposite side of the river—making me aware of a makeshift rock island where Bangladeshi tourists experienced the glassy waters from their nation's end. Unlike the violent reality of border policing represented in media reports and ethnographic accounts, it seemed unexpectedly peaceful, even playful, here.[9]

At the Umngot River, the border was largely unmarked. However, it was most visible as a solid fence at the "India–Bangladesh Friendship Gate" and the Dawki–Tamabil Integrated Check Post in Tamabil, approximately a three-kilometer drive along the border from Dawki.[10] This short drive took us over four hours on the narrow, winding roads of the Khasi, Garo, and Jaintia Hills of Meghalaya. We were stuck amidst a long row of trucks of varying sizes, driven by Khasi, Garo, Assamese, and Bengali truckers employed by many enterprises, carrying limestone and boulder rocks extracted from the Indian hills, and on their way to cement factories in Bangladesh. Damien, a Khasi-Christian and native of Dawki who drove me along the border, runs a tour and travel business in the capital city of Shillong. He expressed that over the years, the border infrastructure in the region has

9   For more, see: Sur, *Jungle Passports*; Ghosh, *A Thousand Tiny Cuts*; and Hussain, *Boundaries Undermined*.
10 Kindly note all names mentioned in the essay are changed to maintain privacy.

Figure 2. Boating on the Umngot River. June 5, 2023. Dawki, East Khasi Hills, Meghalaya./ Photo by author

expanded in his home village, where the river used to gush down heavily to the Bengal plains.
Integrated Border Checkposts are the new spatial instruments of the Indian government that regulate customs, facilitate trade, move resources, and strengthen security by managing the movement of people across the border. At Dawki–Tamabil, a new checkpost-cum-campus primarily includes a passenger terminal that facilitates the movements of vehicles, a cargo terminal, and a warehouse. It also hosts a set of secondary programs like animal and plant quarantine facilities, buffer parking, rest areas for truck drivers, a canteen, and extra space for future expansion. Fenced and gated, this entire campus is surrounded by soaring watchtowers, with BSF guards watching over these daily transactions on the national boundary and scanning for suspicious vehicles just three kilometers away from the tourists enjoying the glassy waters of Umngot River.

Figure 3. Trucks carrying limestones and boulder rocks on their way to the border checkpost. June 5, 2023. West Jaintia Hills, Meghalaya./ Photo by author

The trucks that I witnessed were employed to take advantage of the economically opportune and resource-rich landscape of the region. The Khasi, Garo, and Jaintia Hills are rich in limestone deposits that are easy to mine.[11] Available on the surface of these mountains, limestones and boulder rocks have been heavily mined in the region and moved by trucks and steamers to cement factories for processing. Fifteen thousand metric tons of limestone are estimated to be in these hills, waiting to be transported across India and Bangladesh. At the Dawki–Tamabil ICP, the trucks were primarily operated by the European cement giant Lafarge Holcim—the largest

11 Lafarge Holcim, "Equity Valuation Report on Lafarge Holcim Bangladesh Limited."

multinational cement manufacturing conglomerate in the world.[12] This Swiss-French cement giant has 166 cement manufacturing factories around the world, and one such factory is located along the India–Bangladesh Border, in Chattak, Bangladesh.[13] The Indian trucks that line up along the ICPs, are only permitted to transport and unload stones immediately across the border checkpost and are required to return to India right away. Another army of trucks awaits on the Bangladesh side to transport the stones to factories. This way, the truckers can make multiple profitable trips in a day between the mountains and the border but cannot drive beyond the ICP zone, controlled by the BSF. This well constructed border assembly, at odds with the rope

12 Saikia, "As limestone piles up on Bangladesh border, anger against Congress brews in Meghalaya," *Scroll*.

13 Lafarge Holcim is a Swiss Cement Giant, that has a production capacity of 385 million tonnes worldwide, which doubled after the Lafarge Holcim merger.

hanging between fence posts a bit further south of the checkpost, allows the movement of limestones and boulder rocks, while sifting and backpedaling people to maintain a border.

The discontinuity of the border is most explicit and paradoxical when it meets the infrastructures that intersect it in order to develop alternative channels for keeping capital mobile and people immobile. A seventeen-kilometer-long trans-border conveyor belt is such an instrument that cuts across the border fence at Chattak, Bangladesh and Shella, India. This newly renovated conveyor belt, raised five meters above ground to keep it operational during the flooding season, is one of the longest in the world, and transports mined stones from India directly to the cement factory run by Lafarge Holcim.[14] As an astute infrastructural solution, the conveyor belt moves approximately five million tons of stones without requiring any human movement across the border.[15]

Cement factories and mining sites are themselves also spatial variables that interrupt the functions of the border to create environmental and political imbalances. Lafarge Holcim's cement plant in Bangladesh, valued at $225 million, is entirely reliant on mining operations directly across the border, in India's East Khasi Hills.[16] As rivers around Shella and Chattak change color because of excessive mining and cement dust, Lafarge Holcim has faced a handful of legal issues on environmental grounds. For example, in 2010, owing to a petition filed in the Meghalaya High Court, the cement factory experienced significant setbacks in its ability to mine limestone. A year-long legal battle ended when the company was granted permission to resume mining thanks to demands from the Bangladeshi Government, which had been pressured by the EU, the Spanish Ambassador, and Swiss Charge D'affaires.[17] The Indian Ministry of Environment and Forest (MoEF) initially wanted Lafarge to set up its factory in India, not Bangladesh.[18] They wished Indian cement factories could use the limestone mined in Meghalaya to enrich the Indian coffers. However, the 2010 Supreme Court petition that resulted in the discussion on Lafarge's presence in the region eventually approved the company's limestone quarrying permit after they procured a

14 Derige and Hustrulid, "Replacing the World's Longest Trans-Boundary Conveyor Belt," *Engineer Live*.
15 Bouissou, "Lafarge's India-Bangladesh Cement Project Remains Frozen," *The Gaurdian*.
16 Bouissou, 42, 48.
17 Global Cement, "EU and European ambassadors urge Bangladesh to lift restrictions on LafargeHolcim Bangladesh limestone sales."
18 Lyngdoh, "HC Ban Hits Limestone Export," *The Telegraph*.
19 *The Times of India*, "SC Okays Limestone Supply to Lafarge."

Figure 4.
The cross-border conveyor belt, cutting across the India-Bangladesh border.
1. India
2. Border fence
3. No man's land
4. Cross-border conveyor belt
5. "Zero line" or actual line of the border
6. Bangladesh Shella/Bholaganj (India)-Chattak (Bangladesh) Border post. / Google Earth

no-objection certificate from MoEF through diplomatic pressures.[19]

Instead of an obstruction, the premeditated discontinuity of the border licenses it as an agent that inspires investments where the world of logistics, business supply chains, organizational schemes, economic interests, nationalist state practices, and visual infrastructures of sovereignty collide. The border separates the mining site from the factory where stones are turned into cement dust. However, the border made discontinuous by trucks that cross it on a daily basis, or the conveyor belt that transgresses it, also creates a lucrative condition for cement production between and beyond India and Bangladesh, at the cost of the local environment. Therefore, the border's material construction and its becoming an "infrastructure" are not just situated in the spatial apparatus of the fence but also in these unruly spatial installations that intersect it.[20] Meanwhile, small-scale indigenous mining rights in the Khasi and Garo Hills are still under inquiry in the high court. As a result, the border is shaped by multilateral diplomatic forces beyond the countries which it intended to split.

The presence of Lafarge Holcim's enterprise furnishes a different conception of the India–Bangladesh border. It demonstrates that global forces and capital flows, in addition to the state's authoritative impulses, shape margins in the contemporary global south and require its discontinuity. They interrupt and sometimes exacerbate regional political conditions as people confront them, disfiguring historical bonds. While large mining companies like Lafarge Holcim can procure documents, bend regulations, and receive permissions through international power play, those who dwell in the border region endure suspicion over autonomy and land ownership. Khasi and Garo indigenous groups—as well as Bengali villages etched along the border—have financially sustained small-scale mining, but their citizenship has been increasingly questioned while the process of acquiring documents has been made more and more grueling.[21] Driven by precarity, they move stones for the European cement giant. Others, like the sculler rowing my boat and Damien running the tours and travels business, have found

20 For more on the ontology of infrastructures, see Larkin, "The Poetics and Politics of Infrastructure," *Annaul Review of Anthropology*, 327-343.
21 Saikia, "As limestone piles up."

Figure 5. Limestone-carrying trucks moving at Dawki-Tamabil Checkpost. June 5, 2023. West Jaintia Hills, Meghalaya./ Photo by author

employment in the booming tourism economy in the state of Meghalaya. Tourism has become the Government of Meghalaya's new cash cow, and places like Dawki, once a remote border village, have had to support the surge of people and infrastructures resulting from both tourism and limestone extraction and export. Hence, during our long wait on narrow one-way roads of Khasi and Garo Hills, accommodating two-way traffic, Damien remarked that each truck can feed up to twenty people! Tourists from both sides of the border can edge close to the boundary line, however those who seek to migrate, even occasionally for work, meet relatives, or seek healthcare are met with aggression of the Indian BSF.

The extractive assemblage of the India-Bangladesh border is coated with nationalist developmental rhetoric which aims to achieve time-bound economic targets and establish long-term political authority. Anthropologist Sanjib Baruha defines these as attempts at "nationalizing space" which are motivated by the "high politics" of national security and unconcerned with the rights of indigenous people, local autonomy, and political stability.[22] Given its strategic location, the Northeast has been named as a "Gateway to Southeast Asia" and is being prepared for authoritative infrastructures like conveyor belts, ICPs, and highways that facilitate regional diplomatic relationships. Such structures order the frontier beyond their status as harbingers of development in distant rural locations. Instead, as James Scott posits, development is also introduced to restrict potential insurgent menace.[23] Therefore, he writes,

22 Baruah, "Nationalizing Space," *Development and Change*, 922.
23 Scott, *Seeing like a State*, 116.

Figure 6.
India-Bangladesh border fence. June 5, 2023. East Khasi Hills, Meghalaya. / Photo by author

"planners backed by state power are rather like tailors who are not only free to invent whatever suit of clothes they wish but also free to trim the customer so that he fits the measure."[24]

The India–Bangladesh border fence operates like a screen, projecting the speculative cultures of the borderlands, and simultaneously concealing the unequal regimes of movement. Constructed as a discontinuous line, the border unevenly intersects a culturally and politically complex place.[25] Rather than ordering national margins to secure sovereign power, this border assemblage functions as what architectural scholar Keller Easterling calls "infrastructure space."[26] Such spaces combines apparatuses like the border fence, the conveyor belt or the ICPs for political ideologies to shape extractive and nationalist relationships by maintaining

24 Scott, 146.
25 Agier, *Borderlands*, 56.
26 Easterling, *Extrastatecraft*, 15.

discontinuity. The interrupted border fences negate the officially mapped narratives of the border as a continuous line. It allows entire territories to be reformed in service of nationalist ambitions, and the intermittent fence spatially marking the borderline on the ground only obscures its true will. Therefore, the India–Bangladesh border demonstrates that borders are also plural and discontinuous objects that inspire the growth of global economies and make populist governance operable. A discontinuous border, read as a paradox, can challenge the truism that borders are naturally uninterrupted conditions for national sovereignties, established against the grain in an age of global exchanges. Through such a reading, we can center the ways in which architectural and spatial knowledge are co-opted to make borders inseparable from circulations of global economic power and capital.

18°

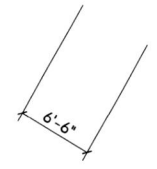

6'-6"

Contortions

Dhruv Mehta

It is incomplete in all these states (it is not something yet), and precisely because the usable furniture is now nothing (instead of something), it evokes fervent interest. Like Michelangelo's *non-finito* sculptures, the incomplete resolution of this furniture allows it to mentally be completed; it is Lacan's *objet petit a*, an object that completes a desire precisely because of its incompleteness. The figure still maintains its identity as furniture—although useless—as it imagines a moment within an endless series of rigid contortions. The movement doesn't extend into the absurd; it is still bound by gravity.

Contortion 1

This project begins with determining what a fetish could be. How does one begin to answer such a question, in which the answer, when arrived upon, always leaves a trace of doubt? Is what has been arrived upon really the thing, that is, a fetish? Even if one arrives at a fetish verbally, the word fails to fully sum up the emotion. It is the interstitial spaces between objects of desire wherein fetishes reside. So what is the object of desire here? It is most straightforwardly cows—but it is also bulls, certain types of architecture, sculptures by Michelangelo, and paintings by Francis Bacon. Which is the correct choice?

All of them.

48   Dhruv Mehta

Contortion 2

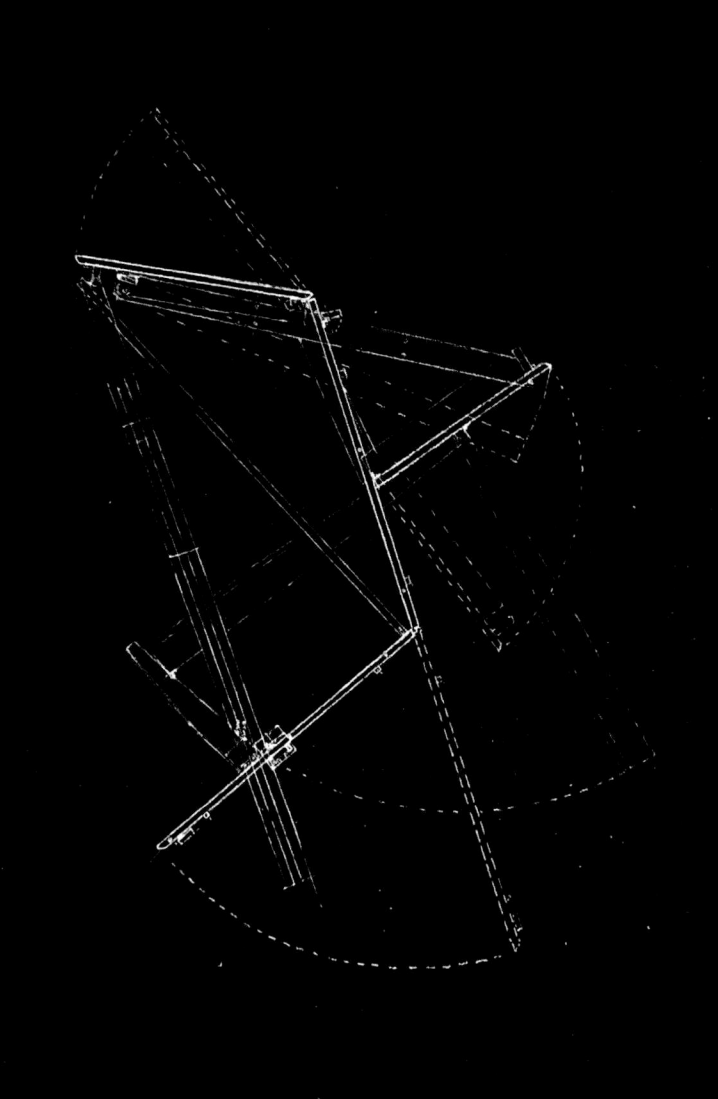

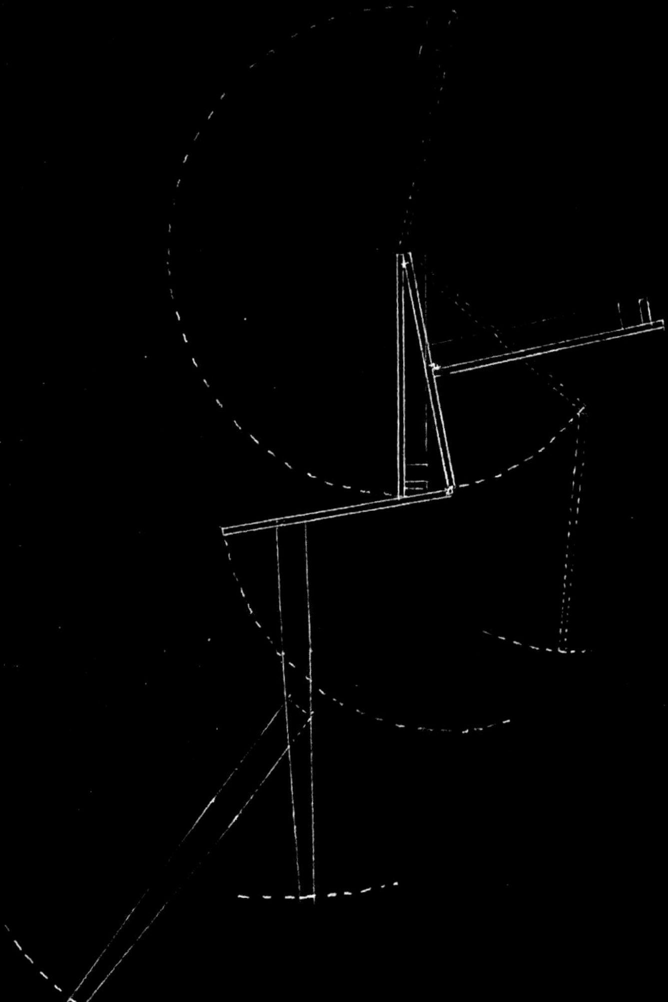

Lying within the gaps between these objects of desire, the fetish is formal. This realization came while pondering Jacques Lipschitz's terracotta relief sculpture *The Rape of Europa* made in 1938. The distortion of the subject/object in cubist works like these not only allows for more information to be communicated, but also acts as a device for generating tension with the frame of the painting or sculpture. Precisely because the bull is constricted within a tight space, a more essential figure of the bovine subject comes through.

If one looks at the plan of Victims by John Hejduk, or the Dominican Motherhouse by Louis Kahn, the same phenomenon can be observed. The bounding of the figures intensifies their affects. But there is also another type of bounding involved, one that doesn't allow the figure to disintegrate when put into such tension with a frame or enclosure. This is the internal tension within the constitutive part of the figure: the limbs to the torso in the case of the bull, the edge connections between the buildings in the case of Kahn, Hejduk, and even James Stirling at Wissenschaftszentrum.

To architecturalize these forces, I begin with a found piece of furniture. The furniture, when constrained by differing frames, starts to morph and contort.

Contortion 3

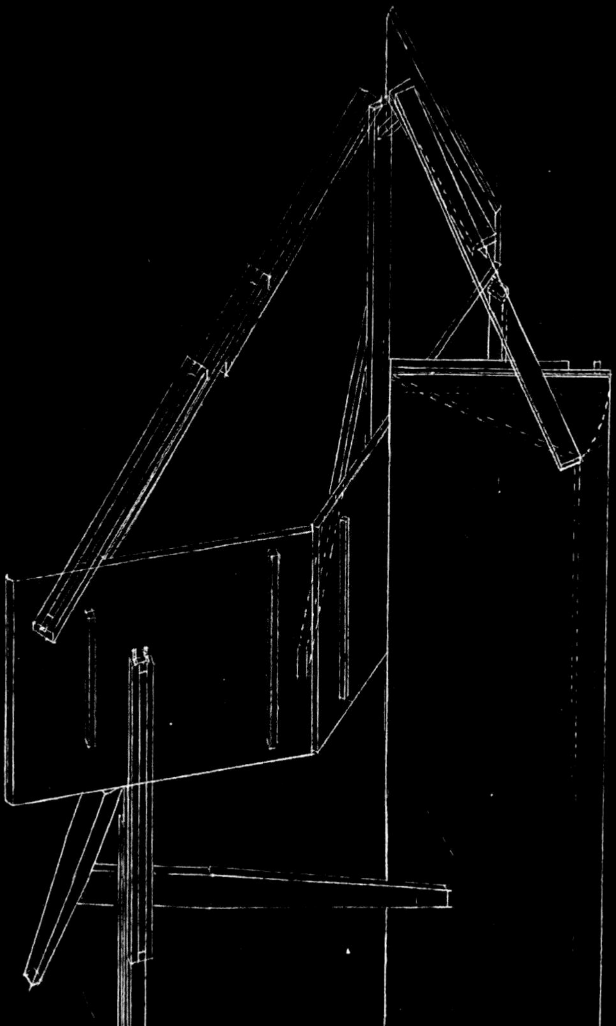

Here is one version of that contortion:

> It is incomplete in all these states, it is not something yet ... and precisely because ... [it] is now nothing, instead of something, it evokes fervent interest.

One thinks of Louis Kahn's Fisher House where the corner window dissolves and involutes to generate a space within the house. In the fetishization of such involution, where the constitutive elements consider the weight and material resistance, the hinge becomes an important device. All points stay connected and individually rotatable. One can imagine, much like Tatlin's *Corner Counter Relief*, the figure, through its contortion, architecturalizes the proximal space. Within a room—or as a room—it problematizes the space contained or around it, and begins to generate architecture.

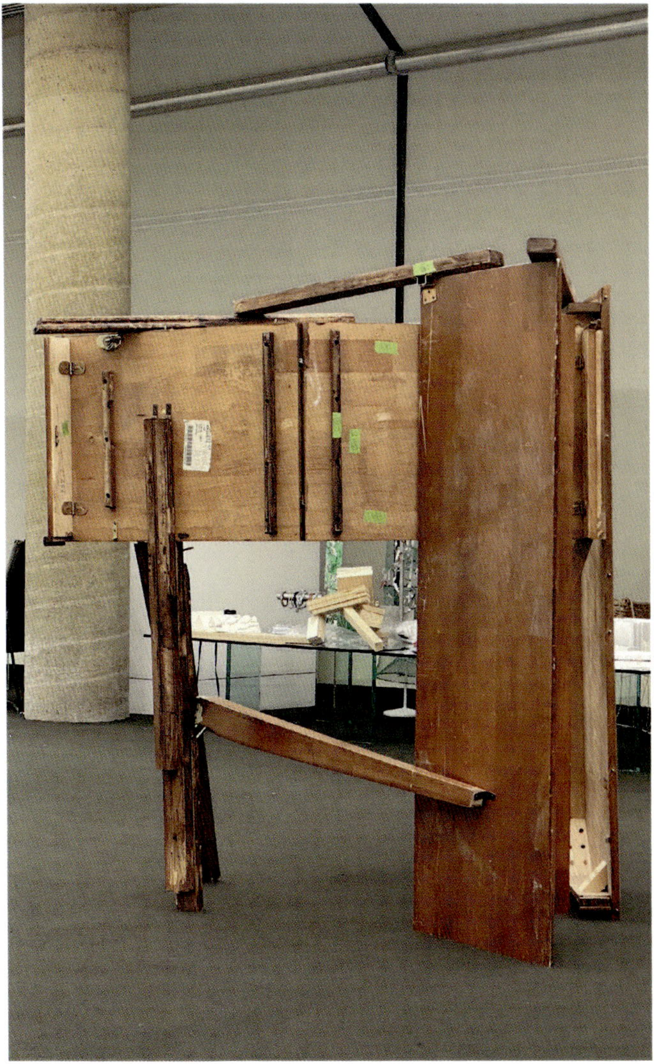

Four Acts: Some Concepts for Queer Histories and Pedagogies of Architecture

S.E. Eisterer

You Can Only Name a Thing You Love
Lately, she has been thinking, that she, mainly everyone, is only scratching the surface of desire.

Have you ever really asked yourself, what fulfillment would look like, spoken, felt, and lived, alive.

Living and knowing is not what they wrote in the books, And quotations are distancing techniques, imprints of discipline, cropped, assigned, half-lined.

Citations, however, are intimate affairs, And language worlds want question marks.

1. Embodied Citation

I want to begin by telling you,
> *It matters what you call a thing,*

which is the first line in the first book by poet Solmaz Sharif.

Over recent years I have learned the most about architectural history and theory from poets. That is to say, seeing poets incantate their own work and the words of those who have passed away gives new meaning to the texts in tandem. Hearing their lines recontextualized and reassembled, they also become endlessly built upon, into something here and there, into something that has been and something new. So I also need to tell you, at this point, that seeing Solmaz Sharif and poet Denice Frohman perform their pieces is different than reading them. And that it was really with the poets and seeing them read that a whole inquiry into the politics of citations began.

Indeed, it was in the moment I heard Solmaz Sharif recite a work of African American poet, professor, activist, and writer June Jordan that I felt both hopeful and at a loss with our discipline, the history of architecture. Because there was no way, I thought, to enliven scholarship like the poets do, that keeps adding and changing in conversation. That quoting in our realms was only cropping, assigning, and half lining, of single ideas, by single authors. Yet, over the months and years I have become intrigued by practices to subvert these tactics, including practices of citation. What about collective knowledge, or hearsay even, of things that are known by context or in bodies or because, you know, you just know?

To which, in a second, without hesitation,
Denice Frohman says,
> *You can only name a thing you love.*

2. Theory Beyond Theory

In 2019, I attended a conference at the University of Pennsylvania with the illusive title "Architectural Theory Now?" I was added as a moderator at the last minute, in part because admittedly I am not terribly steeped in the literature and discourse of phenomenology, whose legacy, it dawned on me at the event, was being discussed. My unfamiliarity with the subject matter was maybe why I seemed to be one of the few people who were perplexed that evening, puzzled that many of the speakers were asking, "Where had architectural theory gone?" There was a sense of misery in the room, that quotable voices and figures that once framed contemporary architectural discourse had outright vanished or receded into the background. As I was sitting to prepare a question for the Q and A, I scribbled down on a piece of paper a short list of people whom I felt my friends, colleagues, students, and I were thinking with. I never got to ask my question that night. Yet, when I moved twice in the years after, I carefully kept bringing the crumpled pink lined paper with the list written in green marker to my next home. The list is 6,000 miles from where I now write, but I prepared a similar one yesterday.

bell hooks
Audra Simpson
Elizabeth A. Povinelli
Sara Ahmed
...
Midnight Sun
Solmaz Sharif
José Esteban Muñoz
Gloria Anzaldúa
Saidiya Hartman
Will Roscoe
N.K. Jemisin
Susan Stryker
...
Angela Davis
David Eng
Denice Frohman
Octavia Butler
Jack Jen Gieseking
Donna Haraway
Wibke Straube
Kim TallBear
C. Riley Snorton
...

I understand that a list is one of the most disembodied ways of citing, especially in feeling an extensive debt. Yet, I would be hard-pressed to point you to a single thought, a sole cropped line, that is citable here. My students and I have asked instead how our understanding of knowledge production would shift if we thought of theorists as people in the world of expanding dialogue. This list is thus certainly neither conclusive nor stable. But at the conference, a list was something I needed. Evidence. To rattle off, or blurt out. To articulate my bewilderment at the panel's sense of insecurity and fear of disorientation, at the sight of a landscape of sea-changing theory—theory far beyond theory—which was creating entirely transformed disciplines. These emerging theories are deep meditations of past and present and intersectional identities in the midst of non-rehabilitative futures and climate catastrophes.

3. Trans* Pedagogy

In a recent event, also at the University of Pennsylvania, organized by Melissa Sanchez, Gwendolyn Beetham, Maria Murphy, and the Center for Research in Feminist, Queer, and Transgender Studies, C. Riley Snorton described what he considers to be the transformational potential of trans* pedagogy. I think of the lecture often in classrooms and architecture reviews because it had something so profound to impart to the pedagogue (vis-à-vis the critic). Snorton understands, if I recall adequately, that transformational pedagogical potential can be supported by the instructors' deep listening; that is to say, pedagogy, conceived in this sense, would be transformational in its attempt at accompanying students to come *more fully into their own voice.*

In parallel to the idea of coming more fully into one's voice, I often turn to writer M Constantine's concept of *voicing*, which I am citing from an unpublished manuscript on June Jordan's politics of language.

> *...developing the concept of voicing; derived from linguistic anthropology but as a pedagogy it has an anti-oppression purpose: to facilitate students' own process of voicing. Which is distinct from "finding one's voice" as a matter of style and (individual) originality. It is instead about deepening our understanding of the various structures of power that have given voice to us, the genealogies that speak through us, and the contradictions inherent in these voicings. [...] Voicing means legitimating voices that have been silenced; means showing silences that have been perpetually made. Voicing reveals erosion, loss, and transformation. Voicing articulates the shame of improper voicing that individuals are made to carry through years of schooling, disciplining, [...] family dynamics. To write through/from it as a way of seeing how it is linked to structures and everyday practices of oppression [...].*

Constantine suggests voicing as a practice that perpetually reflects upon structures of power and grapples with multiple frameworks of marginalization. *Voicing* is at once a place to depart from and a possibility for future solidarities. Like Snorton, Constantine understands voicing not as reifying fixed identity categories, but rather as a form of positionality that is intersectional and transformational. And while voicing asks profound questions about the systems, infrastructure, violence, and privilege of language worlds, Snorton's notion of trans* pedagogy points to the inalienable potential of fulfillment beyond binary constructs of identity by looking inward. Both *voicing* and *coming more fully into one's voice* are processes that allow for transformation while doing the work of positionality. Indeed, it is a form of positionality that is perpetually worked on, but also to be worked from.

When I look at the essays of students in seminars—especially those texts conceived iteratively, through free writes, or that decidedly draw on multiple language worlds—I find both the political labor of *voicing* and the transformational potential of *coming into one's voice* presented, modeled, and taken into so many directions. In the history and theory of architecture, doctoral students mobilize these concepts in various registers; for example, environmental histories of architecture, queer spatial practices, or their own pedagogy. In professional architecture, I have seen students use similar methods to question the foundations of the discipline and how they are taught through precedents, canons, and oeuvres. These works are often acts of tenderness and strength, which is something that architectural historian Sylvia Lavin recently encouraged me to model in public writing, if I ask my students to engage in the labor of voicing.

Staying with work by history and theory of architecture students, for example, I want to tell you about the essay "Pheasant Island, My Amalur" by Guillermo S. Arsuaga. The essay charts the history of a small island at the border of France and Spain, which maintains an alternating sovereignty between both nations every half year. Guillermo wrote about Pheasant Island's metronomic qualities—tidal, temporal, ecological, governmental—and what they reveal about Spain and France's coloniality. He highlighted that no humans are contractually allowed to dwell on this island or to be subjects of this changing sovereignty. In drawing on queer theory, environmental theory, and de-colonial theory, Guillermo pointed to the fundamental fact that Pheasant Island as a material entity resisted simple binaries and legal "fixing," for the meandering river and the tides change geographical outlines continuously. Revisiting the island whenever he comes home, his essay was also interspersed with more personal writing about reapproaching the small landmass. Pheasant Island was where his grandmother—carried by her father, a persecuted socialist militant—crossed into France while fleeing the Spanish Civil War. It was where she returned back to Spain in 1940, nine years older, on foot without her father. And it is where Guillermo goes, with a small boat just to be and sit and listen—an aberration to the legal treaties that reach back into the seventeenth century.

In Euskara, the Basque language which predates Romance languages such as French and Spanish, Guillermo tells me there are distinct categories of words and ways to structure grammar. Whereas Spanish and French bifurcate the world using masculine and feminine nouns, Euskara organizes them in animate and inanimate matter. The animate category includes all entities moving and transforming; it is a disobedient, stubborn category of nouns that unites and is mobilized by language, rivers, islands, plants, and humans.

Summer days are the best ones to visit my Amalur. There are long intervals of Itsasbehera that allow me to walk there. Typically, it shifts. One week you have morning-Itsasbehera, and the following week, afternoon-Itsasbehera. It takes one week for the moon to change its position. That morning I was sure it was a morning-Itsasbehera day; I could see it from my window towards the Ocean. The same Itsasbehera was on the large ocean and the small Amalur. What I didn't know was which of the two banks would be low. Sometimes the sand moves across the Spanish side, sometimes across the French one. Never mind, I thought, anyway it takes me just a ten-minute bike ride from one to the other. Then I realized I might be the first generation to experience Amalur like this. The Schengen treaties allow me to cross to France then walk to Amalur if the tide on the Spanish side is high. What about my dad? My grandma? Maybe it was not Amalur for him then. Perhaps it was, more than it is to me.

Figure 1. Pheasant Island on a summer morning, 2019./ Photo by Guillermo S. Arsuaga

On a June day in 2019, I was having a traditional Sunday lunch at my grandma's, in her house in San Sebastián. I told her that afternoon I was going to Amalur because the Itsasbehera would allow me to walk there. She asked me why I go there so often. "Zer dago hor?" She asked. "ze rez, uharte bat besterik ez," I replied. Then I want to go too, she said. I said: there is nothing to see

Figure 2. Maria in front of Pheasant Island in 2019./ Photo by Guillermo S. Arsuaga

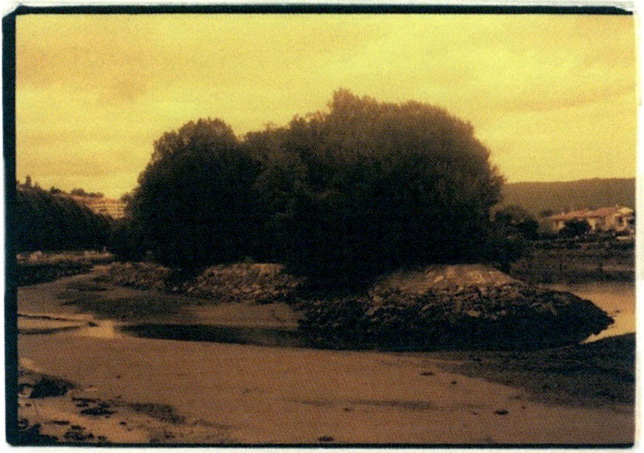

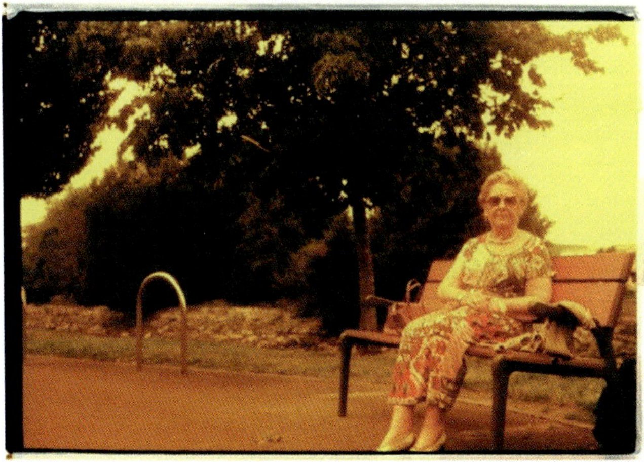

there, they said all these queens and kings got married there, but there is nothing to see, actually it's a made-up island, I think. Well, if you go there so often, there must be something. Take me there. When we were sitting right in front of the island, she told me the story of how she crossed the bridge in front of us twice in five years. Ez dut berriro gurutzatu nahi.

Exposing intimate histories, familial and political, while using the tools of translanguaging—that is moving fluidly between multiple language worlds—makes Guillermo's essay, to me, an act of what Snorton describes as *coming fully into one's voice*. It does so by conjuring ancestral cosmologies steeped in language and histories that defy modern nation states; it insists that these modes of looking and speaking have material ramifications in (built) environments.

Voicings of architectural history as a field, on the other hand, are central when I read M.C. Overholt's consideration of the archive of designer and self-identified lesbian author Phyllis Birkby. In the essay "Promising Subjects: N. Phyllis Birkby and the Writing of Queer Architectural History," M.C. sets out to map Birkby's environmental fantasies against the complexities of confronting queer archives in a method that oscillated between the theorization of historic materials and embodied forms of knowing. In a culminating moment, she reveals to the reader feelings of deep, more-than-scholarly attachment, followed by a sense of loss when archives and figures fail to deliver on a supposed promise—for instance, that of a truly inclusive queer-feminist architecture.

> *I've been thinking about failure*
> *I've been thinking about queer failure*
> *I've been thinking about queer failure as architectural method*
> *I've been thinking about the failures of white queer feminists. The way they deployed the terms "women" and "female" as a tactic of exclusion, even as they were working to make a more inclusive world. Even as we are working. Even as we do deploy.*
> *I've been thinking about Phyllis. She's deceased, so she doesn't know it, but we have a difficult relationship. I've been asking her to do more than she did. I've also been desperately appreciative that she did anything at all.*
> *I've paused on her words with discomfort.*
> *If only she had rephrased that sentence this way… maybe I could be absolved of unease. Of disappointment.*
> *I've been thinking about ephemerality and the failure of some spaces to meet the measure of permanence by which architecture defines itself.*
> *Is queer architecture an oxymoron?*

Along with the sense of attachment, that is both longing and loss, M.C.'s essay itself emerged from an iterative practice between embodied writing and bodily performance. First conceived as a performance in the fall of 2021 as part of a seminar taught by Heather Love and Brooke O'Harra, it became a long reflective essay and, finally, a shorter scholarly paper presented at the Society of Architectural Historians annual meeting in Spring 2023. The long essay probed and, in a sense, advocated for performance as a historical-architectural method that invites other modes of epistemological production. What would its possibilities and apertures become?

M.C.'s and Guillermo's essays are critical to me, because I keep wondering if these feelings and the knowledge about loss, longing, love, resistance, archives, and environmental histories of architecture, families, and nations can ever be told in an "objective" way. And, in any case, Donna Haraway dispelled this notion of objectivity a long time ago, and argued for a view from somewhere (or voice from somewhere?) when she writes that

> *the joining of partial views and halting voices into a collective subject position promises a vision of the means of ongoing finite embodiment, of living within limits and contradictions—of views from somewhere*

Figure 3.
Photo of performance "Queer Archives, Aesthetics, Performance."/ Taken by Maxime Cavajani, December 10, 2021, in Philadelphia, PA, U.S.A.

and against the notion of objectivity. This living with limits and contractions is what I consider central for the training of professional architects today as well. I hear the labor of voicing, the formation of subject position of a full voice, and the halting voices into a collective. These are also expressed in a comment by another student I work with, Jacobie Smith, who has possibly taught me the most in many years of trying to be a better pedagogue. She said,

If you don't understand what I am saying, I am probably not talking to you.

4. The Voice of the (Un)moved Historian

Following a lecture I gave at Columbia University a few years ago, architectural historian Mark Wigley asked me if I believed in the voice of the unmoved historian. Keenly aware of the critique of operative history and going out on a limb, I told him, something rather basic, that no, letting yourself feel what history drudges up is an important tool and that emotive categories can sharpen frameworks of analysis. Wigley then also asked me to say a bit more about what I hoped would be learned by revisiting a history of one avant-garde figure, told from the perspective of the small artifacts and objects that this architect, Margarete Schütte-Lihotzky, had created as part of a resistance network. More precisely, I think he said, I had played a trick in redrawing lines of attention to other objects and positions of knowing and resistance, but I had not said how this would make us, architectural historians, see something different about kitchens and housing projects—in short, the works of modern architecture we already knew (that is, aside from the fact that we had gained insight into the parallel political lives). I always understood this question to be earnest and inquisitive, not a critique, but in fact an act of truly listening.

A first possible answer to this question is that, over the years, I came to understand the core concern of my book on Schütte-Lihotzky not to be biographical really, but rather to be about collectives. In addition, I found myself wondering not so much what people did, but how they led their lives. The project became about decentering the individual and writing towards groups of people. In addition, attention to lives lived meant looking carefully at the economies that sustained these architects' friendships and careers. In a way, I thought, Schütte-Lihotzky's life was a prism to truly look at the history of twentieth-century architecture culture and its constructions, and, through it, ask nagging questions about the politics of resources, labor, and memory.

But I also sensed that Mark Wigley's question was not only about history and methods, but about the field in its present condition. In charting a second possible answer, I want to invoke gender studies scholar Kadji Amin and share a passage that came to me first as an epigraph heading M.C. Overholt's project on Birkby. Amin writes:

> *When a "promising" object fails to deliver, scholars too often compensate by switching gears from idealization to critique, flaying the object for its failure to be sufficiently transgressive or consistently radical. If this occurs early on in a research project, it can initiate the wholesale abandonment of the object that has failed to live up to its promise. Otherwise, we might either sidestep the source of unease, the better to celebrate the object's truly radical aspects, or use it to hone the ego-enhancing aggression of critique, thereby shoring up the critic's position of mastery and political unassailability. [...] scholarship needs to cultivate a wider set of methods and tactics with which to negotiate what disturbs and disappoints and a wider range of scholarly moods than utopian hope, on the one hand, and critique, on the other. Scholars might inhabit unease, rather than seeking to quickly rid themselves of it to restore the mastery of the critic, the unassailability of her politics, and the legitimacy of her trained field expectations.*

In my case, Amin's assertions require voicings to dig deep into the violent, white, hetero-patriarchal underpinnings of discipline and economy conjured by the idea of collective imagination (utopianism, that is) in 1920s architecture and how it has stayed with us in the present. That is, for example, to not look away—as avant-garde architects did and many histories of architecture do—from the thousands of laborers in Russia who had been forcibly unsettled, coerced to work, and killed in abhorrent conditions on construction sites throughout the Soviet Union in the 1930s. On a more fundamental level, I also believe that as a discipline we need to be able to hold and confront violence together with people's intimate and vulnerable moments. In my case, this concerns a generation of architects and artists, some of whom suffered emigration, internment, and death in situations that are so unthinkable that they can only come to us through mediations today. The work then is about the politics of architecture and about the architectural politics of memory, and why, at a centuries distance even, it is still so difficult to see these lives and works clearly. To inhabit these histories with unease and ambiguity as a deliberate rejection of the role of the critic, as Amin suggests, seems to be a possibility, in doing the work of active listening to archives, or in becoming moved as a historian. An entangled and embodied process in the writing of history might embrace a queer politics of designation that honors the mentors who listened, and who encouraged me to remember, evoke, and incantate

you can only name a thing you love.

R3'-7¼"

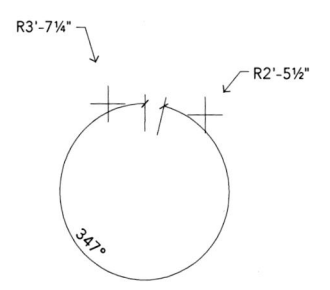

R2'-5½"

347°

الطريق لبيت العيلة
The Route to Beit Al-Eileh

Maysam Abdeljaber

In March 2022, I visited Al Am'ari camp with siblings and former residents Najah (age 62), Nisreen (age 46), and Muhammad (age 44). Najah is one of the eldest among her ten siblings, all of whom spent the majority of their lives in Al Am'ari camp. Their family was forced to leave the camp in 2015.

Al Am'ari camp is situated between the cities of Ramallah and Al-Bireh. Covering an area of approximately ninety *dunams*[1] the camp is one of the smallest in the West Bank. Al Am'ari is currently home to eight thousand residents, with Palestinians continuing to be forcibly displaced—most actively in 1948, 1967, and presently in Gaza due to the ongoing genocide.

1 A measure of land area originating from the Ottoman Empire, currently used in Israel and Palestine. One dunams is equivalent to 0.247 acres.

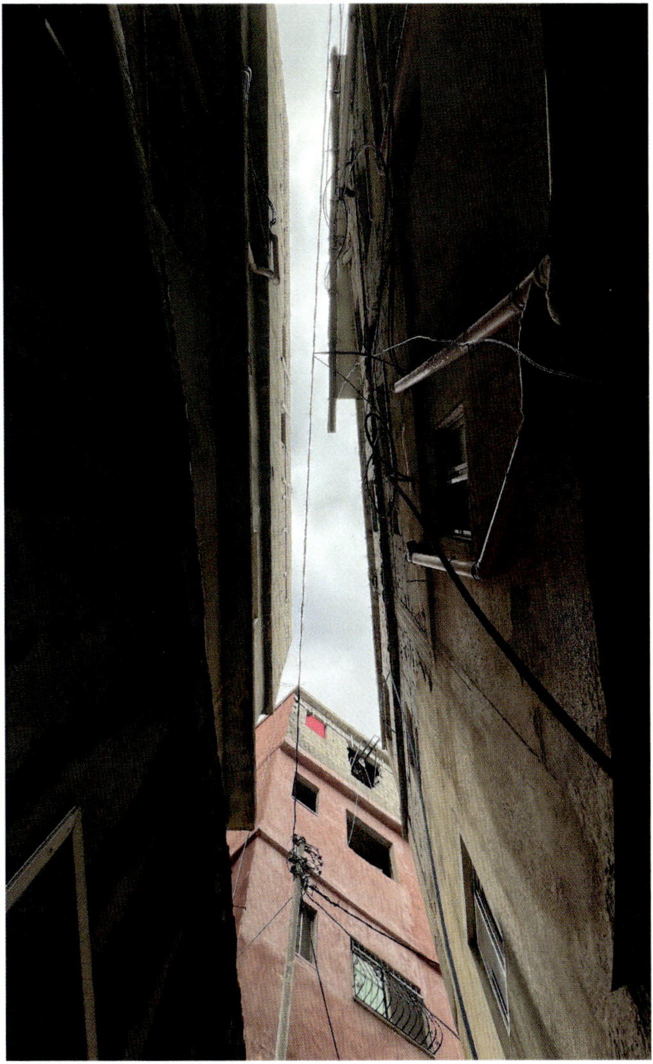

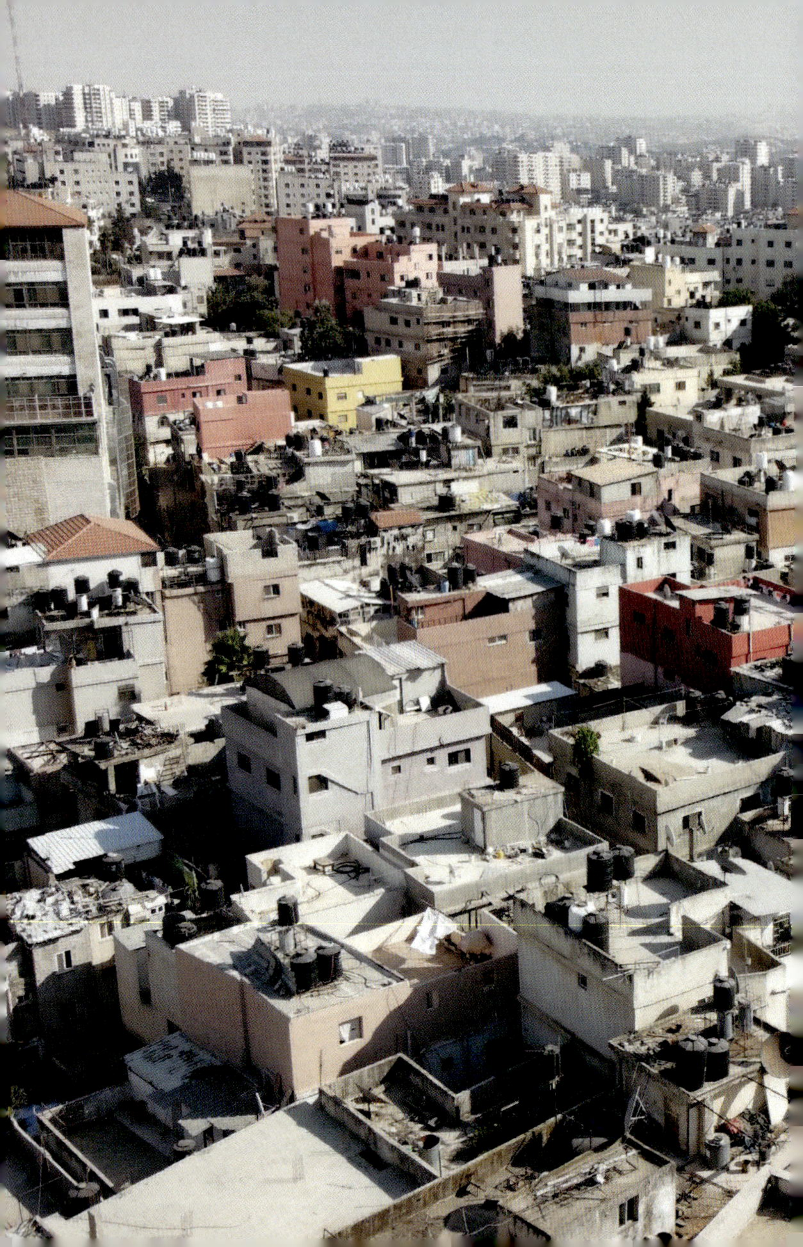

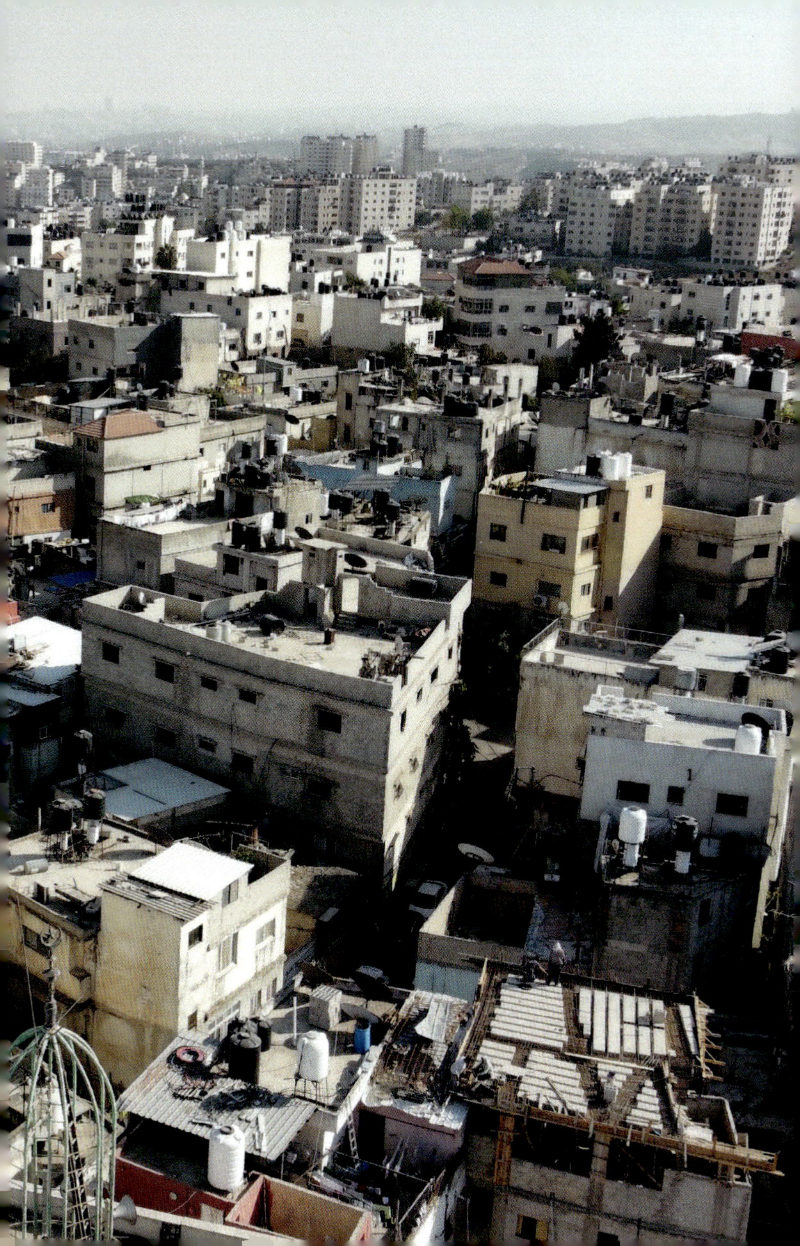

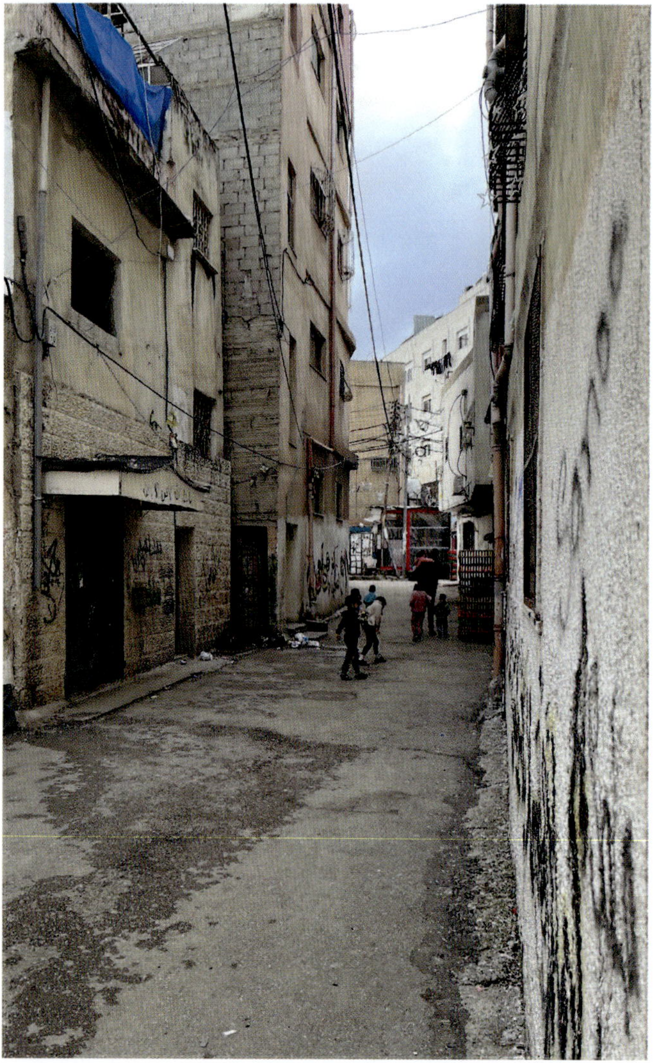

The Route to Beit Al-Eileh

Najah: I was born in Al Am'ari Refugee camp. My mother and father came as refugees to the camp after the 1948 Nakba.[2] They were forced out by the Israeli settlers. Everyone was forced to move into different locations. My parents were first put in a refugee camp in Jamala, Der Ammar,[3] and then moved to Al Am'ari camp shortly after. When they first moved there, they lived in tents for a while and then later they were able to build one living unit.[4]

The *wakaleh*[5] needed to support the units ... our house is one of these living units, only one room at first, it was for my grandpa. When my father got married, he built another room right next to it, so they lived together in two rooms and one bathroom. After my dad started working, he was able to start expanding his home little by little ... adding another room, adding a kitchen, like this.

[2] The 1948 Catastrophe where more than 800,000 Palestinians were ethnically cleansed from their land. This occurred largely in the cities of Jaffa, Haifa, Lid, and Ramla, and led to the formation of Al'Amari.
[3] A village in the West Bank
[4] A room and bathroom provided for each family.
[5] Arabic word for agency, commonly used to refer to a relief agency. In this case it is referring to the United Nations Relief and Works Agency for Palestine Refugees in the Near East, or UNRWA.

However, the land is not our land. The land we lived on was originally for residents of Al-Bireh.[6] They donated their lands to us, refugees. So we had very limited land space that we were allowed to build on. We had to build one room at a time, and if we needed more space, we had to build units above units. Most of the houses were very tight and had multiple floors. The buildings were very close to one another. We couldn't expand outwards.

The streets were tight and broken, we had a poor foundation. It is very old. The sewage system is so close to the homes that it releases bad and toxic smells. We can only make fixes if the UNRWA can support it. Nowadays the UNRWA hasn't been able to give as much support as it used to.

6 The city within which Al Am'ari was established.

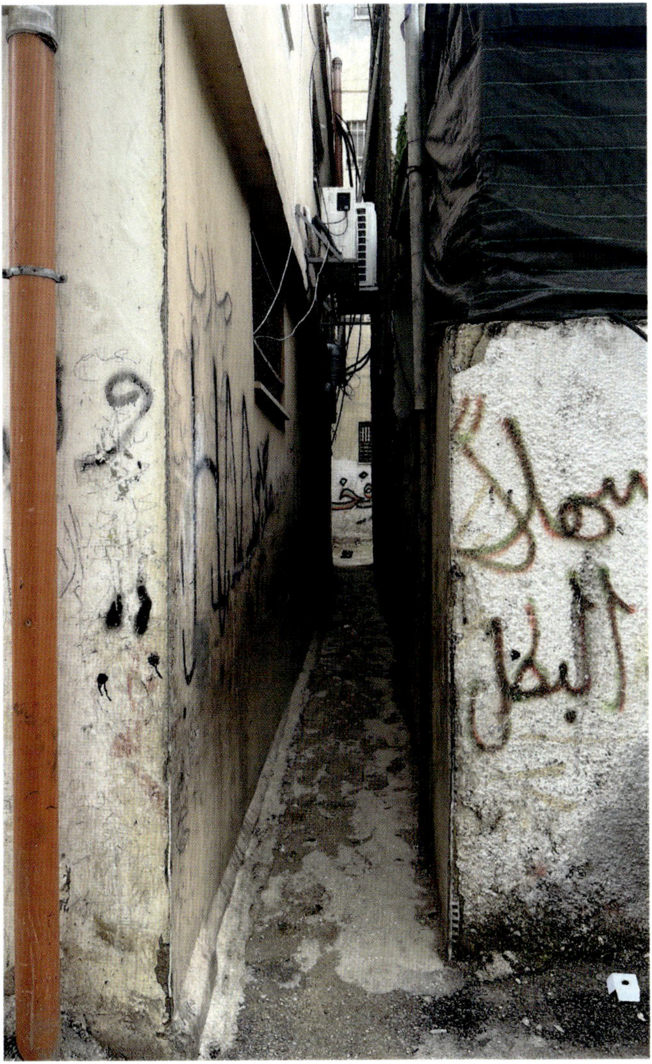
البطل

Back in the day, the refugees used to live on survival packages provided [monthly] by the UNRWA. They supported residents with rice, bread, blankets, etc. Currently, they support limited things, like clinics and schools. But even so, the support is not sufficient for our needs. They stopped providing resources and fixing homes—you would need to be in an extremely poor condition to be eligible for support. Until now, some families still live in one-unit homes, even families with six children, four children. We couldn't grow our own crops because we didn't own the land. Even if we could, we didn't have enough space to grow crops.

Nisreen: The residents opened small stores next to or in their homes, to open businesses such as supermarkets, retail, poultry markets, and so on.

Some stores were so small, like the poultry market. The chickens were left on the side of the streets in cages. They made the camp smell bad. I also remember when we walked in and out of the alleys on our way to school, we had to open our legs to walk through so our feet wouldn't get soaked in the gross water on the ground.

Najah: The sewage infrastructure is poor and there is no proper drainage system in the camp. The homes are very tight, so when it rains the water drains to the lower homes. The homes get soaked and the water causes harm inside, ruining the walls, the floors, the furniture ... because of the humidity and mold, this can cause us to have trouble breathing properly.

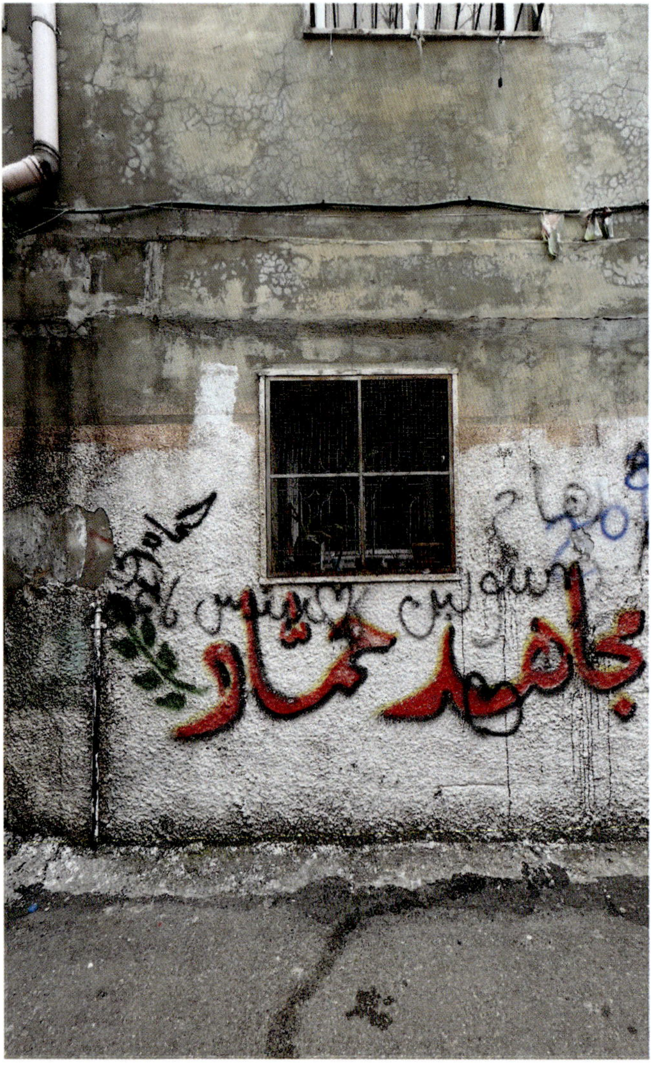
مجاهد حمار

If people want to get medical support, they have the clinic supported by the UN. There are not enough services and insurance. If there are urgent situations like labor, they are transferred to nearby hospitals with some funding support. However, today they usually have to go to hospitals and have to support themselves financially.

All camps in Palestine are bound to face the Israelis who barge into their camp. Because of the occupation, there are always problems between Israelis and Palestinians. Israel would harass civilians or throw tear gas and bombs that cause major injuries and deaths. The camp is filled with families of *shaheed*[7] and political "prisoners," most of whom are young boys.

Nisreen: They would throw tear gas, and people would inhale the gas, sometimes even women who are pregnant would inhale the gas and it would cause major health problems.

Muhammad: Once I was with a friend of mine, we parted ways, he went to work and I went back home. Not even thirty minutes later, they called and told me that "they killed Salem." Sometimes we wake up to gunshots and people screaming. I have a few friends that I grew up with who are currently in prison and have life sentenced by Israel. There's also a widowed mother who lives in our camp, Um Nasser,[8] they call her "Khansaa Falastin."[9] She has seven sons, one of them is a *shaheed* and the other six are incarcerated in the occupation jails.[10]

---

7 A martyr, or someone who is killed because of their beliefs, religious or otherwise.
8 Mother of Nassar
9 Khansaa of Palestine, Khansa is a strong woman who stands strong despite the tragedies she faces.
10 Four days after this interview, on December 20, 2022, Um Nasser's son, Nasser died in the occupation jail due to medical negligence. This means two of her sons have been martyred, and five have been incarcerated.

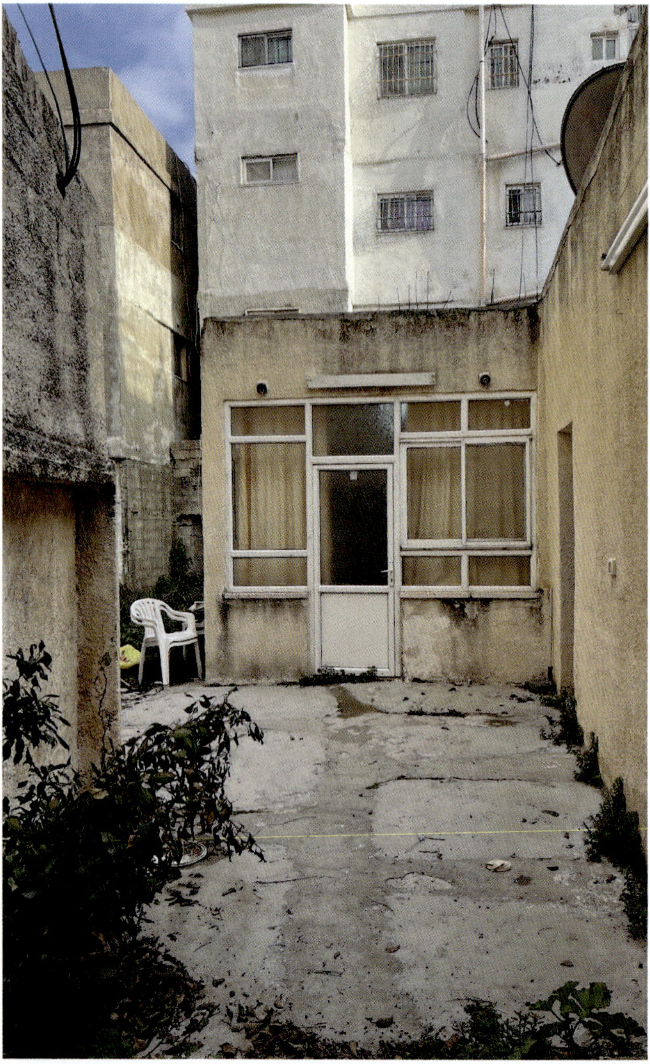

Najah: The best days in Al Am'ari were when the whole family came together during Ramadan and we would break our fast together. And when we have our Suhoor meal, and chase the *musahir*.[11] The best memory! We would get falafel from "falafel abu Jaridah;" they serve the falafel in newspapers instead of bags. The soccer team is very successful, they are one of the best in the nation. There's is a lot of activities like theater for kids, marching bands, and *dabkeh* groups.[12]

Muhammad: My favorite place was the sports complex.

Nisreen: Mine was our front entrance of the house, where I would play with the neighbors.

Najah: My favorite place was my home, the place I lived because it's *beit al-eileh*.[13] We can't forget our childhood and adulthood; thank God for all the good and bad. We lived through the sweet and sour.

---

11 A man who walks around an area beating his drum or chanting to wake up people for prayer and suhoor meal during the month of Ramadan.
12 Traditional Palestinian dance
13 A common Arabic phrase, "The house of the family," refers to the grandparents' home or the main household where extended family members often gather during holidays or occasions.

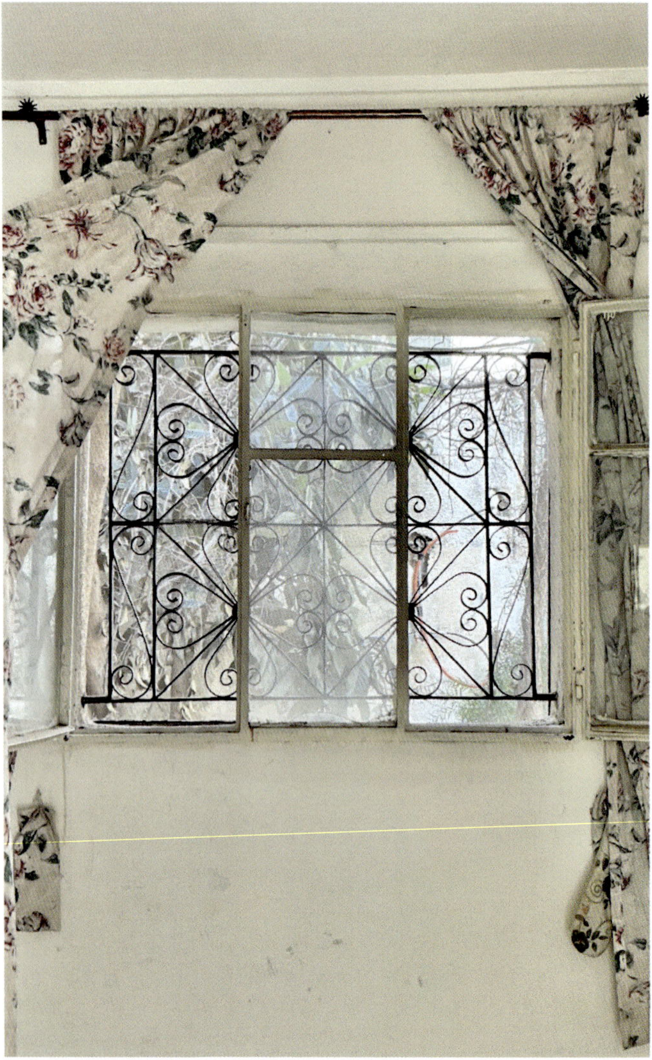

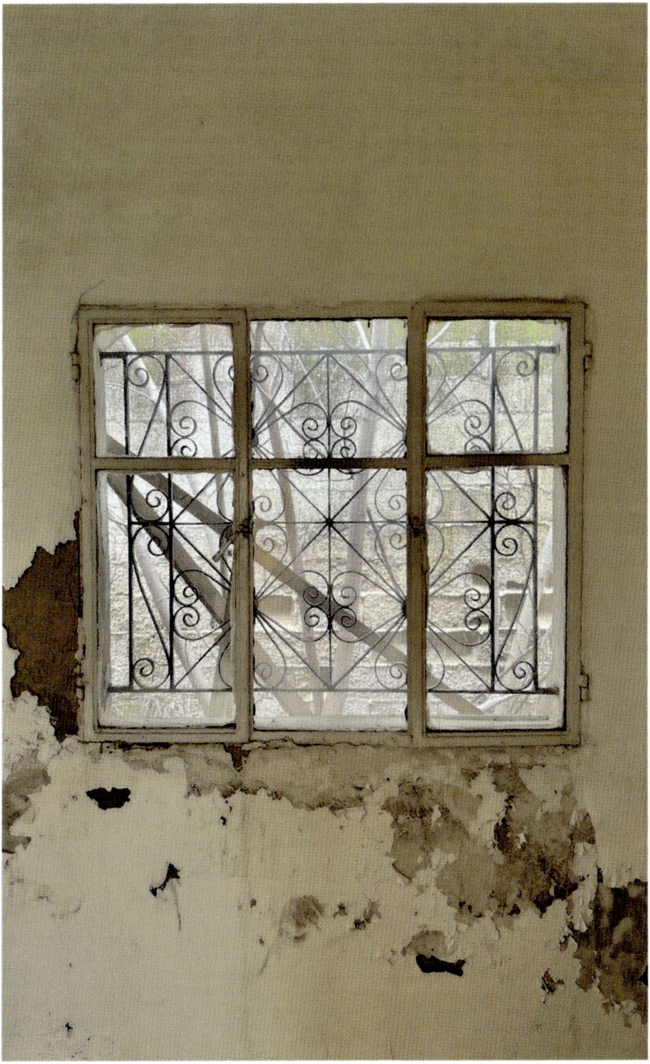

Terrafictions:
On Representation in Landscape Architecture

Tekena Koko

When landscape architecture transformed from tending to gardens and parks into an environmental science, it relinquished its filiations with the aesthetic ideal of the picturesque for the precision of the technical. By the technical, I mean the prevalence of descriptive, orthographic, and technical drawings and diagrams in the practice of landscape architecture—in essence, the conventions of drawing as instituted in the field. Historically, landscape architecture maintained integral and dynamic relationships to a variety of pursuits.[1] The term "landscape" emerged around the turn of the sixteenth century to denote a genre of painting whose primary subject

1 Olwig, "Recovering the Substantive Nature of Landscape," *Annals of the Association of American Geographers*, 630-53.

was natural scenery, while "the picturesque," as an aesthetic category, describes a style of landscape painting imbued with an untamed, rustic allure—a quality notably absent in the refined classical or academic styles of the seventeenth and eighteenth centuries. This genealogical connection to painting through the picturesque implied associations with poetry and philosophy. Landscape architecture was "tied to literary ideas and transcendentalism": practitioners like Frederick Law Olmsted and Horace Cleveland engaged with works of Ralph Waldo Emerson, Henry Wadsworth Longfellow, and Henry David Thoreau, translating literature and philosophy into built forms.[2]

The arrival of photography in the eighteenth century marked the initial departure from the picturesque and its associated painterly gestures, in favor of the technical. Photography offered a technical and indexical framing in lieu of an imaginative construction of the picturesque. As photography supplanted landscape painting in representing the "natural world," so did the term "view" supplant the term "landscape" as a descriptor in the photographic lexicon, and arguably, in everyday language.[3] A second instance of this institutional divestment from the picturesque followed the whims of modernization, during which landscape architecture's tilt away from the picturesque reflected the ambitions of a modernizing society—where the quantitative disposition of its scientific models came to override the qualitative associations that previously framed perceptions of landscape. These changes accelerated

[2] Hohmann and Langhorst, "Landscape Architecture: A Terminal Case?" *Landscape Architecture*, 26-45.

[3] For more on the discussion about this switch in terminology, see Krauss, "Photography's Discursive Spaces: Landscape/View," *Art Journal*, 311-19.

during the post-war years. In 1969, Ian McHarg published his seminal work, aptly entitled *Design with Nature*. In his monograph, McHarg responded to the demands of an increasingly quantitative society by proposing a proto-geographic information system (GIS) as an analytic model for environmental design. A sublime act of institutional reification, McHarg's proposition transitioned landscape architecture away from gardening to assert itself in a scientific and professional capacity. With this transformation, however, the profession decoupled itself from pursuits like the arts and humanities.

In tandem with this decoupling from the arts, the concept of landscape as an aesthetic construct receded, as "landscape" became de-aestheticized into "land" and linked with use-value. This reversal was reflected in the practice of landscape architecture, where *the aesthetic*, lacking instrumental value, was swapped with *the technical*, which possessed the capacity to be descriptive, rather than evoke aesthetic contemplation. From its first degree-granting program established at Harvard in 1901 to McHarg's *Design with Nature* released in 1969, and to the nationwide registration LARE (Landscape Architecture Registration Exam) in 1970, landscape architecture as a profession evolved over a significantly shorter timescale compared with architecture or the arts, which over time, developed theories on aesthetics and representational media. Emphasizing representation formally, critically, and discursively, certain theories of art and architecture have framed representation, for better or worse, as an end in itself, something bearing intrinsic value. In the case of architecture, representation is regarded as something bearing value independent of the utility of building altogether. A case in point is Peter Eisenman's treatise on critical formal autonomy, a polemic on architecture's self-representation of its autonomy from society, which Eisenman considered as a rejection of rampant commodification. I argue for a critical discourse on media and representation in landscape architecture that recuperates its severed links to the arts and recovers the sensibility of the picturesque. While the aim of landscape architecture certainly reaches beyond representation, how we represent implicates how we frame and address field-related concerns.

Landscape architecture's overarching disciplinary program (most prominently, climate responsiveness) might make a project on representation seem frivolous. Nevertheless, such a project could resuscitate its formerly vibrant connection to the arts, potentially expanding our approach to addressing questions pertaining to the built and natural environment. Unlike architecture, landscape architecture has yet to exhaust its project on representation or propose a project that advances beyond a utilitarian framework. Put another way, landscape architecture modernized, yet somehow evaded entry into its *modern*—let alone postmodern—condition. This omission sets the field apart from adjacent practices such as the arts, which evolved through modernism to embrace conceptualism, minimalism, institutional critique, and so on, and architecture, which progressed from modernism into post-modernism and beyond. Of significance here is how these epochs implicated representational practices within their respective fields—in the case of the arts, these transitions were articulated through representation itself. Fraught with contention, these transitions through Modernism, nonetheless, sparked revolutionary changes in the arts and architecture. Could the projective and discursive potential of representation within the discipline be mined further? Could a reclaimed territory of the picturesque, and its associated painterly gestures be the locus for a discourse that advances beyond solution-based tropes?

Projectivity

To argue for a reclaimed territory of the picturesque (and by extension, the painterly) where meaning derives from subjective, intuitive, and poetic participation, I would turn to Rene Demoris. In Demoris's treatise on seventeenth-century French painting, he articulates "the specific and different pleasures" of the *unfinished* draft sketch against the *polished*, fully rendered style. Quoting Roger de Piles, Demoris writes:

> In the *Cours de peinture* of 1708, de Piles wrote about the style of landscape painting, and opposed the *firm* style (*ferme*, with visible touch) to the *polished* one: "The *firm* style gives life to the work, and excuses for bad choice, and the *polished*, finishes and brightens everything, it leaves no employment for the spectator's

imagination, which pleases itself in discovering and finishing things which it ascribes to the artist, though, in fact, they proceed only from itself."[4]

De Piles's comparison of the *ferme* and the *polished* styles echoes the contrast between the picturesque and the technical. The realm of the picturesque, akin to the unresolved, transitory, and fleeting nature of *ferme*-style sketches, withholds definitive content, implying a certain tolerance or "softness." With meaning in flux, a viewer's imaginative faculties are called upon to ponder on a work. In contrast, the resolved and overly determined nature of the *polished* style, like technical representations, precludes the imaginative participation of a viewer and constrains the projective abilities of the work's author.

Softscapes

In landscape architecture, synthetic or inert aspects of the built environment, such as paving, are referred to as hardscape, while natural or vegetative elements are categorized as softscape. This opposition between hardscape and softscape metaphorically tracks the distinction between the technical and the picturesque—the former definitive, the latter, allusive. The following four cases, which were the outcome of a course I taught at USC in Spring 2019, explore soft territories to address the technical-picturesque divide.[5]

4 Demoris, "Body and Soul," in *Painting beyond Itself*, 221-222.

5 I am grateful to the four students from the Spring 2019 Media Course at the MLA program in USC for granting me the permission to use their work for this paper.

The digitally rendered image in Figure 1 depicts trash and found objects sighted during a park visit in Los Angeles. The over-scaled objects comprise a crumbled, past-due utility bill, an eggshell, a toothpaste tube, a toothbrush, a plastic cup, and a medicine pack. In fusing with its material (paper) support, the image establishes a relationship between itself and its support, subsuming the latter into its pictorial realm to convey a narrative on waste.

Figure 1:
Megan Gozini (MLA Student, USC), Untitled.

Figure 2:
Robert Andrade
(MLA Student, USC),
Vague Terrain.

In depicting what appears as fragmented objects in an idyllic landscape, Figure 2 comprises real and virtual models. The digitally rendered foliage served as the backdrop for the placement of two physically modeled wall-like white bars. The bars were digitally scanned and then seamlessly collaged into the rendered scene. Expected medial relationships fall out of sync as three-dimensional objects are falsely flattened into a dimensionless virtual environment. Obscuring the landscape to guide one's view laterally across the picture plane and towards the image's edge, the white bars hint at their extra-pictorial (physical) origin.

The rocklike object depicted in Figure 3 attempts a sort of spatial absence. At some moments, it mirrors its context, while at others, its excisions allow the background vegetation to visually pass through. This attempt at high reciprocity between object and field is further complicated by the act of printing the image on fabric. The fabric disrupts a singular or fixed reading of the image, as boundaries between object and field (vegetation) become inarticulate since the image constantly updates to correspond to the fabric's mutable form (fig. 4).

Figures 3 & 4: Danielle Vonlehe (MLA Student, USC), Untitled.

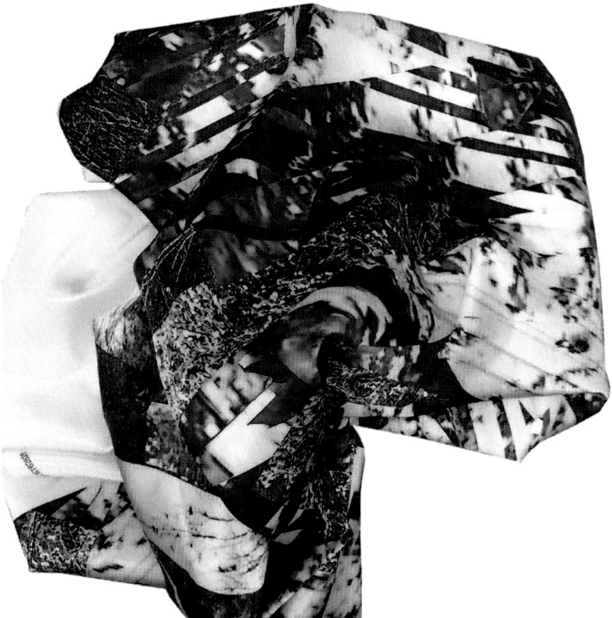

This object oscillates between *representation* and food to assert its post-digital presence (fig. 5). A transparent, hollow container is created by vacuum forming a 3D print of a Google Earth topographic model. This vessel, akin to a petri dish, is filled with a gelatinous medium (clear Jello) mixed with floral clippings from the actual site of the Google Earth model. Afterward, the container is refrigerated to harden. Beyond linking a digital proxy to its real-world source, the inclusion of live flora introduces a durational or temporal dimension to the object. Yet, unlike conventional temporal media, this object's timeline syncs with the decay of the added

Figure 5:
Lisa Cortright (MLA Student USC), Untitled.

flora. This fusion of the digital and the organic, portrayed through the guise of decaying plants, implies vitality and hints at the object's digital transcendence.

Displacement

The cases above radiate a seeming romantic idealism, a quality often absent in the representational techniques of much of today's technical drawings. These representations flirt with the specter of the picturesque and absorb painting's "codes"—its fictive, narrative, and aesthetic devices. Moving away from the conventions of technical drawing, they de-emphasize legibility, forming a sharp contrast with McHarg's or more recent landscape-urbanist representations.[6] In these representations, natural phenomena are reductively abstracted into legible symbols: colors, shapes, and lines that oversimplify their essential complexity. Rather than valorize legibility, the cited examples elaborate on the incapacity to fully account for such complexity. They either conceptually register natural processes such as *decay* or allude to the very *limits* of translating such complexity by acknowledging the difficulty of the task. In other words, they give up, turn inwards, and reflexively gesture towards self-referentiality. These representations depart from drawing to reflect a retreat from *factual* conditions and appeal to an artist's sensibilities more so than to a geographer. They tease out the institutional conditions of drawing—the means through which drawing inscribes, accumulates, and transmits disciplinary

6 The diagrams in McHarg's *Design with Nature* from 1966, when juxtaposed with noteworthy North American Landscape Architecture events or projects—such as the 1999 Downsview Park design competition in Toronto, the High Line project in New York, or the Olympic Sculpture Park in Seattle—employ comparable graphic conventions. These conventions consistently prioritize legibility and continue to influence contemporary practices.

knowledge. Unbounded and siteless, they compete with the convention of drawing, recalling the picturesque's "wildness," and free up space for unruly figures to sneak through. They are at once self-referential in the sense they could be evaluated purely in terms of their formal and aesthetic qualities, yet they engage the broader conditions of their production; that is, they comment on the virtual environments in which they are created, including the relationships between depiction (image) and support and between digital paradigms, food, land, and place. More so than drawings, these representations accrue multiple readings and incite critical reflection. They rely on "belief"—that which a spectator invests in while viewing a work of fiction or art to allow themselves to experience illusion. Irritating the disciplinary codes that authorize drawing, these representations subvert technical and descriptive clarity. They entangle themselves between the arts to exceed the flat plane of the drawing and its incapacity to capture the *density of incidents* or the irreducible qualities of atmosphere, feeling, and sensation.

Is It Art?

In 1981, Stephen Krog's article "Is It Art?" unleashed a brief firestorm of vitriolic debate on the nature of landscape architecture.[7] In light of our discussion, Krog's question warrants a revisit. Moreover, we could rephrase his question, adapting a phrase by Rosalind Krauss: "to what discursive spaces" do the cases cited here belong, art or landscape architecture?[8] Rather than respond emphatically, we could

7 Hohmann and Langhorst, "Landscape Architecture: A Terminal Case?", 26. Also see Krog, "Is It Art," *Landscape Architecture*, 373-76.

8 Krauss, "Photography's Discursive Spaces: Landscape/View," 314.

embrace an ambivalent stance, one positioned at the fluid periphery of landscape architecture and aimed at blurring its discursive boundaries, which would render the question inconsequential. We could embrace an attitude where the descriptive taxonomies—nature and artifice, softscape and hardscape, object and field—are allowed to reach an "ontological tipping point," mirroring the ghost of the picturesque which persists between multiple discursive spaces: the ether and the real, the conventional and the peculiar, and landscape architecture and art.

These cases offer a set of ambitions that link conceptual practices (even those more distant from landscape painting) to locate them within a new discourse on representation in landscape architecture—a discourse at the paper-thin edge of the field. To advance this discourse, I will move beyond Krog's question and pose two more: Could we move beyond the descriptive models that prop up rehabilitative or solution-based tropes toward new models of practice? And could we allow ourselves to absorb extra-disciplinary media to begin to think through representation?[9]

9 The idea of thinking through representation is adapted from the title of a publication by the Institut für Kunstkritik in Frankfurt: *Thinking through Painting: Reflexivity and Agency Beyond the Canvas*.

Scanning Theory: Observations of a Traveling Photogrammeter

Jonathan Russell

June 10th: Seeing the Water

On a windswept beach in Southern Oregon, the intertidal zone is scattered with jutting, water-fractured boulders. Shot through with veins of quartz and sheared at dramatic angles, the rocks seem thrust from the earth, piercing the dark sand. Quietly and methodically, I pace circles around one such outcrop, spiraling closer and closer, never breaking contact. This is not some ritualistic dance but a process of recording and remembering. I leave the beach and within an hour a virtual twin boulder appears on my phone—a high-resolution, photo-textured 3D replica of the real thing. Miles down the road I re-encounter the object's replicated surface, examining the digital double in ways I never could a photo: spinning it around as if I held it in my hands, then zooming down to examine the intricate, weather-drawn details of its rocky surface. I download the model and save it to an online gallery, preserving it alongside other photoscans: a virtual cabinet of curiosities recording snippets of my travels. In June 2023 I visited the United States from Australia and gathered a trail of such digital doubles, experimenting with 3D photogrammetry as a medium for recording and interpreting place. In planning my cross-country trip I was guided by memories of architect, geographer and cultural landscape scholar Paul Groth, who spent a lifetime teaching and practicing the careful observation and analysis of 'ordinary' American environments. In lectures he would gently rail against his culture's blindness to the stories embedded in everyday place, observing that "Americans are like fish who can't see water."[1] My aim, while driving across the country from West to East, was to read the landscape with an open and curious mind, taking every lesson I could from the complex text I was immersed in. Throughout the trip I found myself drawn to 3D photogrammetry: it consistently provided new perspectives on ordinary objects, drawing my eye to settle in spots I might otherwise have passed over—helping me to see the water. Why was this? What makes a photoscan different from a photograph, and what new ways-of-seeing does it open up for the careful observer of everyday place?

1 Groth, "Frameworks for Cultural Landscape Study," *Understanding Ordinary Landscapes*, 15.

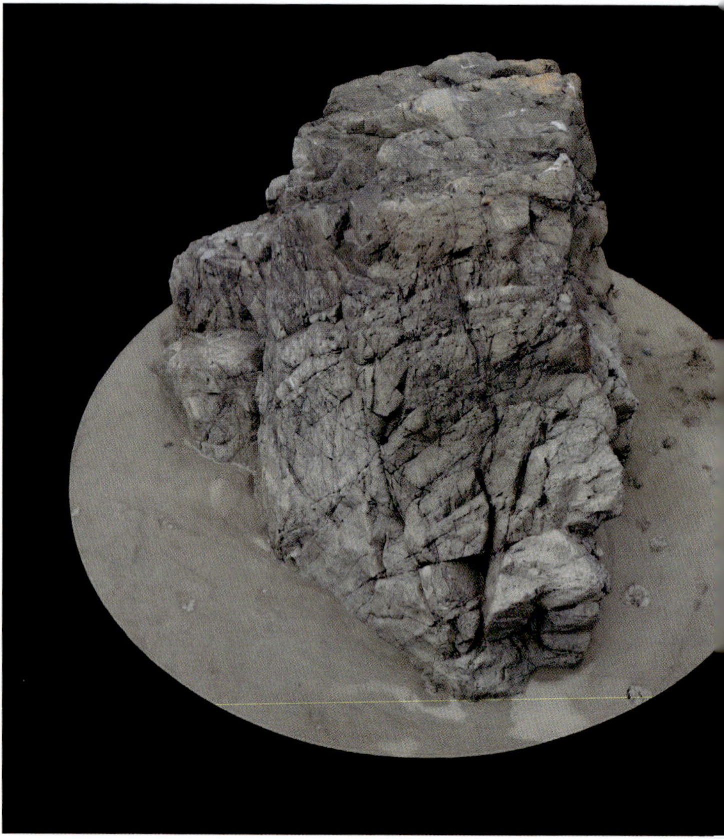

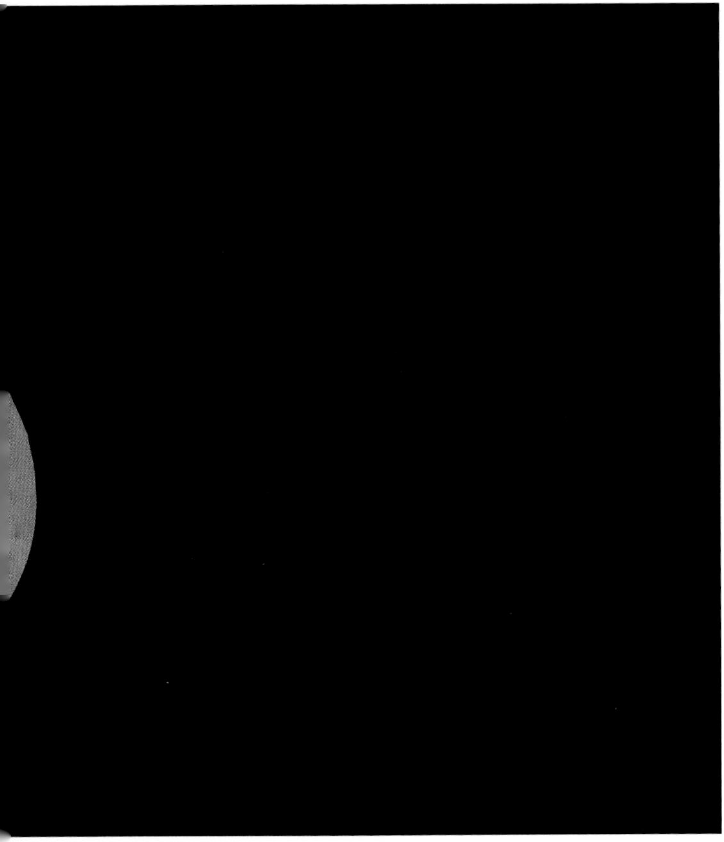

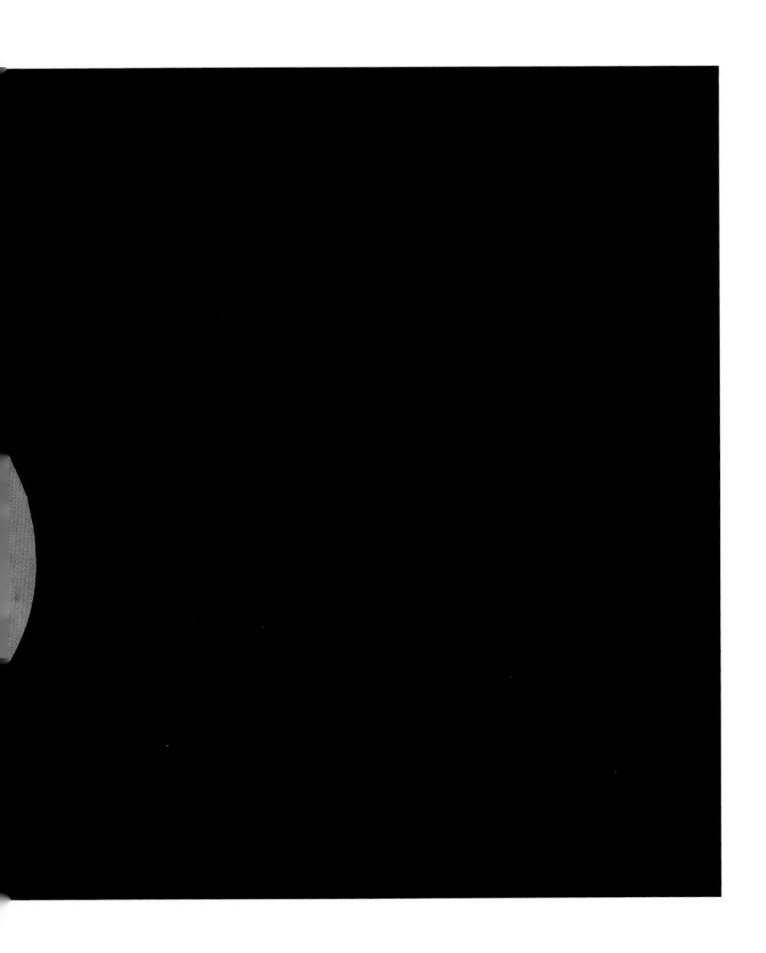

In considering photogrammetry as a technology distinct from photography, we must delve a little into its origins and development. Modern photogrammetry is concerned with the creation of the photoscan—a 3D representation of an object stitched together from 2D images. A crucial underlying algorithm is Structure from Motion (SfM), developed in the 1970s: Like the human brain constructs depth perception from the two flat perspectives of our eyes, SfM algorithms construct three-dimensional point clouds by the serial analysis of multiple images.[2] These point clouds can be rebuilt as the triangulated surface of a 3D model, with the source photos re-projected as textures to create a realistic virtual representation of a scanned object. Crucially, the applications of photogrammetry have grown since the 1970s with its increasing ease of use. Early academic applications were adapted for widespread use in movie visual effects during the late 1990s.[3] More recently, photoscans have become crucial to video game development, where real-world 3D objects are digitally duplicated, repackaged and sold as virtual assets—it is much faster to capture and launder the complexity of real-world objects into virtual space than to model that complexity from scratch.[4] Today, all-in-one cloud-based photogrammetry apps are freely available and easy to use, broadening the potential ranks of traveling photogrammeters: anyone with steady hands and a smartphone can capture a photoscan in minutes, with no special knowledge or expertise.[5] Given this growing ubiquity, there is a pressing need for a theory of photogrammetry. Photography is a well understood and deeply theorized medium, both

2 Ullman, "The Interpretation of Structure from Motion", *Proceedings of the Royal Society of London*, 405–426.
3 Failes, "Mission: Impossible II - a virtual production game-changer".
4 The Astronauts, "The Secrets of Witchfire Graphics".
5 Granshaw, "Editorial: Imaging Technology 1430 - 2015", *The Photogrammetric Record*, 255-260.

for tourists[6] and professional spatial practitioners,[7] but 3D photogrammetry has little such theoretical scaffolding—until recently it was a niche domain requiring specialized knowledge and equipment, and most of the academic literature still focuses on practical applications in preservation, archaeology, and related disciplines.[8] Through the lens of three photoscans captured in June 2023, this essay considers photogrammetry as a medium distinct from photography, and suggests two theoretical frameworks for understanding their difference. Walker Percy's idea of the preformed complex and Umberto Eco's theory of the open work are introduced as pathways toward a theory of how accessible, high quality photogrammetry might change the way we see and understand the everyday landscape.

June 17th: The Garden of Eden and the Preformed Complex

6 Urry and Larsen, *The Tourist Gaze 3.0*.
7 Davis, "Photography and Landscape Studies", *Landscape Journal 8*, 1–12.
8 Marín-Buzón, Pérez-Romero, López-Castro, Jerbania, and Manzano-Agugliaro, "Photogrammetry as a New Scientific Tool in Archaeology", *Sustainability*, 5319.
9 National Parks Service, "Arches NP Park Reports".

Outside the town of Moab in eastern Utah, a hundred-odd cars idle in the mid-June sun. The well-paved road off US Highway 191 carries a million and a half visitors each year past the toll booth and into Arches National Park.[9] Arches is an archetypal example of the twentieth century American national park—a well-choreographed confluence of natural beauty and civil engineering designed to enable mass-scale encounter with the sublime. Comfortable roads penetrate the landscape, guiding visitors along a plateau of towering red rock buttes, eroded sandstone canyons, and the park's eponymous weather-sculpted arches. Park literature welcomes

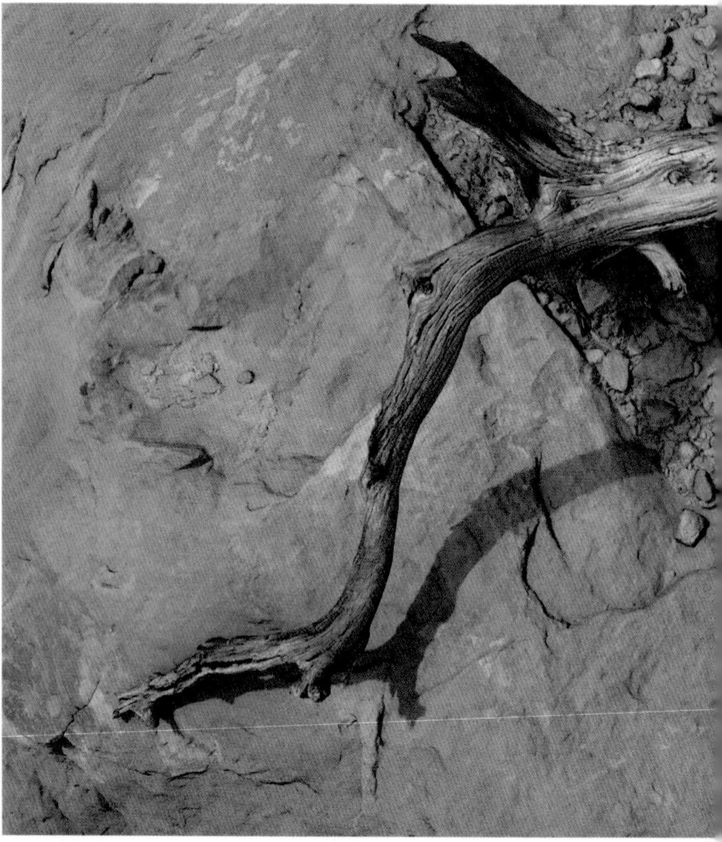

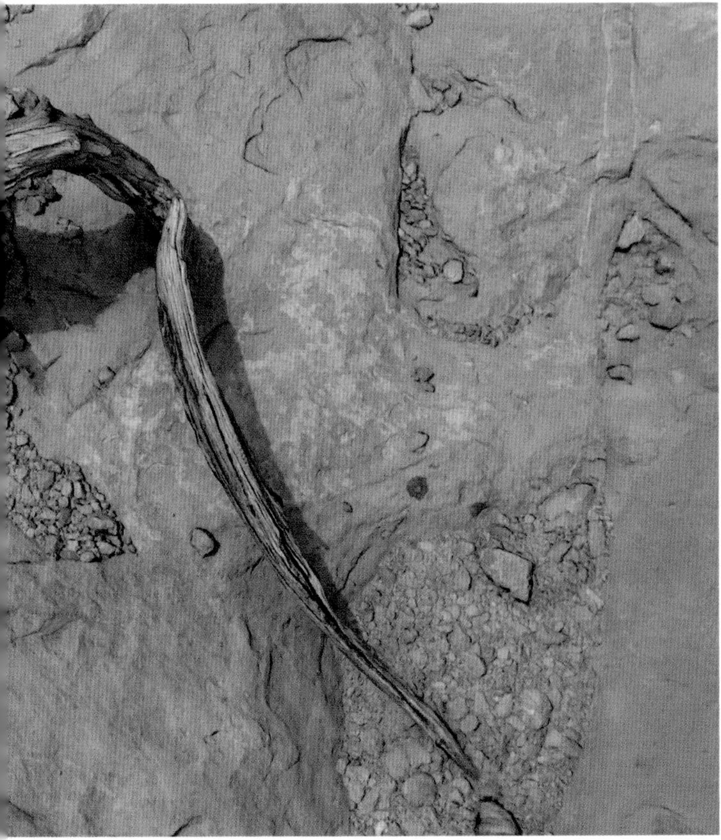

the "Auto Touring" visitor, who can cruise past dozens of attractions with names running the gamut between evocative biblical metaphor (Tower of Babel, Fiery Furnace) and more straightforward description (Double Arch, The Phallus).[10] In the parking lot at The Garden of Eden, I wander away from a cluster of fellow visitors and walk into the sandstone landscape. In a few minutes I am beyond earshot of the carpark, in a small desert wash dotted with low-lying brush and surrounded by towering ochre pillars. My eye catches on a gnarled and sun-bleached juniper branch, and I pull out my phone to start a new photoscan.

Seventy-odd years earlier and several hundred miles down the Colorado River, novelist and philosopher Walker Percy addressed the nexus of national parks, photography and mass tourism in his 1958 essay "The Loss of the Creature". Taking the example of the Grand Canyon, Percy suggests that most visitors never truly encounter the wonder of this landscape on its own terms. Instead, their experience of the Grand Canyon is mediated by what Percy terms the preformed complex—the shared cultural image of the Grand Canyon implanted in their minds long before they arrive. Percy writes that "the sightseer measures his satisfaction by the degree to which the canyon conforms to the preformed complex. If it does so, if it looks just like the postcard, he is pleased; he might even say, 'Why it is every bit as beautiful as a picture postcard!'"[11] Further, Percy suggests that the sightseer's instinct to capture a photo of their own further distances them from direct encounter: "At

10 National Parks Service, "Auto Touring."
11 Percy, "Loss of the Creature", *Forum*, 7.

the end of forty years of preformulation and with the Grand Canyon yawning at his feet, what does he do? He waives his right of seeing and knowing and records symbols for the next forty years."[12] Prefiguring Marshall McLuhan's famous observation that "the medium is the message,"[13] Percy argues that the traveler's way-of-seeing has become distorted and, ultimately, imprisoned by the camera. The subsequent decades have only underscored his insight that photographic mental regimes dramatically mediate our perspective on the world. The familiar lament that we are glued to our phones only part-way captures the situation: we can look away from the screen, but the smartphone's way-of-seeing stays with us. Metaphorically, we are all afflicted with photographer mindset, walking around with a camera lodged in our brain, its lens interposed between us and the world.

In Arches National Park the road chaperones lens-bound traveling photographers through a curated sequence of viewpoints, designed to ensure their experience coincides with the park's preformed complex. The photographer is directed towards vast panoramas and scenic viewpoints, but these are of less interest to the photogrammeter, who is viewing the landscape through a different technological lens. This is not to suggest that the photogrammeter comes closer to Percy's ideal state of direct encounter with place. Instead, the photogrammeter has an opportunity to circumvent the preformed complex because their technological lens points them in a different direction: to capture a good photoscan, the

12 Percy, "Loss of the Creature", *Forum*, 7.
13 McLuhan, "The Medium is the Message", *Forum*, 19–24.

photogrammeter must orbit around their subject, capturing it from all angles. The photogrammeter seeks objects, not perspectives, and in doing so has a chance to see the landscape differently than the traveling photographer.

In the Garden of Eden, a dead juniper branch has come to rest in the desert wash where I stand. About three feet long, it touches the earth in four places—its bounding, craggy topology echoing the rocks around it. My photoscan captures its tone: sun-bleached on one side and dust-stained on the other. Coarse pebbles have collected in a hollow underneath, evidence of the torrential rains that sometimes scour this landscape, and which probably dislodged the gnarled timber and brought it to rest here. The photogrammeter's lens has directed my attention away from the preformed complex of panoramic viewpoints and towards a smaller, quieter, more granular appreciation of the forces and processes that created both this branch and the towering sandstone stacks around it. The traveling photogrammeter has, at least for a moment, displaced the preformed complex and encounters the landscape anew.

June 23rd: The Parking Meter and the Open Work

Founded in 1825 at the summit of the Ohio & Erie Canal, the history of Akron, Ohio parallels that of American transport infrastructure. The construction of large water-powered mills here made the city a key center for processing and transshipment of grain.[14] When the canal's shipping function was superseded by rail and then road transport, Akron's identity was transformed—water from canals was turned to industrial use in rubber vulcanization, and the city began to promote itself as "The Rubber Capital of the World," a key cog in the Midwestern industrial network that motorized America.[15]

Arriving in downtown Akron in late June, I turn off Mill Street and park behind the old Quaker Oats factory, which parallels the railway and lies within a quarter-mile of the Innerbelt highway and the old Ohio & Erie. The mill operated here from 1884 to 1970 before being converted to a retail and entertainment complex, with the site's towering silos repurposed as hotel rooms.[16] Today the building is mostly unused and the small parking lot is empty on a Monday afternoon. Stepping out of my rental car, my eyes settle on a row of yellow painted double-head parking meters lining the curb. I scrounge for quarters in my center console, feed the meter, and pull out my phone to capture a photoscan.

Months later, while reviewing the scan, I tumble into the complex history of this object. Zooming into the front face I spot a small blue plaque identifying this as a "Model N" parking meter from POM Incorporated of Russellville, Arkansas. POM, formerly known as Park-O-Meter, traces its history to the invention of the parking meter in 1935, and has been manufacturing in Russellville since 1964.[17] If Akron, Ohio was the Rubber Capital of the World and

14 Cirtwill, "After Industry," *Midstory*.
15 Cirtwill.
16 Ohio History Connection, "Quaker Oats Company Plant".
17 Miller, "Park-O-Meter", *Encyclopedia of Arkansas*.

Scanning Theory

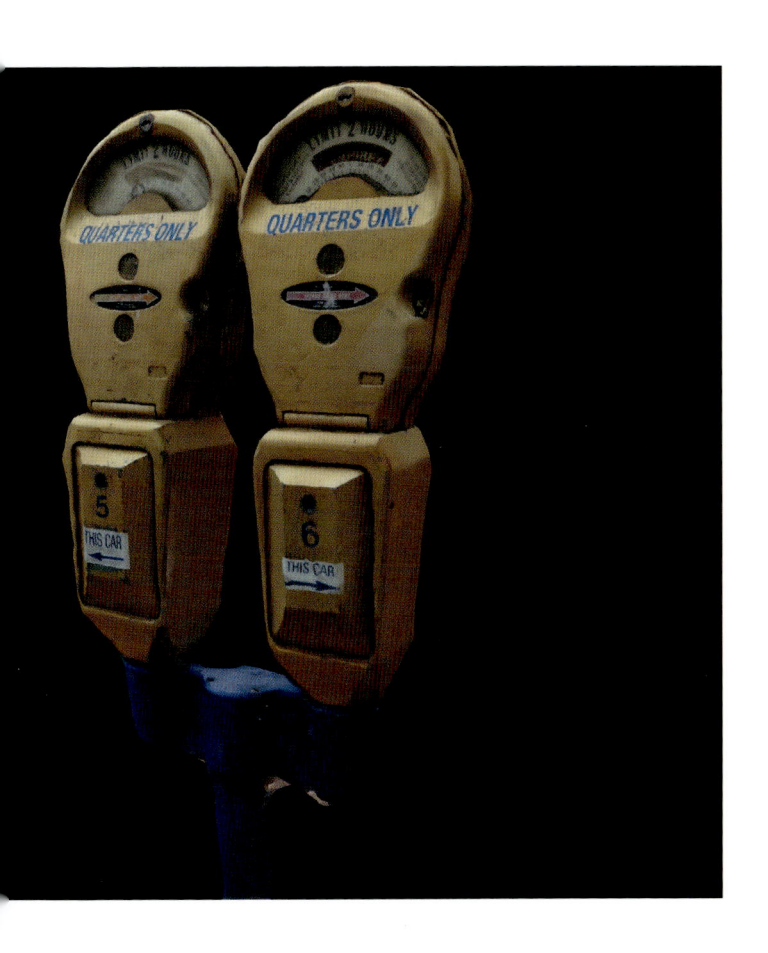

Toledo was the Glass Capital, perhaps Russellville was the Parking Meter Capital: a site of the kind of industrial specialization that was common in 20th century American manufacturing.[18] But the history of an object cannot be reduced to its model number or place of origin. This parking meter is a specific object in a specific place with a specific history. The bright yellow paint on its surface is scratched and pitted, sometimes exposing the raw metal beneath. The meter attendant's key has worn away a circle around the coin vault keyhole, and on the right hand side of the machine the quarter slot is rubbed to a shine by unknown thousands of coins. The photoscan captures the passage of time: the marks, knicks and wear patterns that identify it as unique and emplaced, a commodity object transformed by its environment. This is the beauty of studying the everyday landscape—history at all scales is embedded in the world around us, waiting to be uncovered if we take the time to look closely.

How does a photoscan compare to a photograph as a tool for closely reading an object's embedded history? Without doubt the two technologies are complementary, but it is worth considering the particular value of the emerging, less well-understood medium. A useful theoretical perspective is Umberto Eco's concept of an open work. Writing about visual art in the 1960s, Eco distinguished between art whose meaning is intentionally singular and fixed by the artist, setting it against the open work that deliberately invites a multiplicity of interpretations. Eco refers to a "field of open possibilities" in which "the

[18] Price and Wang, "Explaining an Industry Cluster," *Economic Brief*.

viewer can (indeed, must) choose his own points of view, his own connections, his own directions... ."[19] The photograph and the photoscan, when set against each other, show this distinction in a very literal way: the photographer looks through their lens and chooses a single perspective to represent the object on the other side. In contrast, the photogrammeter records a field of images, a 3D cloud of information that is re-assembled into a more detailed and complex record of the object than any single photo can contain.

The complexity of a photoscan when compared to a photograph is intrinsic to the medium: a photoscan is always three-dimensional, always interactive and always multi-scalar. While a single photo certainly can be semiotically open, the viewer's agency is always constrained by the photographer's choice of scale, perspective and framing. By contrast, in re-encountering a photoscan we are presented with a 3D object that requires interaction and hence requires us to take agency in its interpretation. The object can be rotated, enlarged, turned over, and examined from any number of perspectives. The viewer has agency over the artwork, which invites them to look closely and draw out new meanings from it—including meanings never considered by the photogrammeter at the time of capture. The traveling photogrammeter captures a complex and intrinsically open record of an object, and this multiplicity allows the viewer to interpret and recontextualise the underlying object more readily than the viewer of a photo.

[19] Eco, *The Open Work*, 86.

The oceanside boulder in Oregon, the juniper branch in Utah, and the parking meter in Ohio all point towards the potential of photogrammetry as a medium for seeing, recording, and understanding place differently. My experience looking through the photogrammeter's lens gave me space to step aside from the preformed complex, viewing my surroundings with fresher eyes. After the fact, the intrinsic complexity of the photoscans I collected gave me a more nuanced understanding of these objects than would be possible from a single photograph. The technological frontier of photogrammetry continues to advance, and we might expect to see its use expand in the near future.[20] It is not, of course, a universally applicable medium: photogrammetry works best on singular objects, and often misses context that a photograph might capture. For now, a photoscan also cannot capture sound, action, and atmosphere like video can. Nonetheless, for the thoughtful observer of cultural landscapes, photogrammetry can be a powerful tool with particular potential for architects, geographers, and other spatial practitioners. An architect's eye, freed from the photograph's fixed perspective, can better interrogate the complexity and nuance captured in a photoscan. A geographer can assemble in minutes a multi-scalar and inherently spatial record of place that can be revisited and interrogated much more readily than a single photo. Our disciplines call on us to engage with place deeply and seriously. Photogrammetry can help displace us from ingrained habits of seeing and thinking, prompting us to understand our surroundings anew. With the right tools and the right frame of mind, we

20 Vilariño, Tran, Nores, Frías, and Khoshelham, "3D Mapping of Indoor and Outdoor Environments using Apple Smart Devices", *International Archives of the Photogrammetry Remote Sensing and Spatial Information Sciences.*

can strive to re-encounter place with an open mind and, if it catches the light just right, to see the water we all swim in.

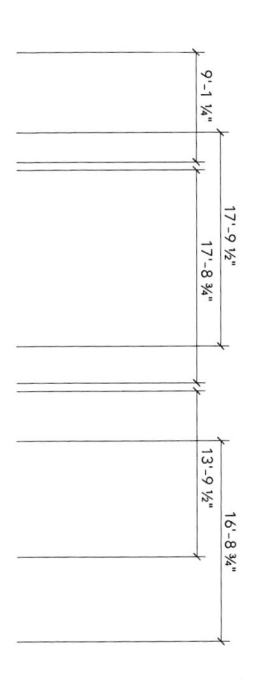

Subtractive Nature

Andy Kim

I have a camera, a Cyber-shot, for amateurs—essentially a point-and-shoot. All I had to do was to make up my mind about where to point it. I began taking pictures of "green spaces" in my neighborhood (between Crown Heights, Prospect Heights, and Park Slope). Some were part of building setbacks, some part of a building's language: framed as planters, unpaved plots, and well-maintained linear grass patches, lush and beautiful in the most conservative way. What was eventually illuminated to me was the precarious existence of urban green space that expresses an arbitrary architectonic relationship with the built urban fabric. They are confusing, and their existence is vague, unstable, unpredictable because these spaces are absent in our urban vocabulary. They are leftover spaces from building footprints, and their size is determined by ready-made zoning. Bureaucratically, there are only two types of private spaces in our city: spaces for buildings and spaces for not-buildings, one with a clear gestalt and one without. And unlike public park spaces, the latter aren't given a clear figure because what "counts" from the point of view of city planning is the footprint of buildings and not "not-buildings," which in the context of Brooklyn are "urban green spaces." Symptomatically, urban green spaces exist as subtractions, as leftover area from lot lines, carved out from building footprints, set back from their envelopes. Urban green spaces, from their very conceptual origin, exist in complete subordination to buildings as negativity.

The images collected here point without pointing—to the historical opacity of "not-buildings" in the city, our positionality to them, and how we have come to collectively imagine these spaces as "less-than-buildings." These images explore the imaginative space of not-buildings as formalized contradictions, as the physiognomy of urban green spaces, as subtractive nature—not as monolith but as many.

glass curtain wall, bench, dark stone, expensive, representation, drawing, model, material, modern, paving, systems, fescue grass (*fescues*), aesthetic, grid, pattern, hatch, abstraction, esoteric, autonomy, richard mier on prospect park, rental at $62 per square foot, rational, texture, plaza st e, prospect heights

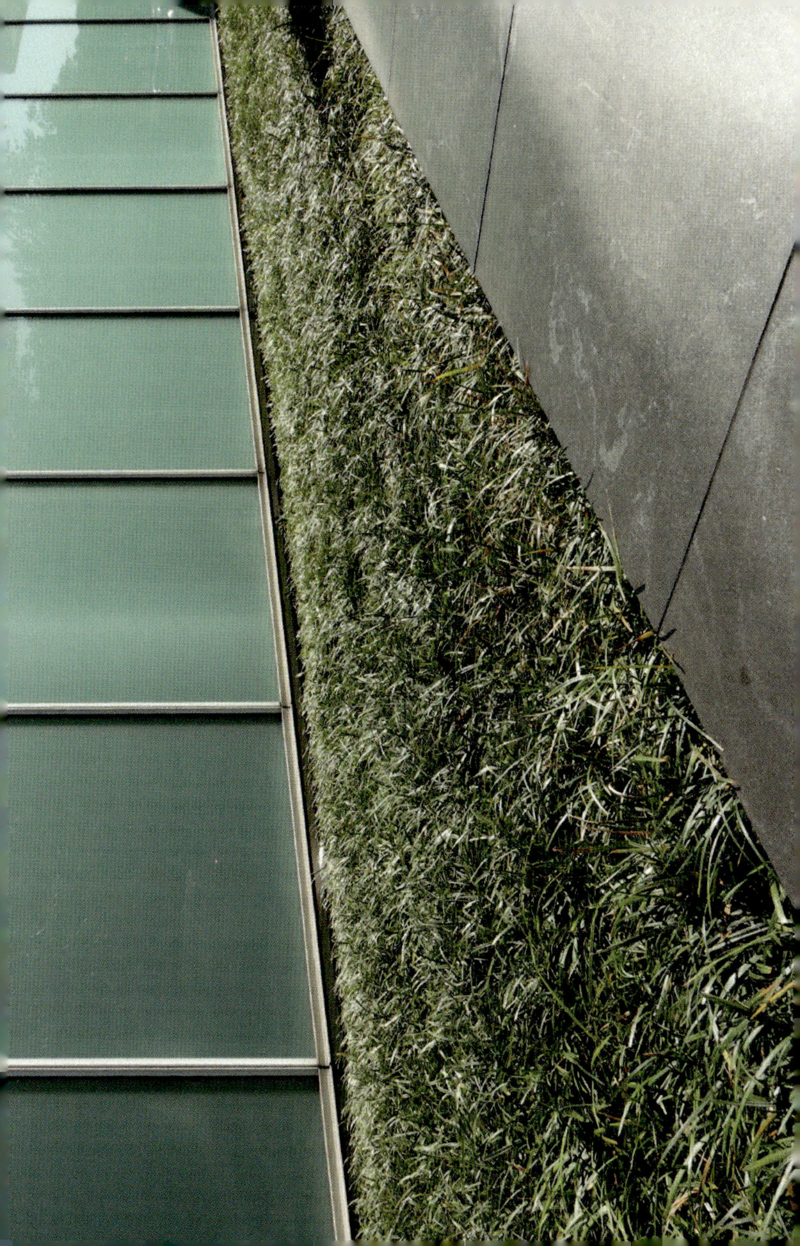

cmu, ryegrass (*lolium*), setback, american, gutter, vacant space, lack, cement, dandelion (*taraxacum*), generic, normal, pervasive, rental at $32 per square foot, default, st johns pl, prospect heights

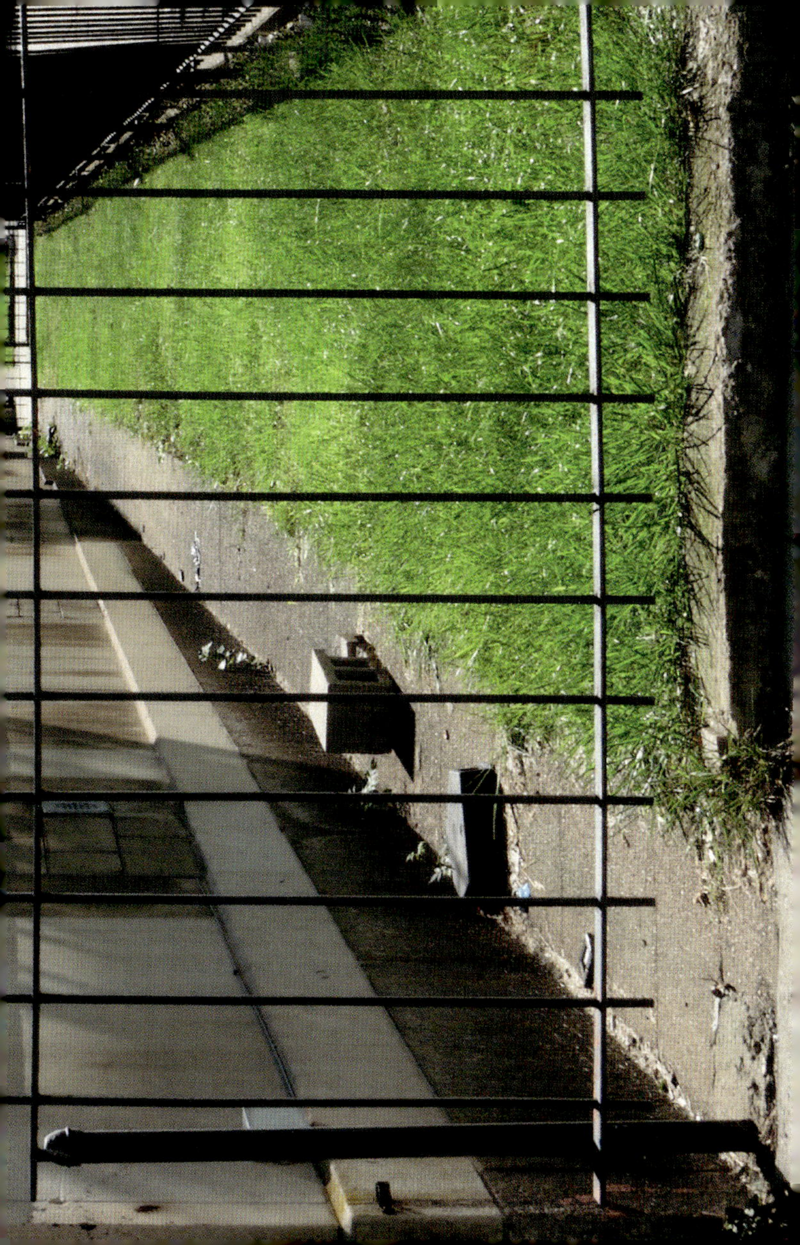

masonry, fence, lush, ecology, biodiversity, wealth, accumulation, birch (*betula*), cosmos (*asteraceae*), ivy (hedera), japanese forest grass (*hakonechloa macra*), coleus (*coleus*), japanese andromeda (*pieris japonica*), touch-me-not (*impatiens*), frost grass (*spodiopogon sibiricus*), plum yew (*cephalotaxus harringtonii*), rental at $49 per square foot, berkeley pl, prospect heights

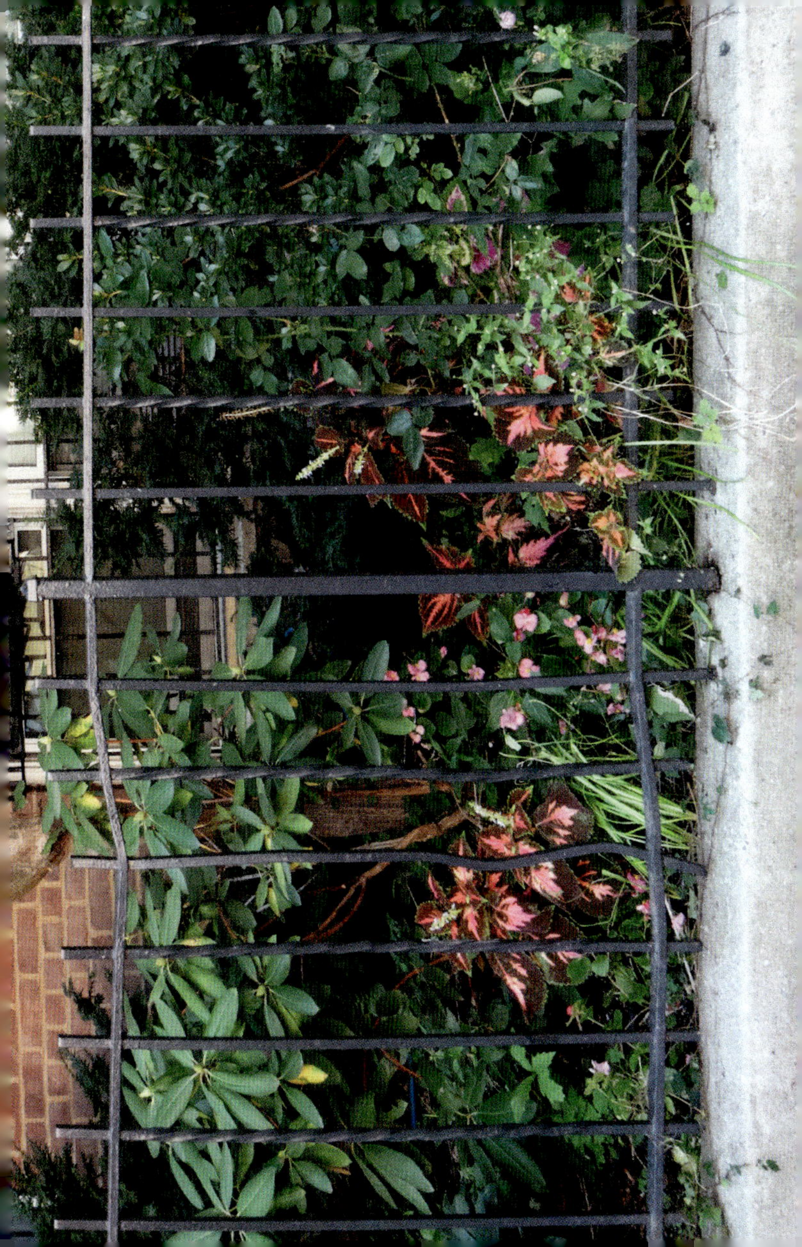

topiary, sculptural, english, picturesque, boxwood (*buxus*), ryegrass (*lolium*), generic, normal, pervasive, default, rental at $30 per square foot, st johns pl, crown heights

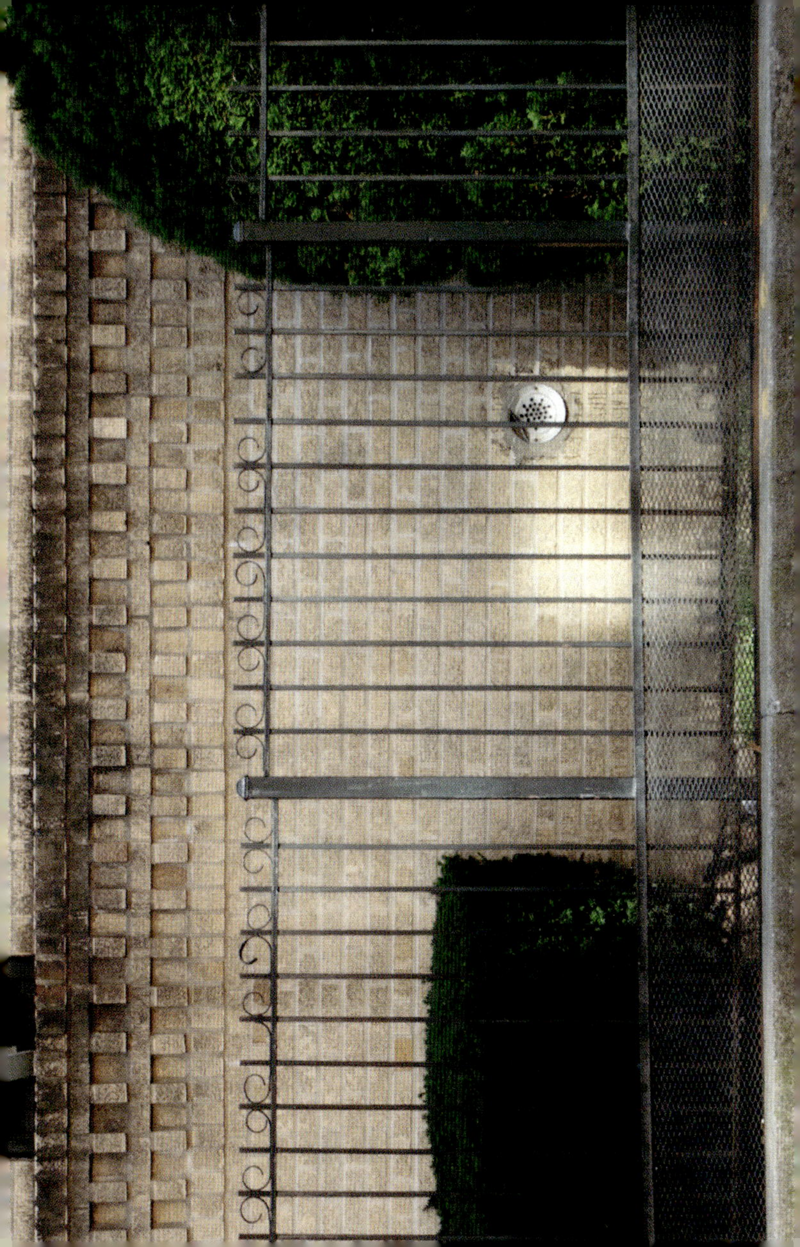

scaffold, orange on mesh, fence, lush, ecology, biodiversity, wealth, accumulation, green painted plywood, birch (*betula*), japanese andromeda (*pieris japonica*), hydrangea (*hydrangea*), low sumac (*rhus aromatica*), japanese maple (*acer palmatum*), co-op, rental at $32 per square foot, plaza st w, park slope

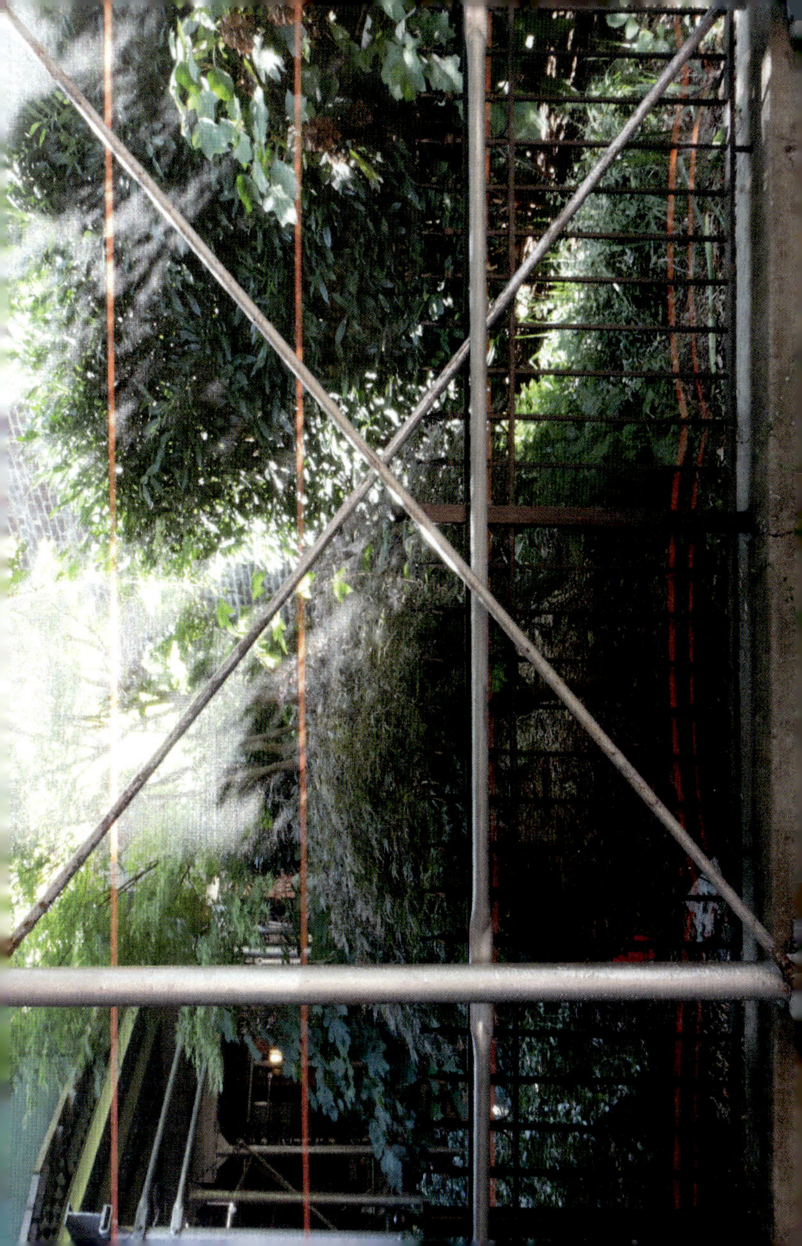

rose guy savoy (*delstrimen*), boxwood (*buxus*), yellow woodsorrel (*oxalis stricta*), black medic (*medicago lupulina*), clearweed (*pilea pumila*), green painted plywood, streetlight (?), under construction, flatbush ave, park slope

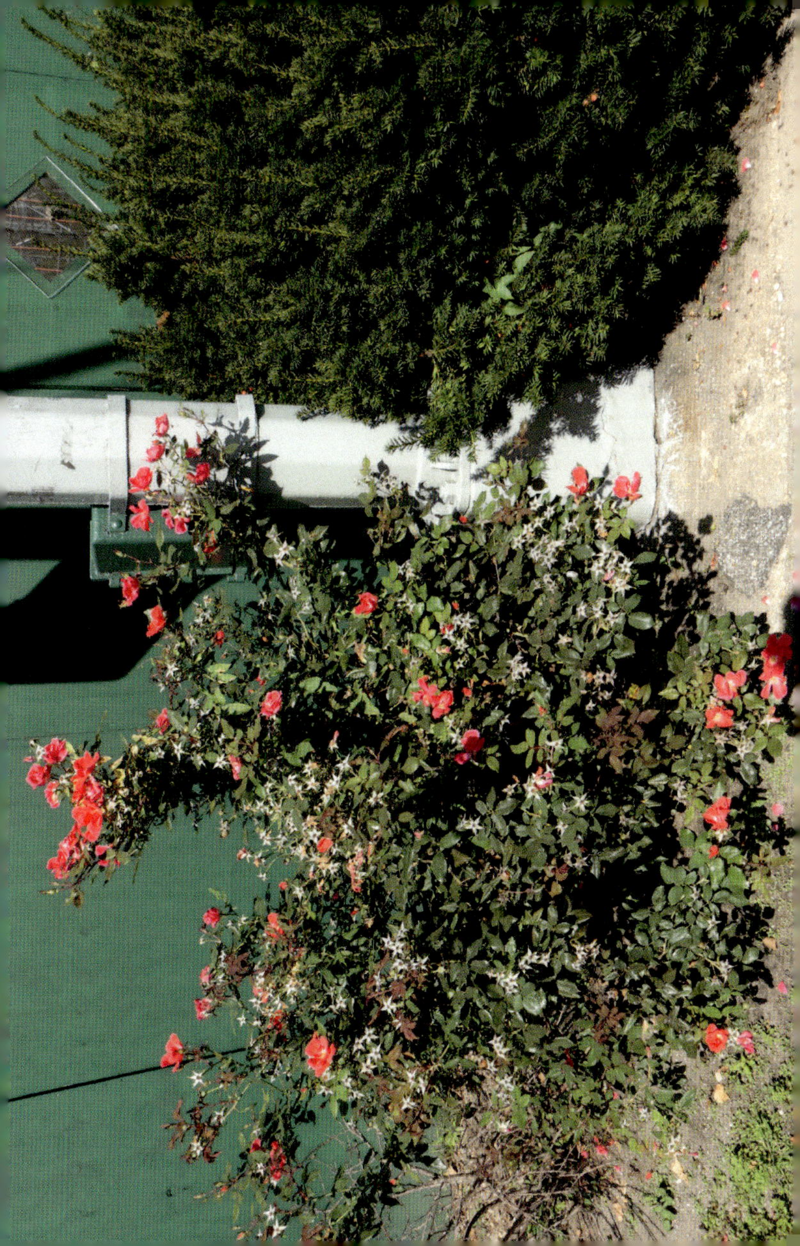

The Poiesis of Miesian Corners

Pavan Vadgama

I am not working on architecture, I am working on architecture as a language, and I think you have to have a grammar in order to have a language. ... If you are good at that, you speak a wonderful prose, and if you are really good, you can be a poet. ... I think it is the same in architecture. If you have to construct something, you can make a garage out of it or you can make a cathedral out of it. We use the same means, the same structural methods for all these things. ... What I am driving at is to develop a common language, not particularly individual ideas.

> Ludwig Mies van der Rohe in lecture
> "Architecture as Language"
> Chicago, 1956

When Mies van der Rohe professes, "I am not working on architecture, I am working on architecture as a language,"[1] he repeats a troped analogy that has persisted since Horace's classical simile *"Ut pictura poesis"*—as is painting, so is poetry.[2] Architecture most fundamentally parallels language through its expression of tectonic vocabulary and grammar. Carrying the mission of modernist liberation, Mies equates architecture to language as it verbalizes Cartesian reason, producing a rational architecture that would inform the creation of modern man. He declares that "good" architects must be "poets," not only deriving their compositions from a universal grammar of structural methods, but recapitulating these standards to generate new, evocative forms.[3]

In Mies's own work, this linguistic negotiation between architectural morphemes occurs most conspicuously at the corners. There, Mies is able to test the veracity of his constructed language, playing with the structural logic of materials, joints, load path convergences, and proportional relationships. Simultaneously, the corner is an aestheticized space: a repository for details, where duality is the essential technique to propel a divergence from the past. Drawing from Schinkel, Mies's corners allow for dual perspectives that hinge frontal to oblique, modern to classical, exclusion to inclusion, and structural disclosure to aesthetic concealment. The following corners from Mies's built anthology can be read as eloquent pivots. Synthesizing semiotic construction and poetic essentialism, these corners perform a dual poiesis: one that materially reconfigures

1 Mies van der Rohe & Puente, *Conversations with Mies van der Rohe*, 56-57.
2 Wagner, "Silent Spaces" in *Meaningful Absence across Arts and Media*, 218.
3 Mies van der Rohe & Puente, 56.

inherited principles of construction, and one that envisions a new form of modernity.

Mies's novel corner tectonics were first inscribed in the iconic Brick Country House (*Landhaus aus Backstein*) drawings for the annual Great Berlin Art Exhibition of 1924. The exhibition showcased a perspective and a plan, which outlined generative grammatical rules for his architectural language. The perspective speaks to a multidirectional flow of space, with walls of varying heights, blocks for fireplaces, flat roofs with clean edges, and vertical glass expanses between fields—an unprecedented formal expression at the dawn of modernism. As uncovered by art historian Wolf Tegethoff, the perspective was produced separate from the plan and could not be directly derived from it orthographically.[4] A fruitful misalignment seeking to reconcile compositional dynamism, the plan depicts freestanding walls with L- and T-shaped corners evolving from the "grammar of the steel section."[5] The structuring of these parenthetical, letter-shaped corners dismantles the traditional arrangement of linearly-connected enfilade rooms in favor of a "neoplastic field."[6] The dissolution of the conventional bi-directional public-to-private flow breaks the legibility of normative social functioning within domestic spaces.[7] Architectural historian Jean-Louis Cohen suggests that Mies's own personal estrangement from his wife, Ada Bruhn, and their two children at this time likely further sensitized him to fundamentally reconfigure spaces for domestic life.[8] A radicalizing pivot, the corner blurs graphemic boundaries between delineated zones

[4] Wolf Tegethoff has speculated that these drawings were not produced concurrently, and that the perspective was produced much earlier than the plan. Tegethoff, van der Rohe, & Dyckes, *Mies van der Rohe*, 37-41.

[5] Mies van der Rohe, Lambert, & Oechslin, *Mies In America*, 195.

[6] Reiser & Umemoto, *Atlas of Novel Tectonics*, 29.

[7] "In the ground plan of this house, I have abandoned the usual concept of enclosed rooms and striven for a series of spatial effects rather than a row of individual rooms. The wall loses its enclosing character and serves only to articulate the house organism." From Neumeyer, *The Artless Word*, 250.

[8] Cohen & Mies van der Rohe, *Mies van der Rohe*, 2nd and updated ed., 176.

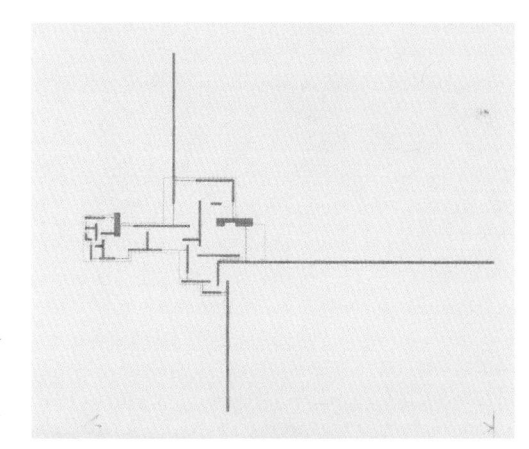

Figure 1.
Landhaus aus Backstein, Foto 2: Reproabzug, Entwurf Grundriss, 1923./ Akademie der Künste.

Figure 2.
Landhaus aus Backstein, Foto 1b: Reproabzug, Exterior Perspektive Brick Country House, 1923, Hall No. 1./ Akademie der Künste.

9 Tigerman, "Mies van der Rohe," *Perspecta* 22: 130

of interior–exterior and service–served, which were clearly legible in his antecedent Potsdamer villas. Through "the breakup of the box" into constituent character types, his corner is troped to its systematicity.[9] The Brick Country House's dissolute corner foreshadows a modernizing language of two-dimensional, planar materials, isolated with gaps at their edges.

While the corners structure an emancipatory modern language, it is no secret that Mies's tectonics hinge on the aesthetic principles and techniques of Karl Friedrich Schinkel (whom he calls the "greatest classicist we had").[10] The interior corners of Schinkel's Altes Museum's vestibule find linguistic mimesis in Mies's drawings. The vestibular corners of the museum shape a transitional, fluid space between the symmetrical colonnade and internal entry rotunda. Aligned with the Lustgarten and Berliner Schloss, the stoa-colonnade's axial frontality is contrasted internally by the oblique path along the staircases to the Pantheon-like rotunda.

10 "Ludwig Mies van der Rohe," in *Mies van der Rohe*, ed. Jean-Louis Cohen, 8.

Articulating an experiential transition from the rectilinear path, Schinkel sought to bring "enjoyment (*Genuß*) and recognition (*Erkenntnis*) of art" to visitors by hinging Roman frontality to Greek obliquity within the museum.[11] By shifting the approach to a forty-five-degree oblique along stairways toward the interior corner, one is forced to wander away from the central axis, around the corner, and into a visual connection with the adjacent riverbank (fig. 3). Like in the Brick Country House, the bracketing and shifting directionality of flow around such corners recalls Schinkel's Romanticist figure, "questing toward new vistas" of enlightenment in their aimless meander away from old society.[12] Mies similarly adopts duality into his vocabulary, contrasting modern with troped classical forms to increase legibility and underscore the novelty of his constructions.

11 Moyano, "Quality vs. History," *Art Bulletin 72*, 600.
12 Ott, "Schinkel and Berlin" in *German Façade Design*, 137.

Figure 3 (left). Altes Museum Berlin, view to the staircase./ Photograph by author, 2024.

Figure 4 (right). Karl Friedrich Schinkel. Altes Museum Berlin: Blick auf das Treppenhaus, 1852./ Staatliche Museen zu Berlin, Kupferstichkabinett

Afrikanische Straße Housing Estate

Mies's subsequent design for the Afrikanische Straße housing estate of Berlin-Wedding is his first formal execution of a corner that seeks to engage as an interlocutor in modernizing dialogues. These four austere residential blocks were constructed between 1925 and 1927, and were his only instance of low-cost public housing. Devoid of any ornamentation greater than a single running course of bricks, the inverted corners at the end of each block became his sole socializing device for modern living. Commissioned by the non-profit social housing association Primus,[13] Mies faced the challenge of designing within the serious economic constraints of the newly-founded Weimar Republic.[14]

Within these limitations, Mies employed poetic syntax to radically depart from the dense, unventilated five-story tenement houses that then dominated Berlin's landscape. His proposal rejected the mandated building line (*Fluchtlinie*) of Hobrecht's Berlin for shifting, setback building volumes.[15] In plan, the series of building volumes create a U-shape, opening to green courtyards at the rear, deviating from the street, and creating front gardens—spatial methods typically reserved for the bourgeois Berliner blocks. With truncated members, not completing the U-form, the volumes shift backward and forward to leave "negative corners," a term conceptualized by architect and author Carsten Krohn.[16] The project's design language resonated with the principles set forth by other Berliner architects influential to Mies,

13 Müller, *Die Friedrich Ebert Siedlung in Berlin Wedding*, 170.
14 Longerich, *Deutschland 1918-1933*, 145.
15 The Fluchtlinie mandates building along the property line towards the street edge. See: Geist & Kürvers, "Hobrecht Plan" in *Das Berliner Mietshaus*, 425.
16 Krohn, *Mies van der Rohe*, 50.

Figure 5.
Häuser Afrikanische Str., Berlin-Wedding, Außenansicht, 1968./ Akademie der Künste.

like Paul Mebes, whose work with the Civil Servants' Housing Collective on Fritschweg turned interior corners into communal green spaces. However, Mies's application of his architectural grammar in the Afrikanische Straße project is unique in that it does not abide with plot boundaries like these earlier models, but instead rebels against them, inverting what would typically form exterior corners and resisting full utilization of the plot as stipulated by Berliner building code. Through the corner, Mies is able to transcend the existing spatial norms of the codified tenement block, and formulate a distinctly modern social, as well as spatial, arrangement.

Staggering in a way that undermines its load-path dynamics, the Afrikanische Straße's inverted corners are not structurally reinforcing, but sharp-angled edges marked by high stress concentrations. As such, they serve solely as an aesthetic gap for the placement of poplar trees as architectural punctuation. The inverted corners of the U, each connected by a single curved balcony, which reads as a formal "hinge," manifest Mies's argument for social space and access to nature as fundamental parts of modern architecture.

Figures 5 and 6, captured by architectural photographer Reinhard Friedrich in 1968, reveal an emphasis on the relationship between structure and experience around corners through a Schinkelian perspective play. The first image, with the tree breaking into the frame, highlights both the frontality of the block and the compositional play with building elements. The second, an oblique perspective of the corner, positions itself against the frontal perspective by highlighting the space for poplar trees in the center and their multiplying beyond the frame. Mies's employment of nature as an architectonic element in conversation with the corner proposes a new nature-inclusive modernism that informs the nature–culture dichotomy within the branches of International Style modernism.

Haus Lemke

Continuing to explore the pivotal power of the open U-typology, Mies developed a series of courtyard houses from 1930 to 1932—his last housing designs in Europe. Haus Lemke, the only built project, is characterized by its extruded L-shaped plan. Perhaps alluding to a courtyard, though not truly enclosed, the form is that of an inhabitable corner which separates and brackets the external natural environment and the organized internal living space. The site, located in the originally bourgeois villa quarter of Hohenschönhausen in the east of Berlin, gently slopes down to an artificial lake. Constructed nature is here employed as a visual foil, providing an external contrast to an anthropocentric modern society. Through the structuring of spatial corners for reflection and dwelling, Mies's vocabulary mirrors and integrates artificial nature into his vision of modernity.

Figure 6.
Häuser Afrikanische Str., Berlin-Wedding, Außenansicht, 1968./ Akademie der Künste.

Figure 7.
Haus Lemke./ Photographs by author, 2018.

Mies incorporates a single, punctual tree at the inner corner, where it is reflected into the house against the glass wall dividing the smaller internal patio-living room, inverting its exteriority against the L that brackets it. In this moment, Mies repeats the sweeping planes of the Brick Country House by placing the glass flush to the outside of the thin brick walls. This gesticulation minimizes the creation of shadow lines caused by roof overhangs or window frames, and produces an artificial flatness that turns the building into a backdrop (*Kulisse*) reminiscent of Schinkel in its originating an aesthetic mission from the corner. From the interior, the view is merged with the wall plane, and the windows selectively frame the landscape, producing picturesque vignettes rather than a seamless connection to the outdoors. This reflection of the landscape within the structure extends Mies's poietic language, hinging anthropocentric interiority and "natural" exteriority to produce a novel modernity.[17]

The modest internal corner of Haus Lemke's L anticipates midcentury modern domesticity. Reflective on one side and opaque on the other, the corners implicate Mies's personal connection to Lilly Reich as he draws influence from Reich's own L-shaped house, the Ground-Floor House, which they developed collaboratively for "The Dwelling of our Time," an exhibit for the German Building Exposition in 1931.[18] Reich's compact L-shaped house connected to Mies's expo pavilion, room-width, floor-to-ceiling glass

17 Krohn, *Mies van der Rohe*, 101.
18 Cohen & Mies, *Mies van der Rohe, 2nd and updated ed.*, 88.

Figure 8.
Haus Lemke./ Photographs by author, 2018.

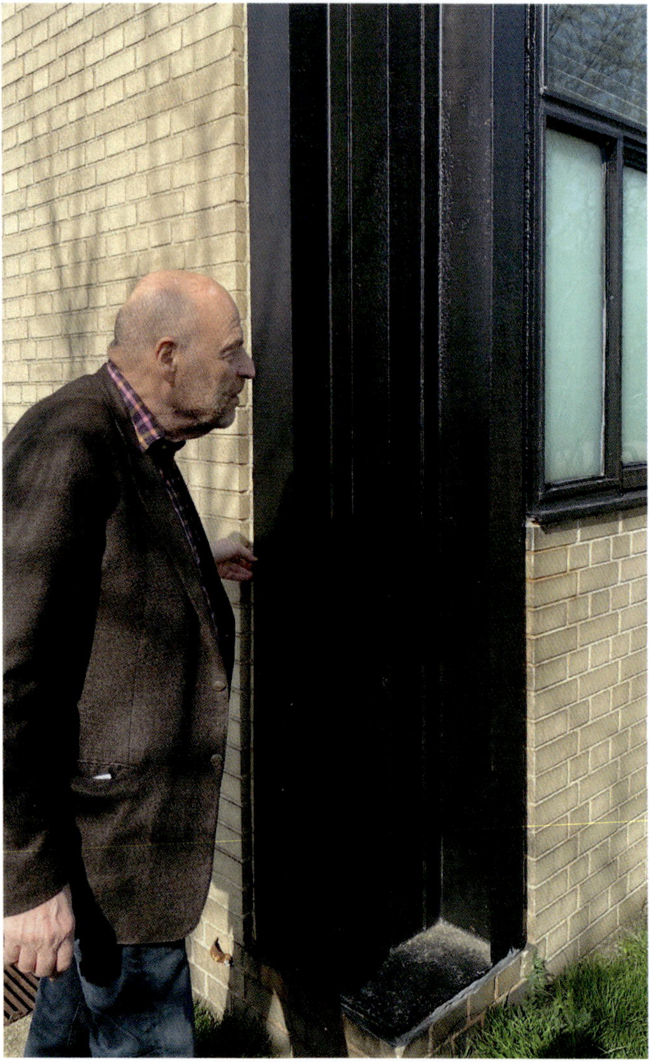

planes are employed in the primary living spaces, each bracketed by a separate L of service and sleeping spaces. The nested L corners of these spaces, legible in the plan, create a sequential arrangement of spaces which fold exteriority into and against the structure. In Haus Lemke, completed simultaneously to Reich's pavilion but only attributed to Mies, perimeter walls extend outward from these corners seeking their own interlocutor. These corners—though detailed as simple English bonds—are intricately woven, both mastering nature and imbricating it into the man-made structure as an integral part of modernizing architecture.

Illinois Institute of Technology

Exiled from the Bauhaus-Dessau, Germany, to Chicago in 1938, Mies's language had to translate in its transatlantic displacement. Expressed through his treatment of corners at the Illinois Institute of Technology (IIT), Mies called upon novel materials to expand his European "international" language into an American global one. Mies collaborated extensively with Ludwig Hilberseimer on the site plan for the new IIT campus in 1956, organizing twenty buildings in various typologies. The corners of the IIT impart structural gravitas in line with his established grammar, yet they are simultaneously repositories of detail, setting the stage for American steel over European brick. Jean-Louis Cohen posits that the industrial Zeche Zollverein in Essen, built by Fritz Schupp and Martin Kremmer in 1932, influenced much of Mies's design of IIT, as he employed

Figure 9. Jean-Louis Cohen at the corner of the Alumni Building, IIT, Chicago./ Photograph by author, 2023.

similar welded steel porticos and steel-girdered walls enclosing brick and glass partitions.[19]

However, Mies introduced an even more rigorous construction technique at the IIT by blending layers of legibility around the I- and H-beams sitting at each corner across the campus. Former MoMA chief curator and architect Terence Riley draws parallels between these corners and those of Mies's earlier, Schinkel-influenced Haus Urbig in Potsdam-Neubabelsberg from 1917, where two plaster exterior columns are offset at the corner to hint at the brick structure behind.[20] In the same language, Mies introduced a vertical channel by cutting out the corner of the building's planar façade where brick would have met brick, as can be clearly read from the Alumni Memorial Hall from 1946 (fig. 9). Within this gap, a protruding secondary "positive corner" of a steel L-profile speaks of an inner I-profile frame. This hint highlights the materially divergent load-bearing structure, expanding beyond the structural quality of the brick as it restricts it to two dimensions. The provocative hinging of brick facade to steel structure, legible through juxtaposition and dissolution, reveals the Schinkelian mission of instruction and clarity within Mies's approach. The base plate at the bottom acts as a plinth, dramatically laying the foundations for a radical turn to a future of modernizing steel over the common brick of his past.

The composition of IIT's corners recalls Schinkel's articulation of "pure statics" through aestheticized corners.[21] On the façade of the Altes Museum, the

19 Cohen & Mies, *Mies van der Rohe*, 2nd and updated ed., 104.
20 Riley, "Mies van der Rohe und das Museum of Modern Art" in *Mies in Berlin*, 20.
21 Moyano, *Quality vs. History*, 594.

stucco coating the corners is demarcated into a rusticated plinth, oversized columns, and a connecting architrave (figs. 10 & 11). The aestheticization of the museum façade symbolizes a particular tectonic grammar, veiling its brick materiality to heighten the perception of structural integrity, clarity, and order. Monumental corners frame the structure and

Figure 10 & 11. Altes Museum Berlin, rear corners./ photographs by author, 2024.

organize internal spaces. This technique arises out of Schinkel's *Anschaulichkeit*, or the "making [of] something concrete through the evocation of clear, moving images."[22] By expressing ideas with precision through material effects, the viewer is able to understand and respond to the essence of the design. Mies, hinging modern American materiality to classical European form, echoes Schinkel and preserves the dialectic tension. In doing so, the corners of the IIT reveal a requisite of the architecture of modernity, to educate the modern man by serving as a foil against existing structures and conventions.

Seagram Building

By 1954, Mies's modernizing language had built its vocabulary of tectonic components, defined the structural logic of its grammar, and questioned the relationship of parts to whole within its poetic syntax. The clear-span structure and high-rise building complex arise as Mies's two methods of originating "a poetry of structure and space."[23] The Seagram Building's mass might suggest a definitive proclamation of geometric uniformity, but its plan speaks a different, more synthetic language. This duality in turn reveals another, more social hinge. In a 2010 interview with the Canadian Centre for Architecture, Phyllis Lambert disclosed that during her collaboration with Mies and Philip Johnson on the tower's design, Mies had been singularly concerned with the superstructure, where his grammar was most visibly implemented.[24]

22 Moyano, *Quality vs. History*, 592.
23 Mies, Lambert, & Oechslin, *Mies in America*, 194.
24 Goldberger, Lambert, & Lavin, *Modern Views*, 25.

The Poiesis of Miesian Corners

153

Denied his architect's permit, Mies returned to Chicago, leaving Lambert and Philip Johnson with the half-constructed project, tasked to "conjure up an interior environment within the space of Mies's structure."[25] Mies's language and the structure provided by his grammar had achieved a level of clarity

25 Lambert & Bergdoll, *Building Seagram*, 149.

Figure 12. Seagram Building, corner of ground floor front elevation./ Photograph by author, 2023.

Figure 13. Seagram Building, corner of tower./ Photograph by author, 2023.

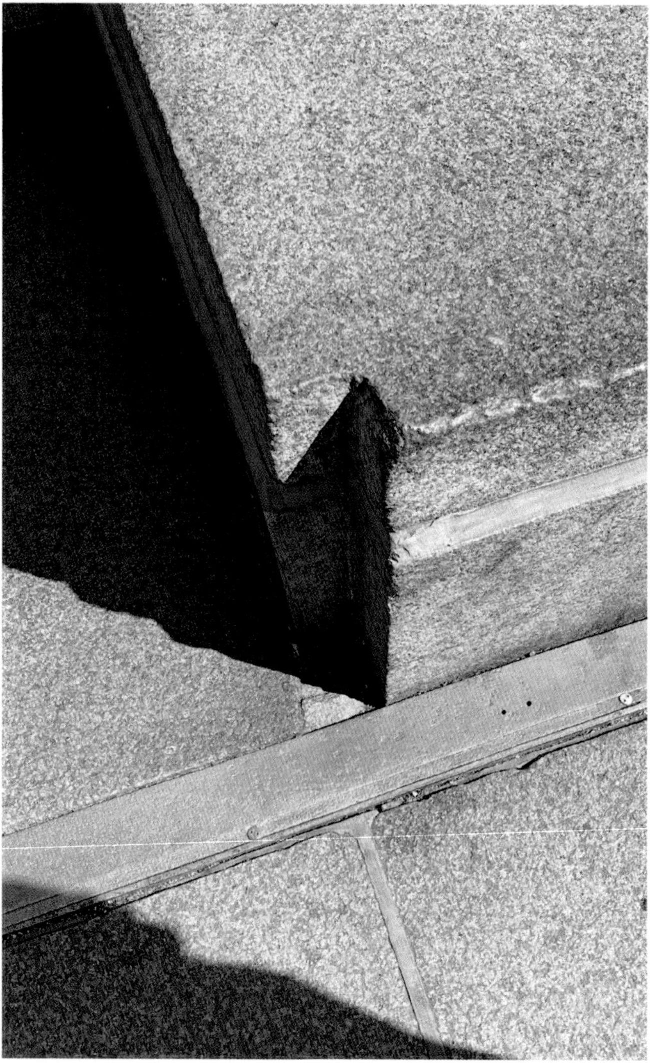

The Poiesis of Miesian Corners

which allowed for the continuation of his work and vision of modernity, even without his presence. The Seagram, characterized by its dual, inter-connected, T-shaped plan, reflects the syntactical brackets of the Brick Country House. The frame of H-shaped mullions in bronze—a material both matte and opulent—stops flush with the corner columns, which are themselves sheathed in a layer of concrete and metal. The volumes are divided horizontally into two sets: a base and a tower, both composed upon a plinth. The base, veiled in travertine and light bands, creates an illusion of buoyancy, as if the entire edifice delicately balances on the visually prominent corner columns. At the corner of the T, where the high-rise transitions into the shorter service tower, Mies orchestrates a material fold—one of the building's corner articulations—marked by a carefully chamfered stone transition. Upon closer inspection, the monolithic stone peels back at the corner, not sitting flush upon itself (*nicht auf Stoß*, as the son of a German stonemason would say) (fig. 12). On close encounter, the viewer realizes every corner unhinges its façade cladding and leaves a gap of discontinuous surfaces, a "phenomenon of splitting."[26] Where the glass façade converges with the structural edge, a corner column ascends in a continuous metallic sheath (fig. 13). Here, the ornamental I-beams, seemingly unanchored, hover at the edge before soaring upwards across thirty-eight stories, optically converging at an ethereal apex in a singular moment of punctuation! This detail is echoed at the smallest scale, such as in the plaza where notched concrete slabs flank the steps, shaping an inverted corner

26. Rakatansky, "Tectonic Acts of Desire and Doubt, 1945-1980" in *ANY: Architecture New York* 14: 39.

Figure 14. Seagram Building, corner of plaza bench. / Photograph by author, 2023.

juxtaposed against the Cartesian grid of floor tiles (fig. 14). The sliding planes dismantle the building's syntactical essence as a singular object, exposing its tectonic vocabulary and material composition. The hinging of the Seagram corner is a material one, and although it operates purely within the discipline and lacks the social implications of the other corners, it is the most blatant "reveal" of Mies's architectonic language. By this point, Mies's language has become so solidified that the corner can manifest itself—it no longer requires an author, or an ulterior motive.

In the poetic lexicon of Mies van der Rohe, corners become more than structural necessities; they are dualistic junctures where narratives of aesthetic authenticity are disclosed as variable and relative. These corners, transcending mere tectonic transitions, emerge as articulate focal points where past and present engage in an interlocution that is integral to Mies's poiesis of a new modern language for a new modern man. Literary critic and theorist Naomi Schor, theorizing on the role of detail in Modernism, has argued it is often relegated to a secondary function as the other against more dominant aesthetic values like form and structure.[27] In Miesian modernism, the corners stand as slight but nuanced turns away from the distinct legibility of International Style modernism, instead conspicuously embedding the often overlooked, debased detail in plain sight. In Mies's orchestration of space, the corner detail makes visible spatial flows, acting as the fulcrum between material syntax and social semantics. The significance of this architectural technique reveals

27 Schor, *Reading in Detail*.

other hinges and points of poiesis, including the connections between the mythical authorial singularity of Mies, and the multiple, pivotal collaborators which are frequently oblique to the canon, such as Lilly Reich, Ludwig Hilberseimer, Phyllis Lambert, and Philip Johnson. These other authors' contributions often steered the refinement of architectural detailing in Mies's most well-known projects.[28]

Mies's built corners, therefore, do not just represent spatial pivots, but also the convergence of creative dialogues—a collaborative juncture. In the construction of these connections, there is an innate poiesis, operating within multiple linguistic registers: the social, the environmental, the disciplinary, the authorial, and the architectural. Mies seldom wrote with words, but his language with corners continues to communicate his legacy.

The author expresses deep gratitude to the late Prof. Jean Louis Cohen.

[28] Cohen & Mies, *Mies van der Rohe*, 2nd and updated ed., 56.

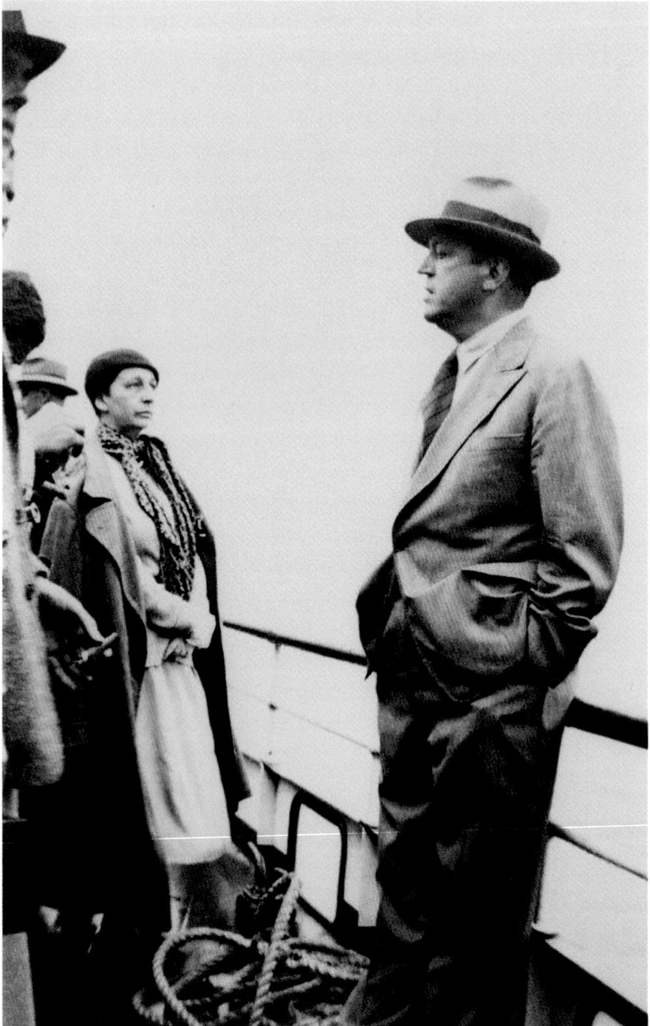

The Poiesis of Miesian Corners 159

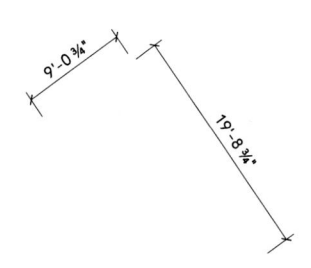

Figure 15.
Ludwig Mies van der Rohe and Lilly Reich on board an excursion boat on the Wannsee, near Berlin, 1933./ Photograph by Howard Dearstyne. The Museum of Modern Art.

Forget LEED: Dollar General to Save the Planet

SALK
Sarah Aziz and Lindsey Krug

Despite societal awareness of architecture's complicity in the climate crisis, it remains challenging to fully comprehend the extent to which it participates in planetary degradation, and how these entanglements might incite action within the discipline. In this essay, we plot architecture's most popular methods for generating environmental consciousness along an imperfect gradient from quantifiable metrics to speculative provocations, and note that they still fall short. On one end of this spectrum, universal green building rating systems like LEED offer a suite of quantitative methods for generating the aforementioned consciousness. On the other end, speculative projects that are visionary and beautifully illustrated might shock people out of complacency but remain unbuilt. While there are lessons to learn from both—technical precision with the former and expanding imagination with the latter—they are insufficient. Sitting at opposite poles, they maintain the divide between sustainability as it is actualized through materials and overly quantitative metrics, and sustainability as it manifests in subjective, abstract, and utopian visions. Both, in their own way, offer unfamiliar and inaccessible solutions and fail to scale beyond the one-off.

To better reckon with architecture's role in the climate crisis and bridge the divide between the technocratic and the symbolic, we propose the use of relatable and widespread building types, a kind of generic alternative. This paper uses ecological philosopher Timothy Morton's concept of the *hyperobject*—a term coined to describe objects so massively distributed in time and space that they transcend spatiotemporal specificity—to foreground a new architectural protagonist that operates at the scale of infrastructure: Dollar General (DG). The unassuming dollar store might seem an unlikely choice. There are few canonical projects that argue for the historical and disciplinary value of copy-paste buildings built and operated by a corporate bad actor, and dollar stores are not without their faults. While they fill gaps in food deserts, they also replace local businesses, reorienting communities around cheap, low-quality products. The supply of plastic goods with little care paid to their use or disposal isn't just a side note; it is a key component of their infrastructure, which works in direct opposition to their ability to operate as a kind of sustainable hyperobject. However, despite the dollar store's shortcomings, its main assets are its familiarity and proximity: the dollar store is uniquely familiar, always nearby in the American built environment, and intimately tied to the everyday lives of hundreds of millions of people. DG is the largest dollar store operator and small-box retailer in the United States, overseeing over 19,600 near-identical stores nationwide. DG is everywhere, making it difficult for consumers, architects, and historians alike to fathom the magnitude of its empire and the degree to which it contributes to extractive practices and carbon emissions worldwide. We advocate for the inclusion of these structures and their shelves chock-full of plastic tchotchkes into discourses touting ecological awareness because such enormous, entangled entities—per Morton—are the very definition of hyperobjects. By positioning America's most prolific dollar store, its buildings, and its stock of cheap tchotchkes as essential artifacts in the planetary canon of a human-altered environment, the DG hyperobject offers new methods for translating and representing complex narratives into relatable metrics, and perhaps new avenues for action.

Sustainability and the Kantian Gap: from U-Values to Dusty Relief, with Little In-Between

The broad cultural crisis fomented by environmental decline trickles down into architecture, igniting disciplinary opportunism and a wide variety of ill-suited pseudo-solutions that fail to adequately translate, synthesize, and depict complex, ecological narratives. This is exacerbated by the gap in impact generated by architecture's methods for responding to environmental awareness, as introduced above. This "Kantian gap," in which the experience of something (the phenomenon) is almost irreconcilable with the thing itself (the noumenon), is omnipresent in our comprehension of architecture's various inputs and outputs when it comes to sustainability. For example, while we may experience thermal comfort as the outcome of architects abiding by LEED regulations (the phenomenon), we never truly perceive the low U-value of a window assembly (the noumenon).

On the other end of the spectrum, with provocative architectural projects offering new environmental paradigms, we can discern the noumenon through seductive images and thoughtful writing, but not the phenomenon because they are either unbuilt or singular and inaccessible, enviable only from a distance for most. For example, in David Gissen's 2010 book *Subnature: Architecture's Other Environment*, he catalogs real and imagined examples of architecture's registration of environmental consciousness. Each project positions subnatural objects, which he defines as forms of nature that are either "threatening" to human existence, "primitive," "filthy," "fearsome," or "uncontrollable," as instruments for reframing the fallout of our anthropogenic activities.[1] However compelling and provocative, the projects—which embrace industrial smoke (Pilot Plant by NL Architects), ossify dust (The Ethics of Dust by Jorge Otero-Pailos), magnetize air pollutants (Dusty Relief by R&Sie), or propagate weeds (Magic Mountain by Cero9)—tend toward the highly specialized, and they primarily offer only technological or conceptual antidotes for ecological crises.[2]

Also in 2010, Timothy Morton published *The Ecological Thought* and introduced the hyperobject. Morton would later expound on this concept in his 2013 book *Hyperobjects: Philosophy and Ecology after the End of the World*, projecting hyperobjects' impacts into contemporary design and aesthetics. Though the term was initially used in the fields of ecology and philosophy, incorporating hyperobjects into the architectural lexicon provides a way to perceive incomprehensibly large things like climate change—the quintessential hyperobject to Morton—which are inextricably linked to the practices and outputs of architects. Morton ventures into architecture, asserting that architects should "design in a dark ecological way, admitting our coexistence with toxic substances we have created and exploited," but offers only one example of such a project, the aforementioned 2012 project by François Roche and Stéphanie Lavaux, of R&Sie, called Dusty Relief.[3] The building has a magnetized exterior and extracts

1 Gissen defines subnatures as "denigrated forms of nature." He writes: "Forms of nature become subnatural when they are envisioned as threatening to inhabitants or to the material formations and ideas that constitute architecture. Subnatures are those forms of nature deemed primitive (mud and dankness), filthy (smoke, dust, and exhaust), fearsome (gas or debris), or uncontrollable (weeds, insects, and pigeons). We can contrast these subnatures to those seemingly central and desirable forms of nature—e.g., the sun, clouds, trees, and wind." Gissen, *Subnature*, 21-22.

pollutants from the air, creating a reciprocal relationship between environmental mediation and building construction. The result is an electrostatic chia pet at the scale of a building: a fuzzy, blobby barometer grown on a standardized, rectilinear frame. Further reinforcing the gap between pragmatism and abstraction, LEED, Gissen, and Morton focus only on solutions that are either difficult to scale, or problematic when they do, against an all-encompassing, monolithic threat: the degradation of planetary systems and humanity's inability to comprehend it.

Dollar General as Hyperobject

Morton leaves us without concrete examples of buildings that assuage our existential concerns within ecological fallout, but the hyperobject framework offers a road map for locating others. Opened in 1955 as a single wholesale store in Springfield, Kentucky, Dollar General Corporation is now present in all forty-eight of the contiguous U.S. states, pulling an estimated forty percent of the nation's consumers to its stores.[4] DG's astronomical growth cannot be overstated: it works against the broader trend of declining brick-and-mortar retail as its fleet of stores tally more than double the number of Walmarts and Targets combined.[5] In 2021, Coresight Research's aggregated data on retail openings in America revealed that DG accounted for almost one of every three store openings nationwide.[6] While part of DG's expansion model has long been to move into areas where Walmart and other big-box grocers won't (providing at least one general merchandise store

2 Gissen, *Subnature*, 54 (NL Architects), 53 (Otero-Pailos), 79 (R&Sie), 158 (Cero9).
3 Morton, *Hyperobjects*, 109.
4 Reuter, "Meet the typical Dollar General customer," *Business Insider*.
5 Corkery, "As Dollar Stores Proliferate, Some Communities Say No," *New York Times*.
6 Meyersohn, "Nearly 1 in 3 new stores opening in the US is a Dollar General," *CNN Business*.

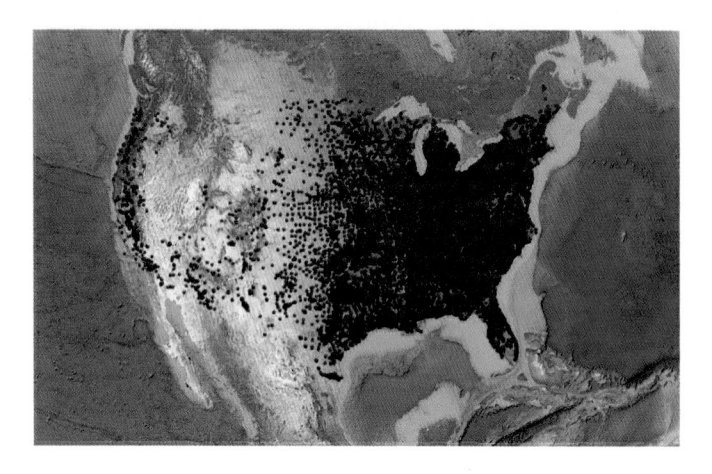

for residents), DG also strategically uses tactics to circumvent the more stringent zoning and permitting rules applied to big-box developments in many municipalities. By maintaining its stores in the "small-box" category under 10,000 square feet, DG avoids regulations that would slow its growth by making new store construction more complicated. While the ubiquitous yellow-and-black signs and beige concrete-block facades are familiar sights for most Americans, it's still hard to grasp how the retail giant ballooned from 7,000 stores in 2004 to nearly 20,000 just twenty years later (fig. 1).[7]

The kind of relentless déjà vu produced by episodic run-ins with Dollar General conjures Morton's notion of the hyperobject, aptly coined during this era of DG's rapid proliferation (fig. 2). Morton tells us that hyperobjects "include thousands of other beings...

7 Dollar General, "In Our Storied History," *Dollar General 75th Anniversary*.

Figure 2. This image, depicting approximately 19,000 Dollar General signposts, imagines the unimaginable scales of the retail behemoth. Seeing them together, we can shift our reading of individual architectures to reading them as a cohesive infrastructure instead./ Image by authors, 2022.

Figure 1.
This map, produced in October 2021, illustrates the 17,831 DG stores in operation at that time. As of January 2024, there are 19,643 stores, reflecting growth of approximately 67 stores per month./ Image by authors with data from ScrapeHero.

8   Morton, *Hyperobjects*, 174.
9   Morton, 1.

[and] end the idea that things are lumps of blah decorated with accidents, or not fully real until they interact with humans."[8] We can read DG through this lens as its stores are too often understood as individual objects rather than relationally as parts of a larger ecosystem. From a distance, they invoke the image of a mom-and-pop corner shop, but upon closer inspection, it becomes clear this is merely one instance of the omnipotent march of the concrete box across America. Morton tells us that "any 'local manifestation' of a hyperobject is not directly the hyperobject,"[9] which challenges the simplistic reading of DG as a bad building, a bad neighbor, a bad lump of blah. We pass one store on our way to work each day. We pass dozens on a road trip from point A to point B anywhere in America. We can never perceive DG in its

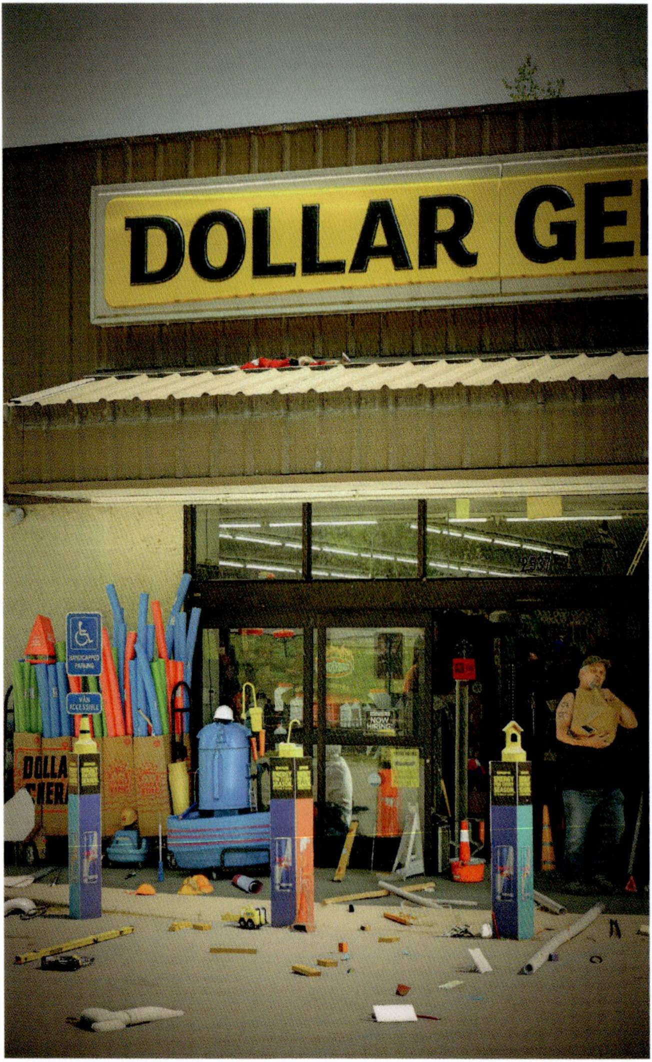
DOLLAR GE
NOW HIRING!

entirety, and its small-box form further costumes the company, conjuring the image of a local shop. Each interaction with DG—each individual building—is merely a refracted morsel of an imperceptibly large, corporate infrastructure. Here, the framing of DG as a hyperobject allows a more nuanced reading of the Kantian gap wherein new architectural protagonists operating at the scale of infrastructure fill in the gradient between the quantifiable and the speculative.

Dollar General's Entanglements with Other Hyperobjects

By reading Dollar General as a hyperobject—a productive reframing of a building type often dismissed in the zeitgeist as merely a commercial nuisance—we can also zoom in on the many scales at which it manifests, from handheld object to global network (fig. 3). Despite its scope, many of the cheap tchotchkes stocked at DG stores are handmade in domestic spaces that double as production facilities with unmonitored workplace safety protocols in China's Zhejiang Province. Despite being an "American" institution, the majority of its products come from Yiwu, a city of approximately 1.5 million people in the Zhejiang. It contains the world's largest small commodities market, a 59-million-square-foot building that displays and sells dollar store goods in bulk. In 2017, documentarian Daniel Whelan offered insights into the lives of a diverse cast of characters in Yiwu's orbit in his film *Bulkland*. The interviews humanize this mercantile behemoth, but the numbers are still staggering. "In May of 2014,

Figure 3.
Typically seen as a commercial nuisance, Dollar General has the ability to produce intimacy with and critical awareness of people, places, and things on a global scale./ Image by authors, 2023.

Yiwu exported 77 million U.S. dollars' worth of small plastic decorations, 44 million dollars' worth of unnamed plastic manufactured products, 36 million dollars' worth of imitation jewelry, and that's just in one month. This is the city the dollar store built."[10]

In America, the spatial consequences of dollar stores are felt nationally, as "approximately 75% of the U.S. population currently lives within five miles of a Dollar General store."[11] If we consider the collapsing of space and time that occurs when you hold one of its objects in your hand and imagine the translation from a domestic space in China to a domestic space in America, a strange, uncanny intimacy and immediacy between transnational production and consumption emerges. Through DG, both populations of makers and receivers rely on this exchange for their livelihood, underscoring the cheapness and precarity that comprise the corporation. However, this is not unique to DG as the majority of America's miscellaneous manufactured items are imported from China.[12] What is unique is the intimacy DG produces through its geographic scope and proximity. Ultimately, intimacy is what Morton says is required to achieve ecological awareness. He argues:

> The no-self view is not a faceless, dehumanized abstraction, but a radical encounter with intimacy. What best explains ecological awareness is a sense of intimacy, not a sense of belonging to something bigger: a sense of being close, even too close, to other lifeforms, of having them under one's skin.[13]

10 *Bulkland*, 0:01:15.
11 Dollar General, "Fast Facts," *Dollar General News Center*.
12 U.S. Department of Commerce, "2022 U.S. Trade with China."
13 Morton, 139.
14 In 2003, a minor from the Mississippi Band of Choctaw Indians was sexually assaulted by a Dollar General manager during a job training program at the store located on tribal lands. The child and their family sued Dollar General and the manager for damages in Tribal Court. Dollar General rejected the premise that they were subject to tribal jurisdiction as a non-tribal entity, despite entering into a voluntary contractual relationship with the tribe through the leasing of the store's property. Following a series of appeals by Dollar General, the U.S. Supreme Court agreed to hear the case *Dollar General Corporation v. Mississippi Band of Choctaw Indians* in 2015. The per curiam SCOTUS

decision issued in 2016 reflected a 4-4 split court, thus simply affirming the ruling of the lower appeals court, which ruled in favor of the minor and agreed Dollar General could be subject to tribal civil law. Despite the ruling being considered a victory for tribal sovereignty, the split within the Supreme Court effectively defers a true decision for a future case and leaves open the possibility for these rights to be denied later on. As it relates to Dollar General, this case is significant in illustrating the insidious "statelessness" of an entity or business like Dollar General. Baked into its name, Dollar General is proud of its company origins as a local general store, a small business on the proverbial Main Street. However, at its current scale and reflected in this SCOTUS case, is the reality that Dollar General wants to have it both ways. It aspires to be a local and

Positioning DG as an object of study elicits an ambiguity of scale that helps illustrate architecture's entanglements with the hyperobjects of environmental decline, such as global warming, labor exploitation, and material extraction. When studying DG, are we referring to the company as a corporation? Or the store, as in the architectural box and its retail layouts? Or the stock, as in the tens of thousands of objects that line store shelves? Because at least one manifestation of DG is situated so firmly in the daily frame of reference for so many people, it is able to reveal layers of itself to us in moments as small as plucking a one-dollar pair of plastic flip-flops off a store rack, or as large as the U.S. Supreme Court issuing its opinion in the case *Dollar General Corporation v. Mississippi Band of Choctaw Indians* in 2016.[14] In Morton's terms, DG is read as a hyperobject itself, while also allowing us to "use this powerful new philosophical approach for finding out real things about real things."[15] When looking at DG, myriad analogs toggle us between intangible forces and tangible things. Its familiarity and nearness help narrow the disjuncture between our own experience of the world and the broader reality of what's taking place. For example, if we want to better apprehend extraction, we can trace a single plastic tchotchke back to an indiscernible pool of crude oil pumping through the Shengli Oil Field underneath the Bohai Sea. Or, to unravel corporate malfeasance and exploitative practices, we can look to the TikTok exposé by Mary Gundel, a former DG store manager in Tampa, Florida, who made national headlines earlier this year for being unfairly dismissed for reporting instances of violence she faced while often working alone in her store. DG is taboo, but because it's proximate and alluring (it's in most Americans' neighborhoods and offers products that range from basic necessities to hedonic goods), its stories enter our immediate experience as we can transpose our lives onto them. The spatial agenda of DG—to build a small-box store on every corner—provides a terrain for inhabiting the gap between phenomenon and noumenon. While DG cannot collapse subjective and objective reality, it provides a reference that lets us float between the two.

Conclusions: Darkly Ecological (and Ubiquitous) Architectures

In her book *Vibrant Matter: A Political Ecology of Things*, political theorist Jane Bennett posits that there's an agency to objects that often go unacknowledged. Bennett writes: "Thing-power gestures toward the strange ability of ordinary, man-made items to exceed their status as objects and to manifest traces of independence or aliveness, constituting the outside of our own experience" (fig. 4).[16] Suppose, then, that intimate encounters between bodies and things facilitate wisdom for ecological intervention. In that case, we may be in good hands with Dollar General based solely on the sheer scale and accessibility of its operations (19,600+ stores!). But DG—notorious for squeezing out small businesses, limiting its stock of fresh food in favor of monocultural options, union busting, and predatory development tactics—has not shown signs, yet, of taking up

... reliable small business in the 19,000 municipalities it serves, but also sees itself as exempt from local oversight and beyond reproach. See: "Dollar General Corporation v. Mississippi Band of Choctaw Indians," *Oyez*.
15 Morton, 15.
16 Bennett, *Vibrant Matter*, xvi.

Figure 4.
In the spirit of Jane Bennett's description of "thing-power," which "gestures toward the strange ability of ordinary, man-made items to exceed their status as objects and to manifest traces of independence or aliveness," this exhibition (designed and curated by the authors) at the University of Milwaukee-Wisconsin's Mobile Design Box Gallery featured high-demand, essential goods purchased in bulk from Dollar General for display in a faux dollar store.[16] Following their exhibition, the products were donated to local aid organizations in and around Milwaukee's Historic Mitchell District./ Photo by Abigail Platz, 2022.

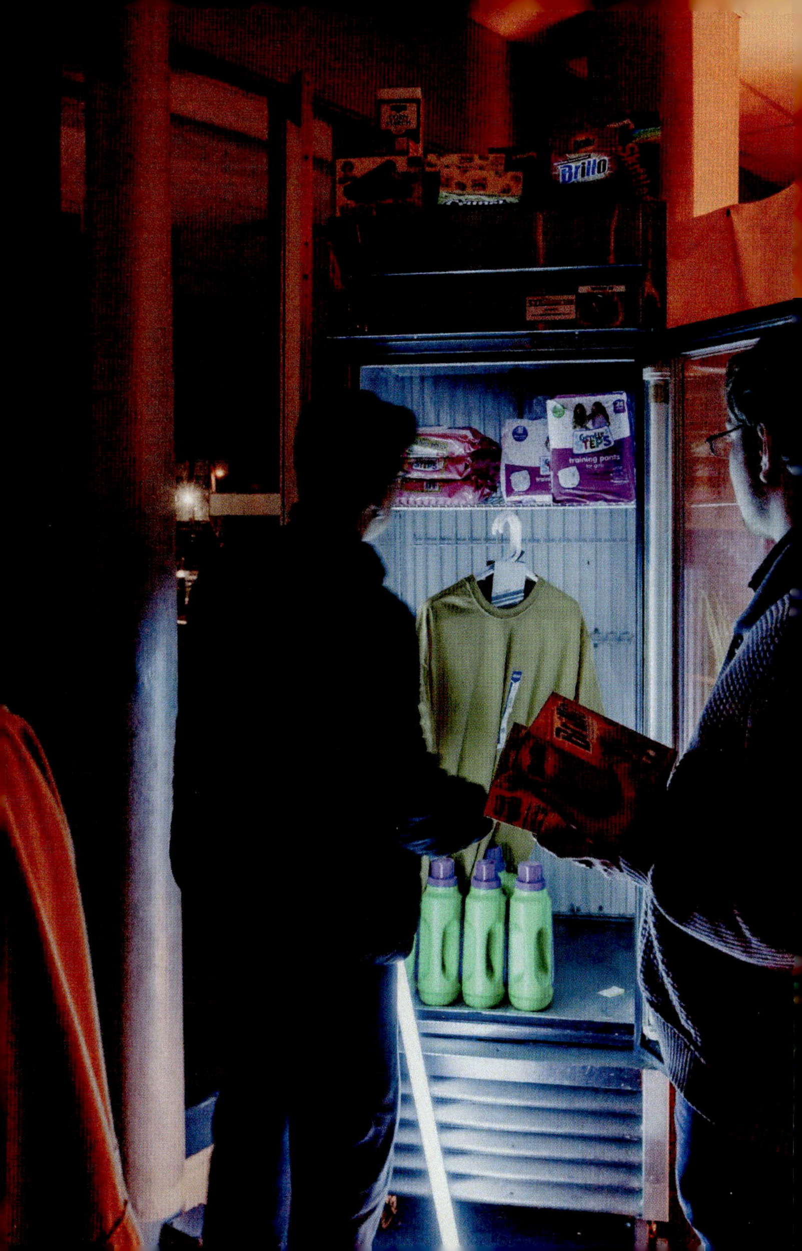
Brillo
training pants

NOW HIRING

FIND YOUR OPPORTUNITY

Apply Today:

DOLLAR GENERAL

SNAP &

the responsibility that comes with this positionality (fig. 5). Morton marvels at his lone example of darkly ecological architecture—R&Sie's Dusty Relief— because of its emphasis on solidity that smartly transcends post-1970s environmentalisms and that era's obsession with equating ecological thinking with regulating flows. In no uncertain terms, Morton asks: "[Why are] flows better than solids? Thinking this way on a planetary scale becomes absurd. Why is it better to stir the shit around inside the toilet bowl faster and faster rather than just leaving it there?"[17] Dusty Relief is participating actively, designing with pollution rather than proposing to push it to a nonexistent "somewhere else," but its technology is purely speculative and leaves us in the realm of abstraction. Buildings that receive LEED certification end up being similar despite their replacement of abstraction with pragmatism. What both types of projects possess in method, they lack in realistic scalability, bending our initial gradient back onto itself to create an uninspiring and seemingly inescapable loop.

DG is the inverse and allows us to occupy this new middle. With its remarkable network of small-box buildings and supply chain logistics in place, what alternative models of climate agency might be possible if DG adopted a method and embraced its presence as a robust, national infrastructure? By writing badly behaved architectures into the canon (and, incidentally, decentering badly behaved architects), we can emphasize contradiction by simultaneously denouncing their participation in planetary degradation and heralding their potential to make a larger

17 Morton, 110.

Figure 5.
Dollar General is notorious for squeezing out small businesses, limiting its stock of fresh food in favor of monocultural options, busting unions, and implementing predatory development tactics, but the scale of its operations facilitates speculation about alternative, radical futures./ Image by authors, 2023.

impact than high-tech, one-off ecological buildings ever could.

Morton touches on changing modalities of scholarship in the time of hyperobjects:

> We are entering a new era of scholarship, where the point will not be to one-up each other by appealing to the trace of the givenness of the openness of the clearing of the lighting of the being of the pencil. Thinking past "meta mode" will bring us up to speed with the weirdness of things, a weirdness that evolution, ecology, relativity, and quantum theory all speak about. This weirdness resides on the side of objects themselves, not our interpretation of them.[18]

Our unlikely protagonist Dollar General is critical in the daily lives of so many but is underexplored in architectural thought and discourse. If architects, educators, and historians are to confront their relationship to ecological harm and still pursue optimistic pathways forward, they must expand beyond the speculative and the niche assemblies of LEED-certified buildings that only few can afford, and embrace the highly franchised, extra-ordinary, and ubiquitous. Luckily for us, Dollar Generals are plentiful, wait patiently, and are *always* close by (fig. 6).

18 Morton, 159.

Figure 6. Reimaging the copy-paste language of Dollar General as something capable of being reconstituted and repurposed facilitates better engagement with ecological harm, and helps architects, educators, and historians pursue optimistic pathways forward./ Image by authors, 2023.

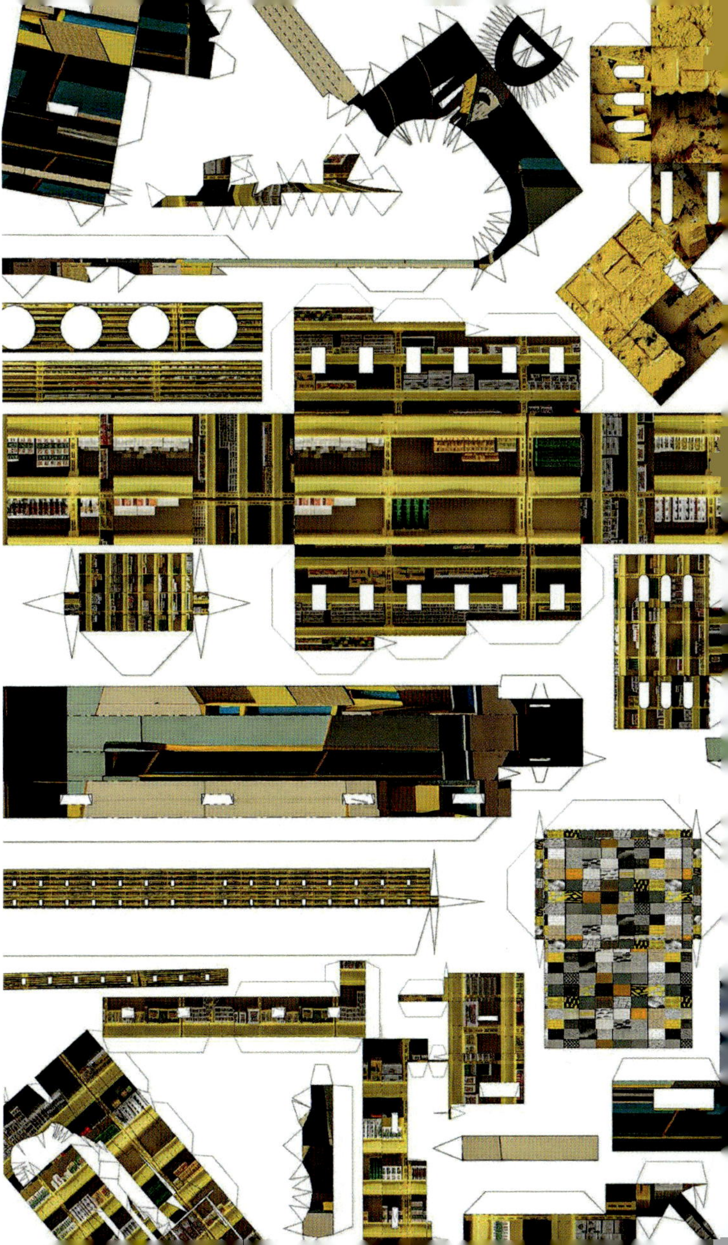

Media on Media: Returning to Jean-François Lyotard's *Les Immatériaux*

Ariane Fong

In 1985, the celebrated philosopher Jean-François Lyotard and design theorist Thierry Chaput curated the exhibition *Les Immatériaux* at the Centre Pompidou. The exhibition spread across 3,000 square meters on the fifth floor of the museum, accessible by its iconic system of external escalators. In the same spirit, cables and ducts were wound through the exposed ceiling of the gallery, with mirrors covering the walls and suspended at oblique angles. A curving, pipelike tunnel connected two sides of the space by way of an outdoor balcony, a kind of detour or shortcut. Initiated by the architecture and design department of the Pompidou, *Les Immatériaux* has become widely recognized as a landmark exhibition of media and information technology, presenting communication as a hallmark of the postmodern era, and well-noted as a touchpoint for many contemporary artists, among them Dominique Gonzalez-Foerster, Pierre Huyghe, and Philippe Parreno.[1]

The exhibition has been studied for the intensity and intricacy of its design.[2] Fifteen years after *Information* (1970) at the Museum of Modern Art, *Les Immatériaux* departed from the language of product development and industrial design and, instead, produced the effects of technology as experience. Walking through the gallery, the visitor was meant to understand their new interests as a postmodern subject. By refiguring questions of formal representation, the exhibition involved the individual as a political subject living in a media-saturated condition, a new material environment. In histories of architectural exhibitions, it marked a turning point where exhibitions and museums began to present and enact the cultural effects of emerging technologies.

Although the curators preferred to call the project a "manifestation," to distance it from historical exhibition practices, *Les Immatériaux* resembled the visual language of world's fairs and product shows, with computers, speakers, headsets, and gadgets on view in vitrines (fig. 1). Among the plastic projectors and grey-and-manilla monitors, the exhibition included architectural models, isometric drawings on paper, glass screens, and one car. One display housed dense clusters of plants bathed in infrared light while

[1] For the artists' interest in the exhibition, see Obrist, "Les Immatériaux," *Ways of Curating*, 157.

[2] Nearly forty years after its opening, the exhibition's documentation has inspired an archival exhibition of its own, hosted at the Pompidou from July 5, 2023 – January 8, 2024. The project generated a digital model of the exhibition space, reconstructed from the catalog's documentation and photographs from the museum's archive, alongside a "virtual exhibition" webpage. See "*Les Immatériaux* (1985): Overview of a postmodern *manifestation* in the Centre Pompidou," Centre Pompidou.

Figures 1 (top) and 2 (bottom).
Installation views of the exhibit./ Images by Jean-Claude Planchet, 1985. Courtesy of Centre Pompidou, Paris

around the corner, spacesuits and other protective garments were posed aloft. A slide projector—a more modest audiovisual device—was presented in a "pop-up" environment, where visitors might slip underneath and join the projector behind the glass.

Images saturated the space with a theater of multi-screen projections at one end of the gallery and a display of monitors and consoles assembled at the other (fig. 2). Nearly thirty radio transmitters governed the space, each broadcasting a different soundtrack tied to discursive questions proposed by the curators. Every visitor was offered a headset, worn to receive messages from the transmitters, which changed recordings as they walked between zones in the space.[3] Outside the gallery, the curators encouraged reflection and afterthought by arranging docent-led group conversations for visitors.[4]

The title of the exhibition referenced the immaterial, the intangible, gesturing beyond the machines, screens, and devices on display, to something else that could not otherwise be perceived. Staging encounters with objects in the space, the exhibit encouraged visitors to question their own relationships with environments increasingly augmented with media. In the exhibition catalog, Lyotard wrote, "the relationship between mind and matter is no longer one between an intelligent subject with a will of his own and an inert object."[5] The curators called these emerging forms and pathways of information "new materials" or "immaterials," identifying plastic relationships between source and subject, sender and receiver.[6]

The exhibition presented media in three forms: as objects in the devices on display; as an environment in the labyrinthine design of the exhibition; and as a form of communication as information shaped by

3 Visitors were required to purchase access to the headsets. Heinich, "Les Immatériaux Revisited: Innovation in Innovations: Landmark Exhibitions Issue," *Tate Papers*, no. 12.
4 Heinich.
5 Lyotard, "Les Immatériaux," *Materiality*, 205.
6 Lyotard, 201.

its mode of circulation. Together in the space, they informed one another, each a component of an apparatus that might constitute a new culture of media. The experience highlighted uncertain aspects of new technology, emergent from their physical supports. Lyotard insisted upon the pedagogical aim of the project: to magnify a sense of unease around the saturation of media and interject within positivist narratives of technological advancement. In the catalog, he recounts his pedagogy simply: "to arouse the visitor's reflection and anxiety about the postmodern condition," a phenomenological extension of his earlier writings.[7]

In *The Postmodern Condition*, first published in 1979, Lyotard presented a formulation of postmodernism as a cyclical phenomenon returning after periods of modernism.[8] The book was, notably, commissioned by the Quebec government as a response to a French report, *L'informatisation de la société* by Simon Nora and Alain Minc, issued two years earlier. *The Postmodern Condition*, though formally an account on technology in post-industrial society, also deliberated the changing status of knowledge, perceptions of legitimacy, and modes of authorship.

Reflecting the periodicity of Lyotard's postmodern condition, the exhibition drew upon the neoclassical tendencies of postmodern architecture by borrowing the classical archetype of the labyrinth. Designed by architect Philippe Delis, the space was shaped by a series of passageways of translucent mesh partitions, appearing as shimmering webbing or

7 Epreuves d'écriture, vol. 1 of *Les Immateriaux*.
8 Lyotard's theory of a periodic ontological condition, rather than a finite period, was distinct from Guy Debord and Henri Lebevre's popular definitions of postmodernism by "spectacle" or "consumption." Lyotard, *The Postmodern Condition: A Report on Knowledge*, vii.

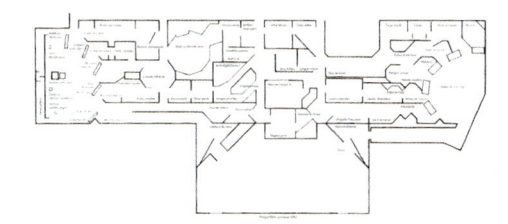

Figure 3.
Philippe Delis, plan of *Les Immatériaux*, 1985.

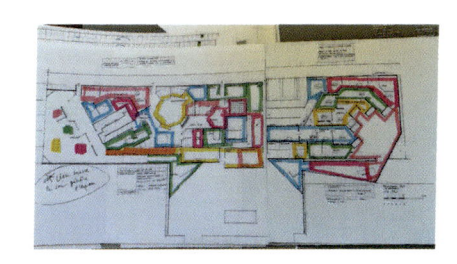

Figure 4.
Chaput's sketches from the exhibition catalog. / Image by the author.

9   The design resembled works of Minimalist art in the preceding decades, as well as Conceptual art's networks of distribution. For an extended discussion of such works in this period. Kraynak, "Dependent Participation: Bruce Nauman's Environments," *Grey Room*, no. 10.

opaque depending on the light (fig. 3). Their erratic plan resulted in a series of corridors that compressed and expanded, creating an interior without end. To shape the labyrinth, Delis designated spaces of interaction into "sites," the areas of encounter, and "deserts," the circulation spaces in between, creating a dramatic staging for aesthetic experience. This *parcours* widened and narrowed space, providing a kind of somatic manipulation or sense of being lost. This postmodern turn to the labyrinth, now purely formal, exchanged the stone of myth for a fabric, textile geometry without poché. This rendering of the labyrinth reflected the poststructural ethics of Lyotard's postmodernism, a material change enacted upon classical form. Delis's labyrinth placed *Les Immatériaux* in dialogue with participatory installation in experimental art of the 1960s, especially works that engage the body of the viewer.[9] The suspended fabric directed the visitor through the space, shaping the physical experience of the exhibition, while the headsets provided an acoustic, discursive layer. In turn, the visitor was immersed in the full environment of the gallery, its passageways punctuated by mediatic devices.

In *Les Immatériaux*, the labyrinth was an architectural intervention on historical forms of object display, reshaping the objects' effects by reconfiguring the space of display around them. Yet, this intervention also represented the sociological anxiety of Lyotard's curatorial conceit. Art historian Janet Kraynak has articulated the tension in participatory installation between "the need (or desire) for reciprocal involvement on the part of the viewer and concomitantly

10 Kraynak.
11 Schneider and Wallis, "Introuction," *Global Television*.

a reluctance to allow for it or, at least, to preclude unfettered access."[10] Apprehensions about the development of a technocratic society coincided with growing concerns around the transmission and export of media. In 1983, two years before the opening of *Les Immatériaux*, the French Minister of Culture Jack Lang had publicly denounced the American television shows as symbols of "cultural imperialism."[11] That same ministry conducted surveys about exhibitions like *Les Immatériaux* to assuage their concerns surrounding the democratization of art.

Figure 5. Installation view of the exhibit./ Image by Jean-Claude Planchet, 1985. Courtesy of Centre Pompidou, Paris

The sociologist Alain Touraine articulated these tensions in *The Post-Industrial Society* (which Lyotard, in turn, cited in *The Postmodern Condition*), writing on "dependent participation" as a precursor of the technocratic society.[12] In Touraine's prediction, "dependent participation" is coerced, requiring consumption of social influence and education within systems of power, leading ultimately to alienation.[13] He, and other sociologists such as Jean Meynaud and Jacques Ellul, were proposing such connections between technological progress, social influence, and political oppression. As Kraynak and Touraine assert, participation becomes a historically dictated persuasion, especially after the emergence of technocratic societies in the 1960s. For Touraine, this emergence was shaped by both technical and social effects, formed by a "knowledge-based economy" and mediatic and cultural forms of control.[14]

12 Kraynak.
13 Touraine, *The Post-Industrial Society: Tomorrow's Social History: Classes, Conflicts, and Culture in the Programmed Society*, 7.
14. Touraine, 7.

Lyotard's cyclical characterization of postmodernism became particularly apt for its development of a social account of technology's effects on knowledge and the transmission of knowledge, or the communication of information. If Lyotard defined the postmodern as "incredulity toward meta-narratives,"[15] the labyrinth was a spatial multi-narrative, an architectural apparatus presenting the illusion of choice that is nevertheless inscribed within a Cartesian framework. It even resonates with the mythic "mastering and possessing of nature," a romantic expression of fighting against fate.[16] Lyotard's argument, here spatial and discursive, told its own narrative of why technocratic society was not only oppressive, but also seductive.

The Centre Pompidou, with its didactic eversion of building systems and embrace of the *mediatheque*, lent its own valence to the exhibition. Famously designed by Renzo Piano and Richard Rogers, it had only opened eight years before and was still a favorite, divisive topic at local dinner parties. The museum, as a democratic yet historically elitist space, illustrated institutional tension between the inclusion and exclusion articulated in Touraine's concept of "dependent participation." The Pompidou's architectural conceit, with its color-coded mechanical systems, further heightened this tension. Within this setting, the curators viewed the Centre Pompidou as a charged space with a public mandate rooted in the celebration of media and technological progress. Against this backdrop, the exhibition designer Chaput's mise en scene hoped to engender widespread critical engagement with new forms of communication.[17] In an interview in March 1985,

15. Lyotard, *The Postmodern Condition: A Report on Knowledge.*
16. Lyotard, "Les Immatériaux," *Thinking About Exhibitions*, 114-126.
17. While Lyotard is remembered as the titular curator of the exhibition, Thierry Chaput is also credited as curator and exhibition designer.

Figure 6 (above). Installation view of the exhibit. / Images by Jean-Claude Planchet, 1985. Courtesy of Centre Pompidou, Paris

Figure 7 (right). Pages from the exhibition catalog. / Image by the author.

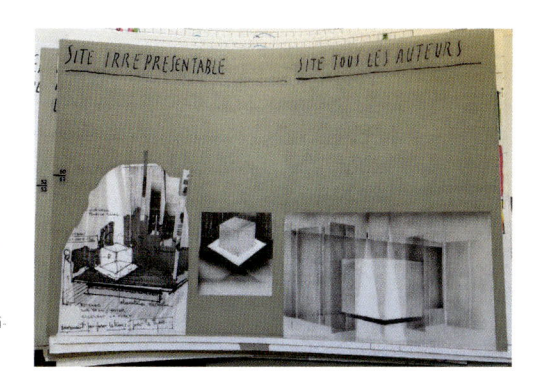

18 "Les Immatériaux: A Conversation with Jean-François Lyotard. with Bernard Blistène," *Flash Art*, no. 121.

Lyotard spoke on the project: "We wanted to exhibit things that inspire a feeling of incertitude,…incertitude about the identity of the human individual in his condition of such improbable immateriality."[18]

Transcribed accounts, photographs from the Centre Pompidou archive, and a two-volume catalog are artifacts of the exhibition. In particular, the catalog was designed to foster reflection upon the profuse experience of the event and offered a semantic response to a mediatic experience. Its first volume, *Epreuves d'écriture*, did so with its own extra-curricular project, a "lexicon of immaterials" which included a seven-part set of instructions sent to thirty artists, scientists, linguists, and philosophers, with contributions from Jacques Derrida, Bruno Latour, and Isabel Stengers.[19] The second volume, split into two halves, the *Album* and *Inventaire*, cataloged the planning and realization of the exhibition in loose plates intended to be rearranged by the reader.[20] They offer fragments of the exhibition—Chaput's sketches in blue pen and pink highlighter (fig. 4), grids of wordplay, charts, force diagrams, and typewritten letters, written by many hands, through many iterations of design. Unbound, the catalog's pages could be reordered and viewed side-by-side, mirroring the disorientation of the exhibition's labyrinth. The permutation of plates in the catalog, an index of the objects on display, was an extension of the exhibition's design into its afterlife.

In *The Postmodern Condition*, Lyotard wrote,

> local tone, drawing, the mixing of colors, linear perspective, the nature of the support and that of the instrument, the display, the museum: the avant-gardes are perpetually flushing out artifices of presentation which make it possible

19 *Epreuves d'écriture*, Vol. 1 of *Les Immatériaux*.
20 *Album et inventaire*. Vol. 2 of *Les Immatériaux*.

to subordinate thought to the gaze and to turn it away from the unrepresentable.[21]

Les Immatériaux developed a phenomenology of technology, caught between invisible information and the material objects that produce it. The lightweight yet maximalist design of the space intensified this relationship in many forms. The presence of media, material and immaterial, was heightened by the installation, which displaced objects from their everyday settings to be shown as devices of influence.

Perhaps the exhibition would foreshadow Rosalind Krauss's observation of the "need for a technologized subject" in the industrialized museum.[22] Bringing together media as object, environment, and communication, the exhibition articulated the historical and phenomenological dependence of information. It interpreted "technologization" as a participatory experience, heightening social and political inquiry surrounding the role of media. In Chaput's design, the labyrinth framed a new condition based upon a classical archetype, as an architectural expression of Lyotard's conceit. The anxieties surrounding information production and their effects on knowledge resonate, cyclically, in today's crisis of information. Its design foregrounded—or perhaps induced—these observations, creating a cultural interface for the postmodern condition.

21 Lyotard, *The Postmodern Condition*, 79. He would reflect further in Postmodern Fables, over a decade after the exhibition, "As the cultural institution proper to the mega-polis, the museum is a kind of zone. All cultures are suspended there." Lyotard, "The Zone," *Postmodern Fables*, 27.

22 Krauss, "The Cultural Logic of the Late Capitalist Museum," *October* 54.

Ten Reasons to Abstract Reflective Ceiling Plans

Ryan Tyler Martinez

1. *Reflective* Ceiling Plans (RCPs) can be tools for *abstraction*.
2. Abstracted RCPs create disciplinary *misbehavior*.
3. Misbehaving within architecture challenges the *conventional* norms of practice.
4. Conventional standards teach architects close *readings* of their work.
5. Alternative readings of color, texture and exuberance trigger productive *conversations*.

191

192   Ryan Tyler Martinez

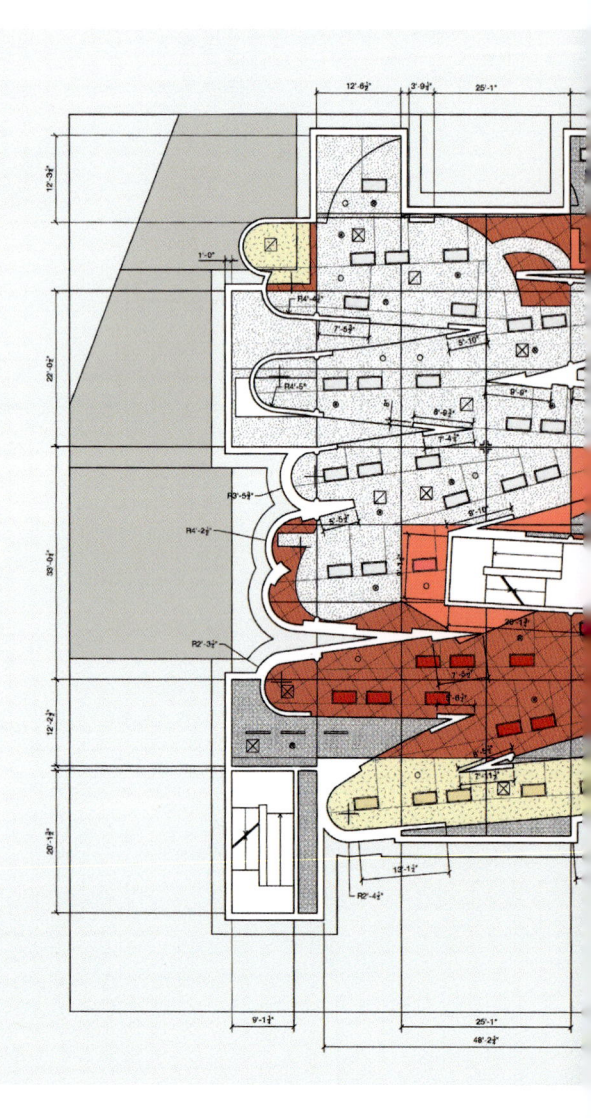

Ten Reasons to Abstract Reflective Ceiling Plans 193

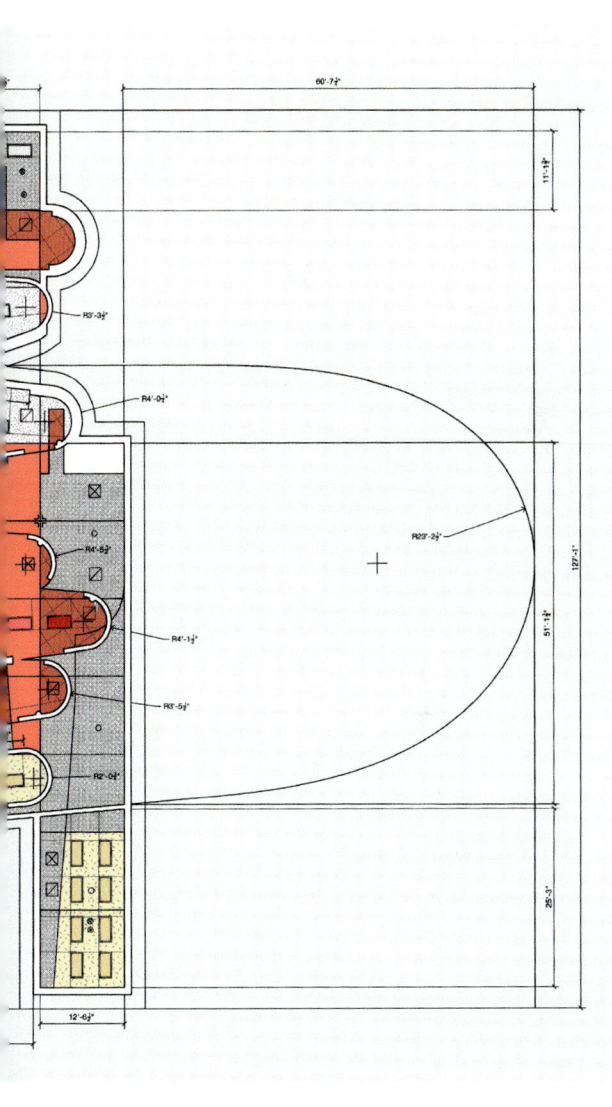

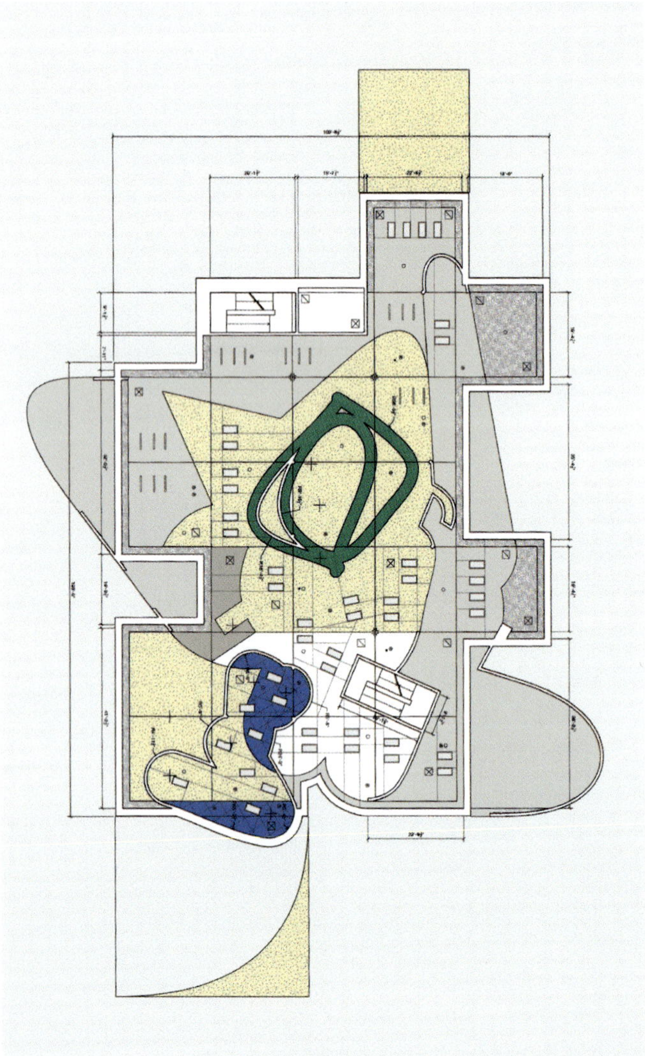

Ten Reasons to Abstract Reflective Ceiling Plans 195

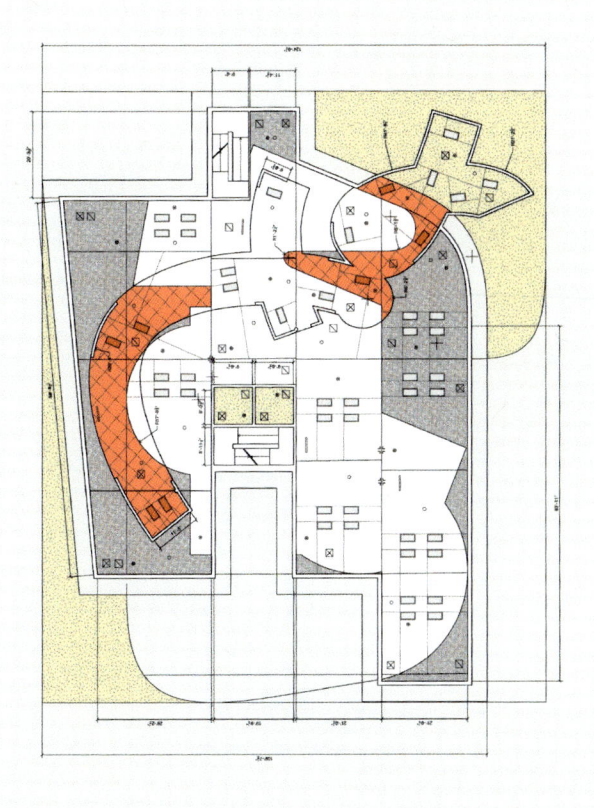

Ryan Tyler Martinez

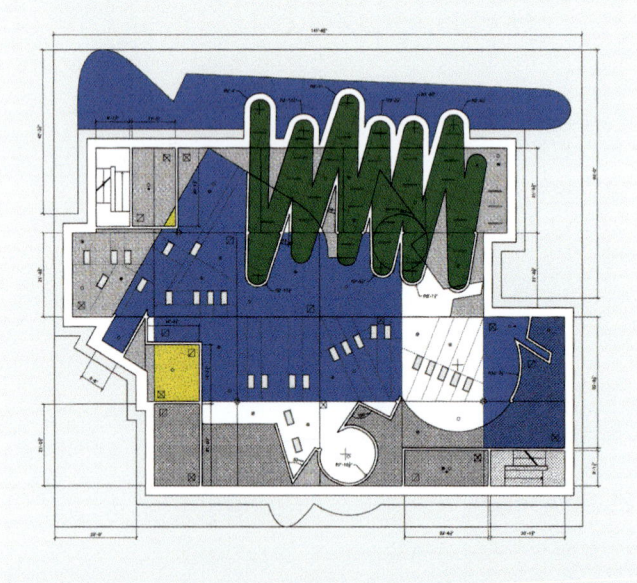

Ten Reasons to Abstract Reflective Ceiling Plans 197

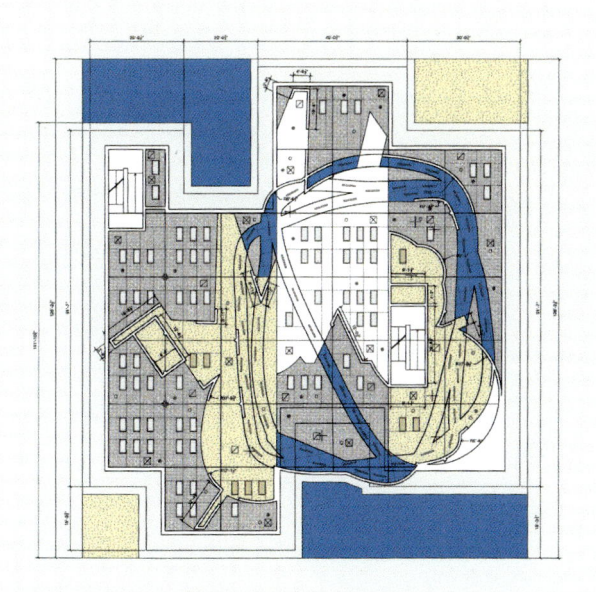

6. Abstracted RCPs raise questions about program organization in contemporary *buildings*.
7. Buildings should look like their *construction documents*.
8. Construction documents engage an architect's representation and *composition* skills.
9. Compositional ambiguity in orthographic drawings can instill *painterly* characteristics.
10. Painting RCPs invites new *perceptions* of details and assembly.

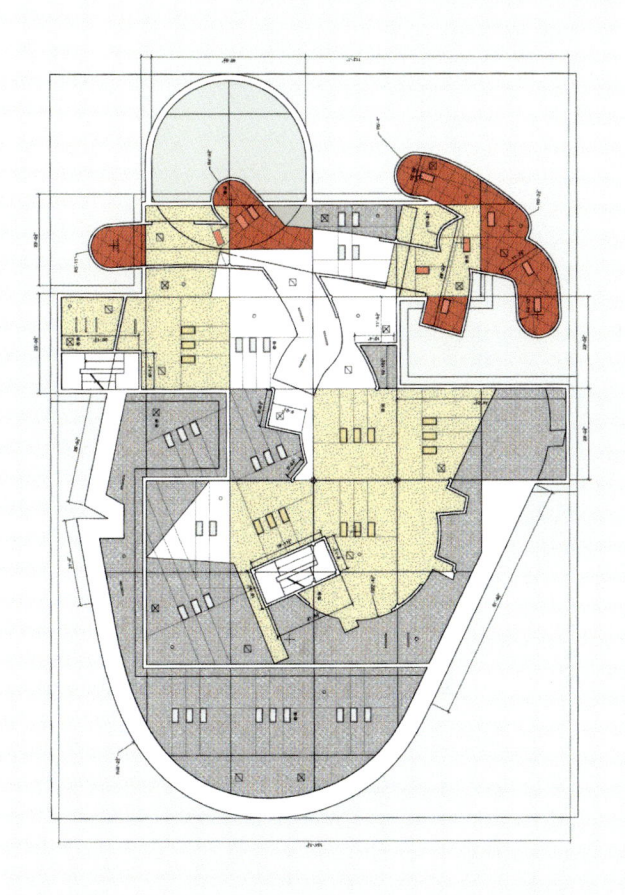

Ten Reasons to Abstract Reflective Ceiling Plans

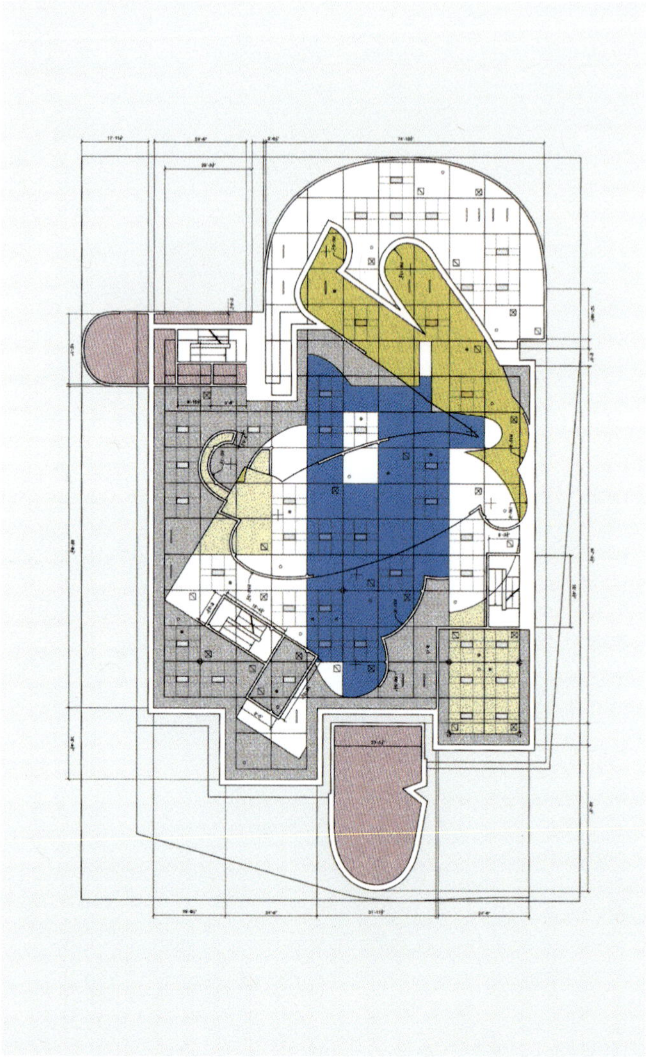

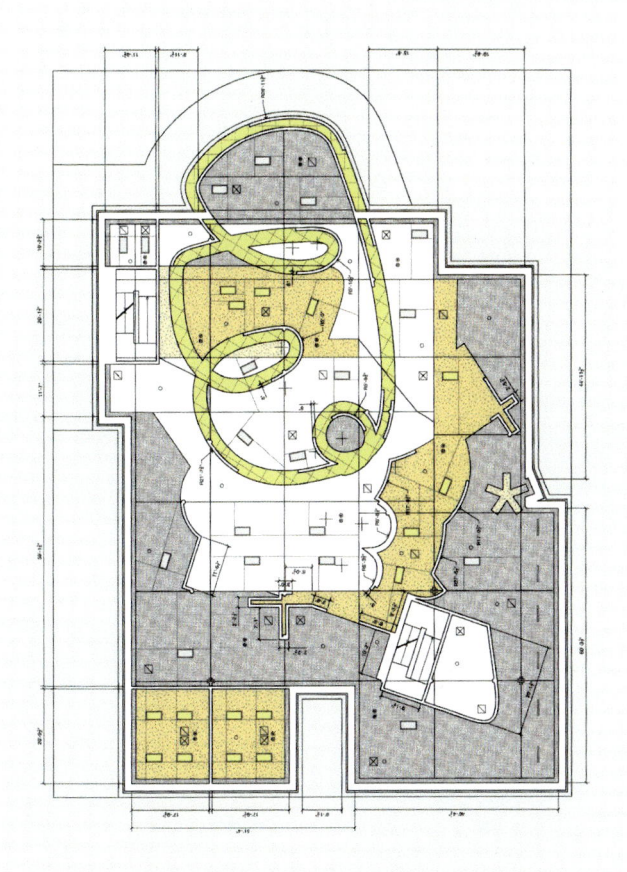

Ten Reasons to Abstract Reflective Ceiling Plans   201

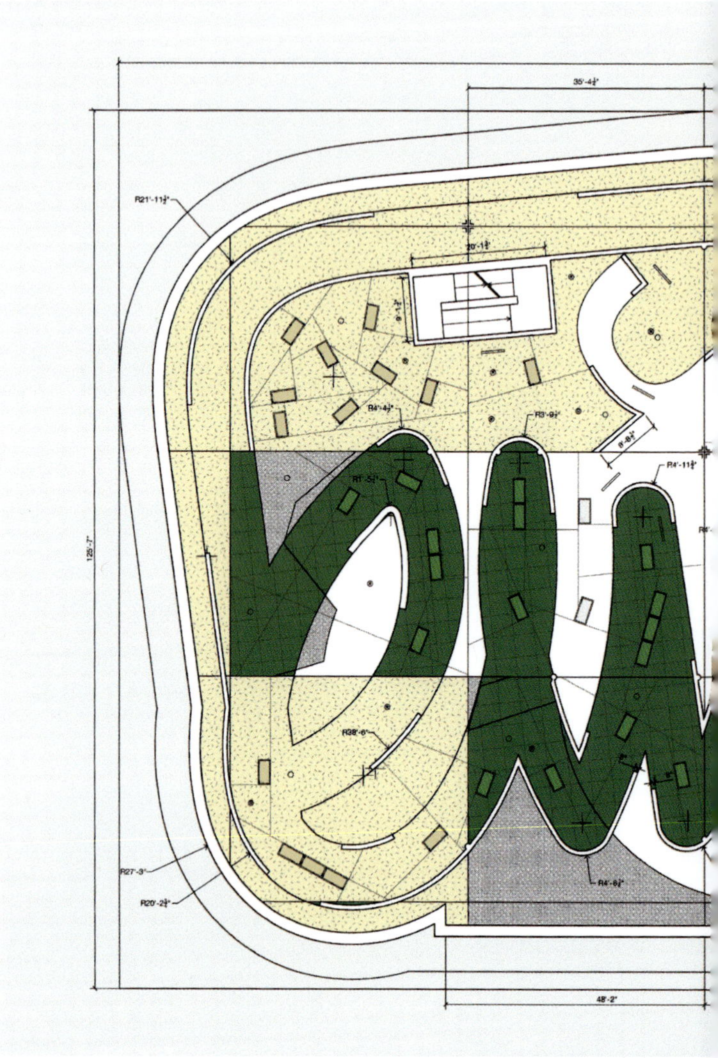
35'-4½"
R21'-11½"
20'-1⅜"
9'-1½"
R4'-4½"
R3'-9½"
R1'-5½"
R4'-11¾"
125'-7"
R38'-6"
R27'-3"
R20'-2¾"
R4'-8½"
48'-2"

Ten Reasons to Abstract Reflective Ceiling Plans 203

Chinese *Xiaoqu*: From Utopia to Dystopia

Zee Ruizi Zeng

Amidst the COVID-19 lockdown in 2019, a controversy emerged among Hong Kong citizens regarding the Hong Kong government's adoption of the term *xiaoqu* in its COVID-19 policies.[1] Originally referring to gated communities with public health and education amenities, the xiaoqu is a prevalent residential typology that has flourished throughout mainland China since the 1950s, particularly in urban areas. While xiaoqu had long been associated with narratives of socialist communal living, the COVID-19 pandemic transformed the term: its connotation became tied to political dystopia as it conveniently served as a unit of governmental

[1] Zeng, "When *YauMaTei* Becomes a Xiaoqu," *Mingpao News*.

control and surveillance on the mainland. Instead of locking down entire city blocks, quarantines were organized around xiaoqus. The residential committee of each xiaoqu collected data of infected residents and reported it to the municipal level. Food and resources were allocated within these same xiaoqu units. Since the term had hardly been used in Hong Kong until 2019, it was apparent that the import of xiaoqu was not simply about using a new word but about adopting a technique of governance from the People's Republic of China.

What is a xiaoqu? Who owns the xiaoqu? Why was it such an effective unit for lockdown control? What is the borderline between public and private inside a xiaoqu? What defines that border? To answer these questions, we need to trace the history and policies of xiaoqu in mainland China and examine the cultural and political implications of this housing typology.

The Blue Collar Dreamworld

Mid-year 1949, Shanghai was relieved from the Chinese Civil War, and simultaneously, industry production began to revive in the city under the control of the Chinese Communist Party. Carrying a long industrial past since the port opening in 1843, in the aftermath of the first Opium War, Shanghai already housed a considerable amount of factory workers. However, dwelling remained an inevitable problem amongst the production workers. Even after the political situation became rather stable, life for them often unfurled in boats or shantytowns on the urban outskirts. By the beginning of 1950, over a million residents shared a similar experience of insecurity in the city.

Seeking to address the issue of blue-collar housing and curry favor with the working class, in 1951, Chen Yi, then mayor of Shanghai, ordered the construction of the first worker's community in China, Caoyang Xincun, on the west side of the Bund (figs. 1 & 2). Allocating ten square meter green space per person, the complex's greenery rate reached an astonishing twenty-nine percent.[2] A hospital, kindergarten, middle and high schools, food market, stores, and cultural spaces were also built within Caoyang Xincun. Chen Yi's vision was succinctly captured in his words: "To serve production, to serve the working people, the priority is to serve the working class."[3]

Though at the time the prevalent discourse of Chinese architecture leaned towards the Soviet Union, the design of the first stage of Caoyang Xincun engaged with the Euro-American ideas of the Garden City and neo-urbanism can be seen. In the head architect Wang Shizeng's memoir, he expressed his early interest in European academic architecture:

> During that time, the studies and attempts in the European and American academic and design circles regarding garden cities and the New Urbanism movement had started to flourish. I was particularly drawn to their emphasis on green spaces, ecology, pedestrian-oriented design, and asymmetrical free

Figure 1.
Bird's-eye view of Caoyang Xincun./ Photo by Fayhoo, 2016.

2 Wang, "Design and Planning of Shanghai Caoyang Xincun Neighborhood."
3 Chen, "Order on 1951 Shanghai Development Guideline."

Figure 2.
Site plan of Caoyang Xincun./Wang Dingzeng, 1956.

Chinese Xiaoqu

layouts. At the same time, the memories of laughter, wind chimes, and growing up amidst the tree shadows in the old alleys of Shanghai have deeply imprinted in my mind. How can I organically blend these two completely different cultural genes in my design practice?[4]

The answer for Wang was a community organization with a more intimate scale—a mid-rise neighborhood system gated community. However, in his 1956 account of the building of Caoyang Xincun, presumably under increasingly oppressive political pressure, Wang relentlessly critiqued his reference to the Euro-American tradition of the neighborhood unit as "reactionary" compared to the Soviet communist ideal of the superblock. In the same essay, he rebranded such a system of denser population concentration as xiaoqu—a term that was just established as the Chinese translation of the Soviet concept of *microrayon*. Originating in the Soviet Union, the concept of microrayon referred to a community settlement that comprised multiple highrises and day-to-day infrastructure (fig. 3). Facilities such as schools, kindergartens, and even hospitals are integrated within these complexes, enabling residents to carry out their day-to-day activities without needing to leave the community. Reappropriating the term, Wang further distanced his project from the idea of the neighborhood unit.[5]

Wang's self-critique of the design of Caoyang Xincun indicated the intricate political tension with which housing issues had been charged at the time. Labeled

4 Li, "The First Large-scale Residential Community in New China—Birth and Planning Design Anecdotes of Shanghai Caoyang Xincun," *Construction Times*.

5 Wang, "Design and Planning of Shanghai Caoyang Xincun Neighborhood."

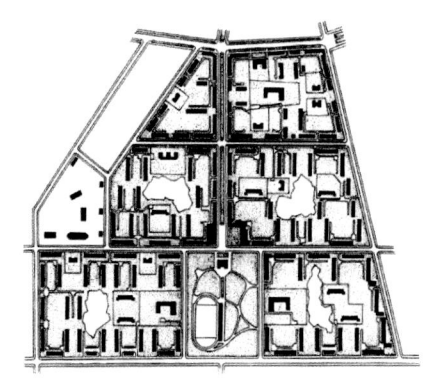

Figure 3.
Plan of a Soviet residential Microrayan./ *Residential Construction in the Byelorussian SSR*, 1980.

as bourgeois, the Euro-American academic tradition of neighborhood units lost popularity in planning under Mao. Yet, partially through a subtle shift in terminology that reconciled Wang's design with the dominant political ideology, xiaoqu as a typology survived and became more associated with the Soviet concept of microrayons, although the spatial organization of xiaoqu was akin to that of neighborhood units.[6] The concept was first introduced to the leadership and architectural experts of China in 1955. The Russian term was translated as xiaoqu (combining xiao for micro and qu for rayon). Publicly discussed in China in a 1958 issue of *Architectural Journal*, the microrayon was considered an ideal and avant-garde urban arrangement for a communist society.[7] Although it was retrospectively stamped as xiaoqu, Caoyang Xincun nonetheless imperceptibly shaped the understanding of such a neighborhood type in China.

6 Lu, *Remaking Chinese Urban Form*.
7 Liu and Togniev, "The Planning and Architecture of Urban Housing Districts," *Architectural Journal*.

Concurrent with the establishment of Caoyang Xincun in 1951 was the issuance of the Central People's Government Finance Ministry Public Grain Stamp, ushering in an era of rationing in the communist People's Republic of China. Up untill the 1990s, rice, cotton, TV, leather shoes, and even cigarettes, were exchanged with their corresponding stamps (fig. 4). Experimenting with Marx's tenet "The nationwide centralization of the means of production will become the national basis of the society constituted by various associations of free and equal producers," new factories started to be operated under the governmental entity.[8] Called work-unit (or *danwei* in Chinese), these government organizations held lifelong employment positions and often rationed social benefits to the employees, including access to worker's residence. The residents in the unprecedented worker's community at Caoyang Xincun were carefully selected, most of whom were "model"

8 Karl Marx, "The Nationalisation of the Land," *The International Herald*.

Figure 4.
Ration tickets used in China./ Photo by Red Guosam Zhu-Guang01, 2018.

Figure 5. Celebrated and praised, workers moving into Caoyang Xincun and walking through the gate of the community, 1952./ *People's Pictorial*, 1952.

9 Luo, "Space Producing and Space Change: New Residential Areas of Workers in Shanghai and the Experience of a Socialist City," *Journal of East China Normal University*, 91-96.

textile or metal workers (fig. 5). From two hundred and seventeen different factories in Shanghai, a thousand and two families were relocated to the gated community, and many of them were awarded "exemplary worker" by the Communist Party.[9] A new class of workers was thus fabricated. Praised and honored, those who lived in the xiaoqu had the same political agendas, cultural beliefs, and social backgrounds (fig. 6). At a time when people were still weighed down by post-war scars, a utopian life for blue-collar workers unfolded within the units where dreams of progress and modernity resided. Radios could be found in the living room, offering a glimpse of the wide world; flushing toilets (which were very rare) were shared among households; children could walk to school in fifteen minutes inside the complex (fig. 7)—a blue-collar dreamland indeed.

Figure 6.
Sign "Long live Chairman Mao," in CaoyangXincun./ Photo by Yang Cheng, *The Paper*, 2009

Serving as an exemplary worker's community, Caoyang Xincun became a site of diplomacy since its erection, receiving waves of foreign journalists and officials. However, the steel fences all around the xiaoqu also announced the exclusiveness of the community. Perhaps it was for the sake of safety, or to further demonstrate the privileged and utopian nature of the community that was maintained and owned by the government. Workers in the xiaoqu established their unique privilege through the fences. On the other side of the wall stood the still bewildered people, who peeked at the life inside Caoyang Xincun with admiration, awe, and perhaps jealousy. It was then the intangible group of the "working class" was more palpably defined—those who were inside the walls.

10 "People's Republic of China Regulations of the Guangdong Province Economic Special Zone."

Figure 7.
Workers' children exercise in the primary school in Caoyang Xincun, 1952./ *People's Pictorial*, 1952.

The Middle-Class Enclave

In 1978, Deng Xiaoping guided the Chinese economic reform *Gaige Kaifang*. From then on, rural youths rushed from villages to big cities to seek opportunities to work at newly founded, private-owned businesses. One of those urban centers was Shenzhen, a city freshly founded after the economic reform, with its advantageous position as a new port in Guangdong adjacent to Hong Kong. As per the "Regulations of the Guangdong Province Economic Special Zone," ratified in 1980, the Chinese government embraced a market economy by encouraging foreign investors to plow into factory establishment and venture capital in the region.[10] Since then, Shenzhen has become a capitalist enclave for free trade and international corporations without contradicting the ideology of the Communist Party. Waves of factories flooded into Shenzhen, especially manufacturers of technology products. Like many port cities in China, Shenzhen completed its fast transformation from a fish town to an economic juggernaut. Of course, such a rapidly growing city needed a rapidly growing housing market that would also boost the economy of the country. Right at the beginning of economic reform, Deng suggested a potential way of housing reform by "allowing private construction or private-public partnerships, installment payments, mobilizing private funds, with the state providing materials."[11] As one of the pilot zones, Shenzhen was the first city to experiment with Deng's idea. In late November 1987, a piece of land sized 8,588 square meters by the city reservoir was bid for a fifty-year land use right, which marked the earliest case of commercial land use in China (fig. 8).[12] On this sold plot, the first privately planned commercial xiaoqu came into being. Like a worker's xiaoqu, Donghu Liyuan is a gated community with amenities like outdoor green space (sixty percent of the total area), an outdoor gym, running paths, and a community center (fig. 9). Though certain infrastructures such as hospitals and schools, which are

11 "Sector: Big Event," *Urban and Rural Planning*, 151.

12 "The 1987 Participants Recalling Events: 'First Land Auction' Driving Constitutional Amendments," *Shenzhen News Paper*.

Figure 8.
Luo Jinxing, the manager of Shenzhen Real Estate Company (the one holding number 11 sign), acquired the land use rights of a residential land auctioned by the city government, 1987./ Photo by Chen Zhishan, Xinhua News Agency, 1987.

Figure 9.
Bird's-eye view of Donghu Liyuan./ Image captured from Lianjia Maps, 2024.

usually public and government-owned in China, cannot be introduced into this private development, the planning is similar to that of a well-equipped community in the Mao period.

Modeled after the socialist utopia of collective living, Donghu Liyuan promised a tight-knit environment with comprehensive services that could keep up with the management intensity of a worker's xiaoqu. The first private property management company in the country was therefore established (fig. 10). In an article that highlighted the xiaoqu property management at Donghu Liyuan for the first China Happy Community Model Award, the private company was acknowledged as the "Property Management Model."[13] According to the award committee, the property management in Donghu Liyuan successfully fostered ground for "faith and spiritual pursuit." The commodification of communal care was thereby disguised and justified by the abstract idea of transcendence.

In an overnight bid in early 1980, the apartments were sold out instantly. Eventually, the success of Donghu Liyuan and other similar developments drove an amendment to the Chinese constitution in 1988 that states "land use rights can be transferred per the legal provisions."[14] From then on, xiaoqus mushroomed and became the most prevalent type of housing in Chinese cities. Housing the rising middle class that managed to accumulate wealth through the economic reform, the gated xiaoqu, yet again, came to define the state-of-the-art social stratification in China. Subsequently in 1994, China launched the Housing Reform, which officially declared the total privatization of the housing market in China and shifted the responsibility of housing construction from the state and work units to individuals.[15] Emerging out of the dream of an idealistic communist utopia, the worker's xiaoqu donned the cloak of capitalism.

13 "Donghu Liyuan, Our Community of Happiness," *House and Real Estate*, 65.
14 "The 1987 Participants Recalling Events: 'First Land Auction' Driving Constitutional Amendments," *Shenzhen News Paper*.
15 "State Council Decision on Advancing the Reform of Urban Housing System."

The Undercurrent of Carework

As private housing became increasingly prevalent and the economy more liberalized, the collapse of the centralized system of housing rationing raised anxieties about social control. The mechanism of residential segregation in the work-unit era made it easier to implement political agendas and manage social discontent, whereas in commercial xiaoqus, there was no equivalent political organization.[16] To tighten control over urban populations, the government passed "The Organization Law of Urban Residents' Committees of the People's Republic of China" in 1989, which required neighborhoods to establish "residents' committees" (*jüweihui* in Chinese) to "assist the people's government or its dispatched agencies in carrying out work related to the interests of residents, such as public health, the one-child policy, relief for entitled groups, and youth education."[17] The establishment of the *Organization Law* formed the basis for administrative control over xiaoqu communities, where even private property managements are subjected to governmental policing and surveillance through Residents' Committees (fig. 11).

It was also the same year when "The City Residential New Development Community Management Regulations" was approved by the Ministry of Construction of the People's Republic of China, which stated that every xiaoqu should establish a xiaoqu Representative Committee to "represent the property owners and occupants within the

Figure 10. Property management company of Donghu Liyuan./ Image by *Sohu News*, 2021.

16 Lu, *Remaking Chinese Urban Form*, 68
17 "Order on The Organization Law of Urban Residents' Committees of the People's Republic of China."

Figure 11. High alert: two active members of the residents' committee on duty watching a strange man./ Photo by Wu Qiang, from *Wu Qiang's Photography Collection*, 1982.

Figure 12. Xiaoqu's fences reinforced by steel plates during the Shanghai lockdown./ Photo by author.

Figure 13. Shopping Stamp during the Shanghai lockdown, "Your shopping window is 18:00-18:30, May 19th."/ Photo by author.

residential community, safeguarding the legitimate rights of property owners and occupants," while also bearing the responsibility to "subject to supervision and guidance from the real estate administrative department, relevant administrative authorities, and the Urban Residents' Committees."[18] Therefore, by the end of 1994, the hierarchy of power had found its way into every xiaoqu. A private developer would purchase "the right of land use" from the government, and build a new xiaoqu for sale; the xiaoqu residents would establish a Representative Committee, which would work with the developer to hire a property management company; both property management company and the xiaoqu Representative Committee are then subjected to the supervision of Urban Residents' Committee, which usually oversees two to three xiaoqu complexes; the Urban Residents' Committee then supports and implements governmental rules and administrative standards.

The chain of power goes down to the most basic level in everyday life in xiaoqus, not only providing care and security but also imposing law and order. In the COVID-19 era, the xiaoqu functioned as a tool of intensifying control. To enforce quarantines, the gates of xiaoqus were mounted with metal barriers (fig. 12). When the supply chain was disrupted, the rationing era seemed to be back—with stamps that only allowed one to leave thew xiaoqu limited times per day (fig. 13). Food seemed to arrive at wealthier xiaoqus first, and Coca-Cola became a circulating

[18] "The City Residential New Development Community Management Regulations of People's Republic of China."

currency.[19] Inside these gated xiaoqus, every resident endured an unreal jump from utopia to dystopia.

The Conscious, Unsettled Dystopia

On July 1st, 2022, the "zero-COVID" policy suddenly collapsed in the aftermath of grass-root protests in Shanghai, the last city to maintain lockdowns (fig. 14). Released from their xiaoqus, many residents described their experience of the pandemic as an unresolved, dissolute dream—three months of their life were swept away in quarantine, and without any confirmation, they reattained their hard-to-defined, elusive freedom. And what happens now?

The gated xiaoqu remains the most popular option for urban housing in China. In fact, according to the latest report of *Shanghai New Real Estate Public Notice* in June 2023, all twenty-six developments are gated xiaoqus.[20] Ironically in 2016, during Xi's first term as the Chairman of China, there was a call to dismantle the walls of gated xiaoqus under his administration.[21] However, these very walls played a significant role in enforcing control under COVID-19 policies. This paradox underscores the complex interplay between policy objectives and real-world outcomes—with China's current law, it seems a vicious circle to continue developing gated communities. According to the codes, developers have the responsibility to maintain the roads, greenery, and infrastructures within their developing area, leading both developers and residents unwilling to make their complexes public. In the meantime,

19 Hu, "Shanghai City Dwellers Develop New Bonds as They Barter Goods amid Lockdown," *Global Times*.
20 "The fifth batch of concentrated listing for new properties in Shanghai in 2023," *Shanghai Real Estate Exchange Center*.
21 Central Committee of the Communist Party of China, "Several Opinions on Further Strengthening Urban Planning and Construction Management Work."

the continued development of gated xiaoqus even after COVID-19 also reflects the cushioned, overly dependent citizenship that the architectural type has come to foster. Indeed, the xiaoqu diversifies the urban landscape, concentrates urban care provision, and gives everyone within the complex a bit of green and security in the extremely dense city—something a regular apartment complex in the U.S. hardly achieves. However, what does this extra comfort cost? And given the exclusiveness of the xiaoqu, who can really enjoy this level of comfort?

In September 2023, sponsored by the Shanghai government, Caoyang Xincun welcomed journalists in its recently built museum. In a short news article about the museum, the original idea of the microrayon was still advocated and praised.[22] Once a utopia, now a dystopia, xiaoqu as a unique architectural type has witnessed the vicissitude of Chinese society, from socialism to capitalism, from post-war to post-pandemic traumas. Perhaps, the gated communities exemplify how care work can often simultaneously lead to multilevel surveillance. Yet, it was not until the pandemic that one began to realize the bio-political intensity that xiaoqu has long embodied. As the veil of control lifted, citizens in China confronted a society forever changed. This time, one must ponder: how will this conscious, unsettled dystopia manifest in the future residents' daily lives?

22 "Entering the 'Village History Museum' to see the more than seventy years of history of New China's first workers' village," *The Paper*.

Figure 14 (next page). Shanghai Urumqi Middle Road protest rally. November 27, 2022./ Photo by Philip Roin, 2022

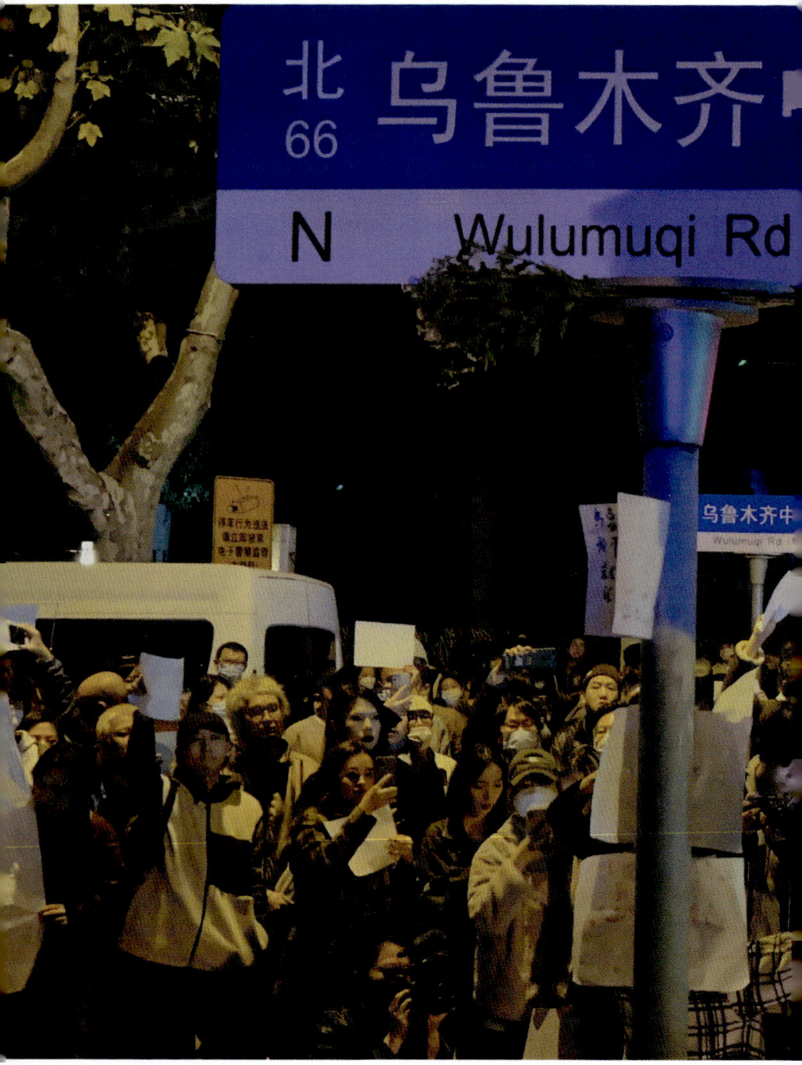
北
66
乌鲁木齐
N Wulumuqi Rd
乌鲁木齐中
Wulumuqi Rd

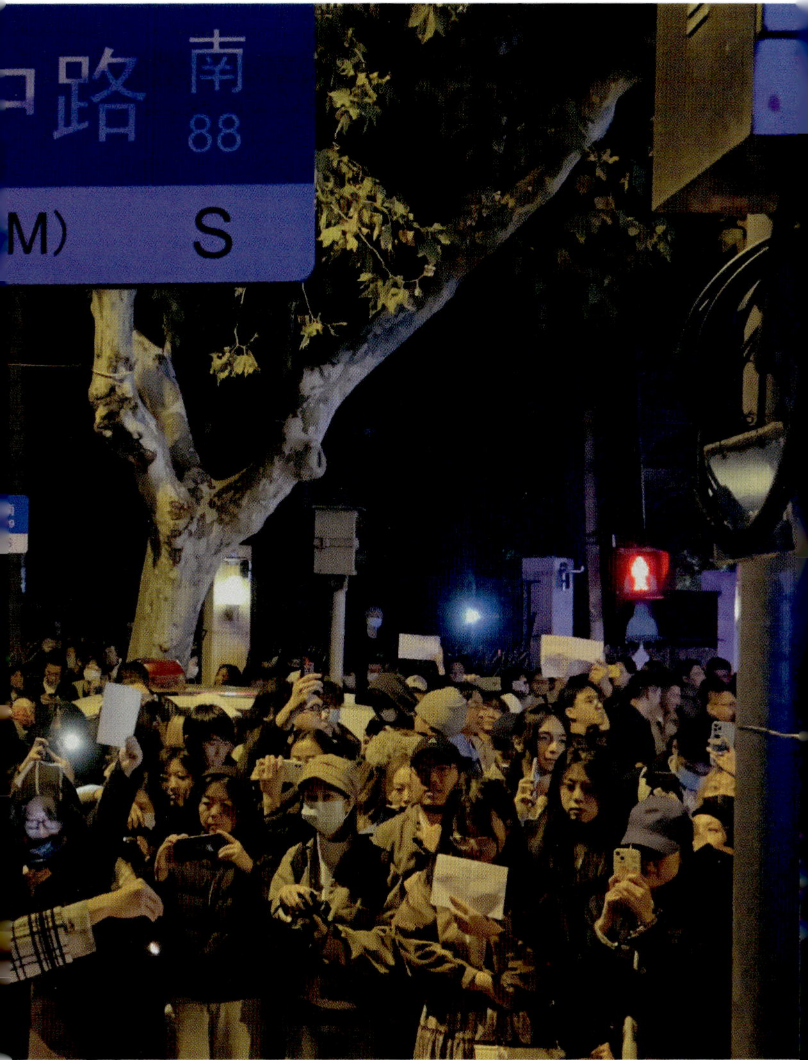
路
南
88
M)
S

Reimagining Cultural Narratives: Sumayya Vally on Architecture, Biennales, and the Global South's Voice

Guillermo S. Arsuaga and Shivani Shedde

Restating the significance of "orientalism" remains an impossibly crucial task. Edward Said's monumental theorization of orientalism as a category of knowledge conceived and weaponized through Europe's encounter with the Orient has shaped decades of scholarship and debate. This epistemic framework, embedded within an intricate web of stereotypes, generalizations, cultural misrepresentations, and power relationships, crystalizes itself in the material realities of oppression and violence that continue to play out with historical gravity in the built environment. Indeed, demystifying the tropes of orientalist exoticism and categorizations of backwardness goes beyond an analysis of discourse and ideological semantics. Rather, Said's meticulous dissection of the "orientalist" lens through which the "West" views and engages the "East" challenges us to confront how these tropes are internalized in the former colonies where the enduring legacies of colonialism, settler colonialism, or neo-fascism shape space.

Figure 1.
Sumayya Vally at the Islamic Art Biennale./ Copyrights Marilyn Clark.

How does architecture intervene? Sumayya Vally, who is based between South Africa and the United Kingdom and is the founder of Counterspace, provides a compelling argument to define other domains to re-evaluate and re-contextualize our understanding of the Global South. By countering orientalism through Arab, diasporic Asian, and African cultural narratives that coexist with politics and materialities of space, Vally thoughtfully offers insights into the evolving discourse and practices within architecture. In doing so, Vally's work is concerned with the realm of the everyday, the "demos," rather than the state. In our conversation, we delve into the complexities of her work: her perspective on how architecture embodies cultural identities and demands a deeper understanding of history; the ways in which the experience of space forces solidarity across sanctioned borders; and how architecture might provide an avenue to reclaim forgotten narratives.

Vally's curation of the Islamic Arts Biennale (IAB) 2023 emerged as a critical cultural event to dispute the assertions of orientalism. Organized by the Diriyah Biennale Foundation and hosted at Jeddah's Western Hajj Terminal from January 23 to May 23, 2023, it marked a significant moment for the spatial and temporal reinterpretation of Islamic art, showcasing an array of works around the theme of *Awwal Bait* (the first home). Linking non-contiguous spaces of the Islamic world through their connected histories, the Biennale's subthemes, *Hijrah* and *Qiblah* (migration and sacred direction) brought together artists who responded to an imaginaire of communal space and cultural identity across land and sea.

***

Guillermo S. Arsuaga (GSA) + Shivani Shedde (SS):
To begin, we would like to refer to a quote from the IAB press release: "Movement is at the heart of an Islamic form of thinking, one that traces the trajectory of ideas between people and places. It is a methodology that feels resonant with the tradition of the sahabah, the name given to those who offered companionship to the Prophet (PBUH). Companionship in journeying brings into dialogue the landscape, lived space, and experience of a community, defining their ties and sense of belonging." Reflecting on this sentiment that is at the heart of the IAB, we were wondering if you could take us through the two terms that drive the curatorial project, Hijrah and Qiblah, and how histories of migration and directionality shape the notion of Awwal Bait, the first home?

Sumayya Vally (SV): My practice is centered on this idea of thinking about diaspora and diasporic logics as fuel for finding design forms, and creative expression for architecture that shapes our built environment and cultural technologies as we know them.

Most architectural designs and artistic expressions we have inherited are preserved in Western forms, often focused on immortalizing or "petrifying" things. However, in Islamic and African cultures, and among other southern traditions, preservation of legacy and history involves living with things. We honor traditions through festivals, rituals, community gatherings, and collective memory. This energy was something I wanted to inject into the biennale at an epistemological level.

The definition of Islamic art, as we understand it, originates from seventeenth-century France and is inherently colonial. When we say "Islamic art," we visualize arabesques, mosaics, and drums—forms we associate with Islamic art, but rarely question their origins or contemporary relevance. These traditions are indeed beautiful and have evolved from culture, but we often revere them as if they stem from faith.

Thinking back to the early days of Islam, the Prophet (PBUH) and his companions focused on practices and simplistic ways of life. Honoring traditions and practices was done through experiences and oral, performance, and ritual-led cultures. My aim was to contribute a new definition of Islamic art to the Biennale—one that is living, relevant, and resonates with Muslims today, while also recognizing the diverse practices and traditions of Islamic culture globally.

Islamic teachings have influenced various forms of culture and radical politics of love, as seen in the example of Malcolm X. These ways of thinking can contribute to our creative worlds within decolonial frameworks, offering different forms and creative inspirations if we consider rituals and practices as generators for creative thinking.

The term Awwal Bait, meaning first house, is the theme for the first Biennale. I was involved in this project from its inception and was part of all the processes, including site selection and infrastructure setup. The challenge was to create a universally resonant experience while also celebrating Islamic diversity. Being the first edition, it laid the groundwork, so I chose elements that everyone could relate to.

Awwal Bait refers to the Kaaba in Mecca, the direction Muslims face during prayer. I wanted to explore this literally, considering how the entire world has moved through this region due to pilgrimage, resulting in a cultural hybridization that I wanted to reflect upon. This concept of the "first house" explores the construction of spiritual belonging and community, and reflects on the principles of belonging that we return to after movement and displacement.

The term Qibla, or the sacred direction, signifies the Kaaba as the center of our rituals. It's a metaphorical point of unity that connects us with those who pray in the same direction—past, present, and future. The exhibition explores this theme across different scales, from the atomic level to the infinite, covering the effects of the call to prayer, ablution, body in prayer, gathering in prayer, and the experience of the Kaaba itself.

The theme Hijrah, meaning migration, explores the site's experience of diversity and movement. The site of the Biennale—the old airport terminal where pilgrims landed—had a significant influence on this theme. My own memories of visiting this site as a fourteen-year-old pilgrim, witnessing the global gathering under its canopy, greatly influenced the energy I wanted to bring to this section. In this section, we explore how we construct home and belonging after movement, the impacts of cultural exchanges due to migration, and how different cultures have been absorbed and embodied in the region. Jeddah itself is a cultural hybrid, embracing influences from around the world—Indonesia, Malaysia, Africa, India, and the subcontinent—which is reflected in the Biennale's outdoor works that serve as gathering spaces, emphasizing the principles of belonging such as food, sound, celebration, work, worship, collective memory, and collective imagination.

GSA + SS: Looking at the pieces exhibited, we were particularly struck by James Webb's "A Series of Personal Questions Addressed to a Boat that Sailed its Last Journey on the Red Sea" (fig. 2). It recalled Christina Sharpe's work "In the Wake," in which she writes about the sea as the forgotten space of modernity, and also as a space of alienation and violence; for her, the object that captures the intense wreckage brought by the sea in an age of globalization is the slave ship. Could you talk a little bit about how the concept of Hijrah might articulate two competing versions of mobility or migration, and perhaps complicate the binaries that seem to be presented in Indian Ocean vs. Atlantic histories?

SV: I think you're spot on in that we see these histories as binary, but they're completely interconnected. Also, this might sound a little bit cheesy, but I am from a place in the world where the two oceans meet in South Africa, and at that point, you can witness two vast bodies of water—the Indian Ocean and the Atlantic—coming together. Our local history is steeped in the knowledge of items that came from the sea, and from many different parts of these waters.

Figure 2.
A Series of Personal Questions Addressed to a Boat That Sailed Its Last Journey on the Red Sea, James Webb./ Courtesy of Diriyah Biennale Foundation

I frequently find myself listening to Thabo Mbeki's "I am an African" speech when I long for home. It serves as a touchstone, a return to my roots. His words paint a vivid picture of diverse convergences, encompassing histories from both seas. He integrates these multifaceted experiences into his identity by proudly declaring, "I am an African." He refers to the Malay slaves, and how the marks from the beatings they endured are symbolically etched into his own body. He discusses the Europeans who arrived, their impact on the land, and includes these narratives into his identity as well.

Often we compartmentalize these histories, but in reality, due to human migration, they overlap and intersect. Of course, there are specific nuances and unique moments in different historical periods, and diverse entities possess their own character. However, there is a shared sense of unity when we view these events as parallel occurrences. A straightforward example would be how the discovery and felling of trees in the UK led to advancements in shipbuilding, which in turn increased global travel. These developments occurred concurrently in many regions. Due to the processes of colonization, despite regional differences, similar power dynamics and tactics were enacted.

Figure 3.
Prototype of a Reassembled Mosque, Yasmeen Lari./ Courtesy of Diriyah Biennale Foundation

The sea serves as an ideal metaphor for the confluence of people, the intersection of movements, and the commonalities in our histories and cultures. Similarly, Jeddah's port, with its long history of global movement, has seen diverse influxes of people due to pilgrimage, trade, and beyond.

One particularly poignant thought I often contemplate is the story of the West Africans captured and enslaved during their return journey from pilgrimage. These individuals were central to the genesis of jazz and blues music in the Americas. The sounds that emanated from their bodies—their voices—found their way into different cultures and movements through successive generations. Such meeting places have always been conduits of connection, binding people and their histories in numerous profound ways.

GSA + SS: *It's interesting that you describe the term Hijrah as an Arabic word referring to "emigrating," "passing" or "coming." In South Asia, as you might be aware, the term refers to the third sex—neither men nor women—though this would loosely translate to transgender in English, this community often self-identifies as belonging to a gender that is not necessarily in*

the state of transition. That got us thinking about a politics of refusal, as characterized by Moten and Harney, for communities to assert their will and not to give in to imposed colonial orders, but to be actively inhabiting spaces of the undercommons. Is Hijrah a methodology of fugitivity?

SV: Absolutely. Even if we interpret the term Hijrah as referencing migration, it brings to mind identities that are migratory or diasporic, or those that are hybrids, encompassing facets of east and west, north and south, irrespective of our individual orientations. This concept particularly resonates with me, given my interest in Nigeria and how my own identity is hyphenated. The potential inherent in the amalgamation of diverse elements within a single identity is immense. It allows a resonance across geographical boundaries. In my work, which includes my architectural projects, I'm constantly contemplating how this hybrid identity can be a position of power. I don't know if it's necessarily born out of fugitivity, but I'd argue it arises from a position of ambiguity and cultural intersection. This allows us to find common ground with a wide array of individuals, even beyond the cultures we directly embody. I believe cultures inherently resonate with each other, and many of the pieces at the DNA that various artists have contributed also embody this concept.

GSA + SS: Just to add on to that, this notion seems particularly resonant in your recent project: the winning design for the Asiat-Darse Bridge in Belgium (fig. 4). In this project, you've managed to materialize migration histories through the figure of Paul Panda Farnana, while simultaneously invoking the symbol of the boat—rather, a series of boats—as a physical embodiment and emergent representation of these submerged histories, perhaps even colonial histories? Could you elaborate more on your process of materializing fugitive histories through architecture?

SV: Now, let me peel back the layers and delve deeper into the intricate narrative of our project in Belgium. The competition brief was for a pedestrian bridge in a town called Vilvoorde—a place I hadn't previously known or understood well. Initially it appeared to be a straightforward pedestrian bridge design, but the context of the task prompted me to think deeply about our approach.

Naturally we began to explore the town's relationship with migration due to its significant location by the sea, which witnessed immense movement. With my curiosity piqued, I started linking this to the Congo because of Belgium's historical connections with the region. We embarked on extensive research and discovered a figure named Paul Panda Farnana. It was fascinating to learn that this relatively obscure personality hailed from Vilvoorde during the era of World War II.

Paul Panda Farnana was an exceptional individual. He was a genius who studied horticulture in Vilvoorde, and significantly shaped the landscape of Belgium. Furthermore, he expanded his work to the Congo, where his efforts played a substantial role in defining its landscape as well. As a Pan-African, he convened numerous conferences with Du Bois and several others across Europe. During the war, he served Belgium but faced severe brutality—a common experience for Congolese soldiers in the Belgian ranks. This hardship spurred him to become a more pronounced advocate for fair wages for the Black populace in Belgium. His work significantly influenced the legal frameworks in the region.

Despite his monumental contributions, Farnana remains relatively unknown. When we introduced him to the jury, only one person had heard of him, and she wasn't aware that he hailed from Vilvoorde. This inspired our architectural response to think about water architectures.

Figure 4. Asiat-Darse Pedestrian Bridge./ Courtesy of Counterspace.

We found inspiration in the boat structures of the Congo—dark, hollowed-out timber structures that often cluster together, serving as platforms for activity, gathering, and trade. We admired this sense of unity, and it influenced our design. Conceptually, we thought of these structures as linked boats, both for structural stability and symbolic representation. Each boat—in homage to Farnana's work—would carry plant species related to his research.

Following a diasporic pattern, there would be a main structure accompanied by ancillary boat structures. These additional elements would float along the riverbank, anchoring at specific points developed in collaboration with the project's landscape architects. They would assist in the pollination and rewilding of previously industrial zones, serving as a metaphor for landscape healing.

A bridge is more than just a structure connecting two points in space and time, and we wanted our design to reflect that expansive idea. Since our proposal's development, local newspapers have run stories about Paul Panda Farnana, generating interest even before the project's public announcement. To me, this feels like a gift, an opportunity to honor an overlooked story through my work.

For those who consider my methods far from traditional architecture, I hope they'll see that there is always architecture waiting to be discovered in overlooked places and stories. It is the architect's responsibility to deeply comprehend the site because, in crafting a building or structure, we are communicating our interpretation of that place.

GSA + SS: *Let's revisit the topic of biennales. These large-scale exhibitions have changed the way art is made, seen, and discussed, particularly regarding self-representation. When in the context of historical decolonization and anti-imperialist struggle, it doesn't seem premature to say that one of the legacies of the Islamic Art Biennial, the Sharjah Arts Biennial, the São Paulo Biennial, the Kochi Muziris Biennale and so on, is a sense of continuity of the radical cultural, political projects of the Third World that reinvigorate connections, and highlight common lived experiences. And yet, there is an anxiety that while these biennales do offer a space to represent and excavate hidden histories, they may simply be enacting and perpetuating a perennial, almost ethnographic interest in "local cultures." What challenges do you foresee in ensuring that these spaces do not perpetuate hegemonic views, as is often the case with extractive knowledge practices?*

SV: First off, I am wired to be inherently optimistic and hopeful, so rather than seeing any of these challenges as a source of anxiety, I see them as windows of opportunity. I think that southern territories and conditions have been victim to ethnographies, extractions, reductions even for so long, that right now is the most opportune moment to undo all of that and take ownership of our own narratives. To put forth worlds and write histories in our own image. That said, I think it's important to ensure that the custodians and curators of these knowledge practices are reflective of the work and their contexts.

Platforms like biennales and pavilions are important for us to fiercely protect and actively shape and question, because they are platforms for imagining the future. I do not believe that the Islamic Arts Biennale sought to or merely "showcased" local culture. I set out to create and contribute a generative definition of Islamic art—rooted in the oral, the aural and the ritual—and the artists responded and contributed their visions and questions for the future. How can something so plural become hegemonic? Perhaps it is defined solely by an outside gaze. We have not had an opportunity to see ourselves reflected this way. And I'd say, as much as it is an open hand of welcome to others, it is also imperative to have these opportunities to imagine from us for us, to think about how we unpack our ways of seeing and being in the world and how they can not only "solve" crises our world is facing, but look at paradigms from entirely different perspectives and thereby offer different imaginations so needed in our world.

GSA + SS: In its conceptual framing, the Biennale works hard to showcase a poetics of solidarity. Could you talk about some of the art that has been showcased?

SV: Indeed it does. Given the Biennale being rooted in these shared practices, rituals, and ways of being, I felt a deep sense of solidarity resonating from across the works and participants. Hijrah means migration. I was thinking about Jeddah as a nexus of cultural production and exchange because it has witnessed so much movement because of the pilgrimage. It has embodied and absorbed the cultures of the world in its own culture, and it has transmitted its own culture to the world. I was also thinking about the ways we construct 'home' and construct belonging after movement, often after displacement. Our Islamic calendar is marked by the moment that the prophet undertook migration—when he migrated from Makkah to Medinah because he was fleeing persecution. This most contemporary of conditions—that of movement—is something that is so resonant with the world and so many populations, Muslim and otherwise.

I wanted to reflect how communities are constructed and reconstructed—what are the ingredients of community? Sharing in prayer, work, food, sound, celebration, loss, memory and imagination.

But that is also a theme throughout the Biennale. I consider pieces that evoke that sense very strongly, the below come to mind.

Through performance, sculpture, and installation, Igshaan Adams' piece, *Salat al-jama'ah* (fig. 5), explores aspects of politics, race, and religion as they have affected both his personal history and that of his community.

Figure 5.
Salat al-jama'ah, Igshaan Adams./ Courtesy of Diriyah Biennale Foundation

His intricate woven artworks employ a range of natural and synthetic materials, but many draw inspiration for their form and pattern from traditional Islamic textiles. For this work, he acquired a number of used prayer rugs from close friends and family living in the Bonteheuwel district of Cape Town, where many Black and Colored families were forcibly moved by the apartheid authorities in the 1960s. Well-loved and worn, each rug records the imprint of its owner's body in the act of prayer over many years. Adams has interpreted these patterns of wear using beads and semiprecious stones to create a series of new textile pieces. In combination they form an impressive composite work that speaks of the value of collective worship.

A big part of what the Biennale aimed to demonstrate is that Islamic practice is rooted in collective rituals and experiences of community and belonging.

In a celebration of the humble everyday prayer, Joe Namy's *Cosmic Breath* choreographs the call to prayer from eighteen different, often unexpected locations, across different time zones. These include, for example, a petrol station in Jakarta, a parking lot in Detroit, the side of the street, a chip shop in Cape Town, to name a few. He's recorded these and choreographed them so that the call starts at the same time, reflecting on the idea of cosmic breath—that every second of the day the call to prayer is being called somewhere on Earth, because it moves with the movement of the sun. And there are five a day, so when we stand up in prayer, we're joining this undulating rhythm and this undulating call. We're joining with people who do the same. So many of our practices are not able to be held in traditional archives because they're not written forms. They're oral, passed down from generation to generation, from body to body.

Figure 6.
Islamic Arts Biennale, scenography by OMA./ Copyright, Marco Cappalletti, courtesy of OMA

For their site-specific installation, *anywhere can be a place of worship*, Syn Architects have designed an enclosure that recalls the humility of this first *musalla* ("a place to pray"), reminiscent of the courtyard of the Prophet Muhammad (PBUH).

The walls are formed from local palm reeds woven together by Saudi artisans, recalling how temporary prayer spaces were once created along travel and pilgrimage routes. Gaps in the walls allow glimpses out to the immediate landscape where indigenous plants bloom, evoking the historic gardens of Madinah. Light from above falls on a slit that stands for the *mihrab*, emphasizing the role of the sun as a compass, determining the direction as well as the times of prayer. Simple maintenance—raking the ground and compacting the earth that supports the walls—is performed each day. Without these acts of care the structure would disappear entirely over time. Like ritual prayers, they construct and sustain its identity as a musalla and as a civic space. Like many of the works under the Hijrah theme, the work itself is an invitation for gatherings.

Maintaining the Sacred by Dima Srouji studies the destroyed stained glass windows of Al Aqsa Mosque. The piece is a reconstruction of those windows, working alongside stone masons and glass blowers from Palestine. The abstracted glass shapes in the window's stone frame make reference to society, geography, history, theology, and time. They include allusions to the landscape surrounding the Haram al-Sharif, the destruction of the windows, and bullet holes in the mosque wall. They also draw on traditional motifs used in Ottoman colored glass, as well as a catalog of other Islamic geometrical and plant motifs. This sculpture honors the Aqsa Mosque precinct as the largest Palestinian public space in Jerusalem, and the courage and perseverance of the people who use it.

GSA + SS: Conventional orientalist thinking often characterizes the Islamic world as anti-modern and timeless, filled with communal and sectarian conflict. This perspective has contributed significantly to the persistent rise of Islamophobia, aided by numerous wars with neo-imperialist objectives. Currently, this issue is most acutely evident in Palestine—a place that is home to many religions besides Islam. How do you perceive the urgency of organizing such a Biennale and how it aims to challenge and subvert the entrenched power structures and narratives within this historically deep-rooted discourse?

SV: Right now, in the context of so much emergency, we need the emergence of different voices more than ever—to bring about difference in the face of the status quo. There is a temptation to solve the emergency by replacing it with solidity, but sometimes that solidity is complicit in being part of the problem. As much as architecture is about creating solidity, too often that solidity tears people apart—making walls, imposing infrastructure, erasing history. We need to recognise the power of our craft to represent who we are in form, to convene us so that we coexist.

The Islamic Arts Biennale presented a profound opportunity to see ourselves (people of the Muslim world) represented in a way that portrays our diversity and cultural hybridity. Of course it is an open hand and invitation for all to experience Islam, but we cannot overstate the power of a platform like this—to speak from this particular set of voices from around the world. It is an opportunity for artists to realize works that would not be possible elsewhere, both in its scale and in what it is doing. In most contexts we operate in we have to do the work of explaining the context first, leaving very little room for deep nuanced work to emerge. Here, we operated with an audience who has a base level understanding of the context, and it allowed the artists freedom to really interrogate the subject matter they were working with and express unprecedented forms of expression for the artworld. It did that and it still remained accessible to an outside audience, which is proof that we can do this work in other contexts. That is profound because there are so many perspectives from other cultures and ways of being which our world, and all its challenges, can learn deeply from.

The works in the biennale are experiential: they put forth an entirely different definition for Islamic Art, rooted in the experiential, the oral, the aural, our ritual practices and the ingredients and infrastructures of gathering and community, in a way that doesn't sit within the traditional sense of the gallery or museum. This project puts forward worlds that are resonant with our lives, and come from different bodies of knowledge that can push forth the future of museums and creative practice differently.

This is a platform to ask questions about architecture: what is a gallery and who is it for? How does it operate for different kinds of people? What is a truly public space? It was really essential for the project to take root in other places and to situate media, thinkers, work and programme from different realms into the same platform. This is a key part of the way I work, which is about trying to bring in the vibrancy and expression from other things to imbue architecture with some life and some magic.

The region has the opportunity to shape the future of cultural typologies differently. I sincerely hope that my project demonstrates that. I hope the region will not look to imitate the grand cities and projects of the West, but work from the inside out to develop entirely different worlds because we are deeply in need of them.

Figure 7.
Anywhere can be a place of worship, Syn Architects./ Copyright Laurian Ghinițoiu. Courtesy of Diriyah Biennale Foundation

Say Hello, Wave Goodbye: The Concrete Aspirations of the Pearl Bank Apartments in Singapore

Joshua Tan

When self-governance from British rule was achieved in 1959, Singapore was on the verge of a "severe socioeconomic crisis" with about half a million people living in "degenerated slums" and "squatter areas."[1] Anticipating this imminent housing shortage, the newly elected People's Action Party (PAP) established the Housing and Development Board (HDB) which swiftly produced 120,00 housing units from 1960 to 1970 in two Five-Year Building Programs.[2] The programs were highly successful, exceeding the expected target by more than ten thousand units.[3] However, this number included many "emergency" units built to rehouse residents who had been

[1] Castells, Goh, and Kwok. "The Shek Kip Mei Syndrome," *Studies in Society and Space*, 209.

[2] Yeh, *Public Housing in Singapore*, v.

[3] Yeh, *Public Housing in Singapore*, 9.

displaced by fires and new developments. With the mitigation of the housing crisis by the end of the 1970s, Cheang Wan Teh, the Singaporean Minister of National Development, argued that the one-room "emergency" flats had outlived their usefulness, and their "standards" were now deemed to be too low.[4] Subsequently, HDB was tasked to "restructure older housing estates" by upgrading units and relocating residents.[5] Social historian Kah Seng Loh observed how this rapid—albeit controlled—process of demolishing and rebuilding housing became a significant aspect of Singaporean modernity in *Squatters into Citizens*.[6]

While Loh focused on the (re)development of public housing, I am interested in how it extended into private housing developments. As crisis turned into success, scarcity made way for abundance—a transformation with material implications for the housing landscape of Singapore. The end of the 1960s marked two significant moments for Singaporean housing. First, the new housing town of Toa Payoh, which began construction in 1965 as part of the second Five-Year Building Program, neared completion. Built on reclaimed swampland, it was the first to be completed entirely by the HDB and, as such, was an important testimony to the political legitimacy of the ruling party.[7] Second, in 1969, the third Government Land Sales Program implemented by the Singaporean Urban Renewal Department (URD) allowed public land to be sold for private residential development for the first time. This eventually led to the construction of Pearl Bank apartments. Despite it being a sale

4 Singapore Parliamentary Debates, 998.
5 Goh, "Ideologies of 'Upgrading' in Singapore Public Housing," *Urban Studies 38*, 1589–1604.
6 Loh, *Squatters into Citizens*, 215.
7 The name Toa Payoh, a mix of the Hokkien dialect and Malay language, actually means "big swamp."

to private developers, the URD continued to maintain strict regulation over the design and finances of the project. As such, Pearl Bank apartments may be seen as one of the earliest case studies of government intervention in private housing.

By comparing Toa Payoh housing and the Pearl Bank apartments, I connect the desire for upward mobility with the demolition and redevelopment of housing. They provide a lens to understand the development of housing today in an economic context that increasingly sees housing as an investment rather than a home. While this phenomenon of real estate development is all too common in neo-liberal economies today, what differentiates the casestudy of Singapore is the strong government intervention—in both political will and resources—that dictated the relationship between housing and the economy. This relationship has long been used as an example of Chalmers Johnson's "developmental state" theory, a model of capitalism which is characterized by state-led macroeconomic regulation and planning.[8] With Pearl Bank apartments, I demonstrate that this housing strategy was not limited to public housing projects like *Toa Payoh*,[9] but also included the private. The apartments are interesting for another reason. Despite being modernist in style—an explicit homage to Le Corbusier was made—like the first HDB blocks in Toa Payoh, the architect of Pearl Bank apartments cited a return to traditional modes of living as the design's innovation. In other words, nostalgia for the past was used as the modernist development's appeal. Establishing HDB's development of

[8] Johnson, MITI and the Japanese Miracle.
[9] Lee, Productivism, "Developmentalism and the Shaping of Urban Order." and Wang, Urban Policy *and* Research 26.

Toa Payoh as a baseline for housing development, my analysis will trace how Pearl Bank apartments was used to establish the aspirational through legislation and design.

Toa Payoh: Addressing a National Crisis

For the newly independent island state of Singapore in the 1960s, the problem of scarcity was existential. The state's anxiety over resource security, finite land, and economic development was demonstrated by a national narrative of self-sufficiency and the public messaging of limited resources.[10] Economic growth through industrialization was believed to be the only way for Singapore to "survive."[11] Public housing was intricately tied to this goal. With its establishment as a statutory board,[12] HDB solved the housing shortage by constructing affordable housing for Singaporeans.[13] Though the functions of HDB has changed over the years, two primary functions can be observed.[14] The first was to develop "housing and related facilities" for sale or rent to people with low or middle income. The second was to manage and maintain the conditions of the housing estates.

Through HDB, the Singaporean state encouraged home ownership to ensure its citizens had a "stake" in the nation.[15] Public housing flats were sold on a ninety-nine year lease to citizens, incentivizing regular and formal employment by requiring consistent mortgage payments which in turn helped fulfill the state's promise of improving the citizens' standard of living.[16] Furthermore, as economic historian James

---

10 Chua, "Singapore as Model," *Studies in Urban and Social Change Worlding Cities Modeling*, 30.

11 Ong, *The Economics of Growth and Survival*, 7–14.

12 A statutory board is an autonomous government agency established by an act of Parliament, giving it greater fiscal autonomy and flexibility in its operations compared to regular government departments. See "Singapore: A Country Study," GPO for the Library of Congress, 1989.

13 Quah, "Why Singapore Works," Public Administration and Policy, 18.

14 Yeh, *Housing a Nation*, 3.

15 Chua, "Maintaining Housing Values under the Condition of Universal Home," *Housing Studies*, 766.

16 Salaff, "State and Family in Singapore," *International Journal of Urban and Regional Research*, 33.

Lee has argued, linking social security with home ownership also allowed "balanced socio-economic development" to be possible while encouraging asset-building of the citizenry.[17]

Figure 1 (left). Photograph of the Façade of Toa Payoh Flats./Courtesy of Christian Chen, Unsplash.

Figure 2 (right). Standard Unit Plans of Toa Payoh Flats./ Courtesy of Author.

[17] Lee, "Productivism, Developmentalism and the Shaping of Urban Order," *Journal of Sociology & Social Welfare*, 128.

The Toa Payoh flats completed in 1970 were the first prototypes of the HDB for the massive urban developments to come. They were white and repetitive with strong horizontal accents (fig. 1). Varying from ten to twenty storeys tall, the housing blocks could be categorized formally into linear slabs: L- and Y-shapes.[18] Their units were accessed through a single-loaded corridor then ran along the length of the building. The housing units were designed to meet the United Nation's standards of occupant density—one person per room was ideal while three or more people per room was overcrowded (fig. 2).[19] By 1970, an average of 2.41 persons per room seems to have been achieved.[20] Concrete was the material of choice, a decision justified by economic constraints.[21] This simplified style would soon associate the housing projects with brutalism.[22] Given limited resources, this housing minimum was sufficient to establish the state's goal—political legitimacy.[23] By the end of the decade, however, with the housing crisis largely contained, the priorities of the state would extend to the aspirational by way of private housing.[24] To understand its sway over the private sector, this paper turns to Pearl Bank, a private development that was nonetheless intricately tied to the state apparatus.[25]

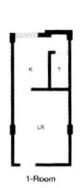

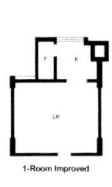

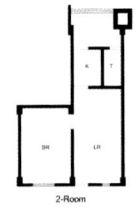

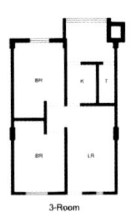

18 Singapore: Housing and Development Board, *First Decade in Public Housing*, 26–37.
19 Yeh, *Public Housing in Singapore*, 27.
20 Yeh, *Public Housing in Singapore*, 35.
21 Khim, Soh, and Alan, "Alan Choe The Housing and Development Board's first architect-planner, and founder of the Urban Redevelopment Authority," *Speaking Truth to Power: Singapore's Pioneer Public Servants*.
22 Goh, "The Pioneer Club."
23 See Chua, "Political Legitimacy and Housing" and Yeh, "Housing a Nation."
24 Wong and Yap, "From Universal Public Housing to Meeting Aspirations for Private Housing," *Four Decades of Transformation*, 96 and 108–111.

1-Room

1-Room Improved

2-Room

3-Room

Pearl Bank: Aspirations for the Future

At the time of its completion in 1976, Pearl Bank apartments was the tallest and densest residential building in Singapore at thirty-eight floors (fig. 3). Although stylistically similar, its design was considerably different from the early modernist public housing projects in Toa Payoh. Rather than simply providing the minimum, Pearl Bank apartments demonstrated the benefits of social mobility. While it was a private development, the state continued to exercise its control over the design with legislation and regulation.

It began with creation of the Urban Renewal Department (URD) within HDB in 1966.[26] The aims of the URD were to provide a "healthier environment" and "make better usage of the land" which involved "clearing slums," "comprehensive planning for traffic and circulation systems," and designing of public housing and other amenities."[27] The Land Acquisition Act which passed that year allowed the state to acquire privately-owned land for the purposes of development.[28] The Government Land Sales Program in 1967 implemented by the URD allowed the resale of this land to private developers.[29] Its third sale in 1969 was launched exclusively for residential development, making possible the construction of Pearl Bank.[30] Architectural historian Lee Kah-Wee observed that the URD would prepare models and plans of potential architectural schemes for private developers. While the general language of the design guidelines was loose and alternative schemes could

[25] For how this was deployed in public housing, see Kong and Yeoh, "Housing the People, Building a Nation," *The Politics of Landscapes in Singapore*, 94–117

[26] The URD was the successor of the Urban Renewal Unit which had been created to work with the 1962/63 United Nation Urban Planning experts. Kong, "Conserving the Past, Creating the Future," 22–25, 28.

[27] Kong and Yeoh, "Urban Conservation in Singapore," *Urban Studies*, 248.

[28] For the criticisms of this act, see "Land Acquisition Act," ed. *The Statutes of the Republic of Singapore*, 38; Yeung, "National development policy and urban transformation in Singapore."

[29] Lee, "Regulating Design in Singapore," *Environment and Planning: Government and Policy*, 148-151.

[30] Singapore, "Pearl's Hill," *National Library Board Infopedia*.

Figure 3. Photograph of the Façade of Pearl Bank Apartments./ Courtesy of Gigi Ling, Unsplash.

be proposed, the URD "reserved the right to make all decisions" and were "judged on the overall economic return and design merits offered."[31] Early schemes essentially followed what the URD proposed but later projects like Pearl Bank would deviate significantly. Nevertheless, the level of control public authorities continued to expect of private projects demonstrated that even private development had to be in line with public objectives—aesthetic, economic, or otherwise.

Pearl Bank was also one of the earliest examples of Strata Title Ownership after the Land Titles Act (1967). This new act allowed housing units to have separate titles of ownership within the apartment block. Residents would collectively own or lease the land it was built on.[32] Pearl Bank held a ninety-nine year land lease and was one of the first private housing projects that had similar tenure terms as public housing instead of the usual freehold private ownership.[33] This allowed the state to accumulate financial returns from leasing without the costs of undertaking development. Simultaneously, it would allow the private sector to satisfy the aspirations of the middle class for better housing. The Land Acquisition Act, Government Land Sales Program and Land Titles Act demonstrate that even private housing projects were politically significant for the state.[34]

Pearl Bank can be seen as part of this larger economic project to link housing with economic development. To achieve this, it invoked a return to traditional modes of living while offering an intermediate step to demonstrate economic success.

31 Lee, *Regulating Design in Singapore*, 149, 151.
32 Lee, *Where the House Begins*, 11–12.
33 Huat, Public Housing Residents as Clients of The State, *Housing Studies*, 52.
34 However, this level of state involvement in both public and private housing projects had its drawbacks. It became increasingly difficult for the state to distance itself from responsibility when there was a misalignment of consumption expectations and disposable incomes. The state was prompted to lease and sell public land as well as offer subsidies to retain local talents in Singapore when misalignments occur. See Huat, "Public Housing Residents as Clients of the State," 52–55.

Pearl Bank was designed by Tan Cheng Siong of Archurbanics (now Archurban Architects Planners). The architect adeptly relied on existing social valuations of property types, a promise of accommodating larger family units, and a design that re-interpreted the communal networks of traditional village layouts. It contained two hundred ninety-six housing units that would house one thousand five hundred residents.[35] Its cylindrical form contrasted with the linear concrete blocks of Toa Payoh. Two-bedroom, three-bedroom, and four-bedroom apartments were offered. Eight penthouse units crowned its top, all of which were offered to civil servants and statutory board employees by the Urban Redevelopment Authority (the successor of the URD) in 1979.[36]

Pearl Bank's design can be considered a middle class aspiration because of three factors. Firstly, Pearl Bank was an intermediate form between the simplex units of Toa Payoh and the upper-class terraced houses in Singapore. Due to the scarcity of land, terraced houses, shophouses and bungalows—often termed "landed property"—were of premium value.[37] In 1970, landed property was just over a quarter of the total housing stock.[38] Tan wanted to overcome the idea that "terraced, semi-detached, and bungalow houses" were "superior," by showing the luxury of living in multi-levelled apartments in the sky.[39] While the apartments were inspired by Le Corbusier's Unité d'Habitation (1952), rather than employing duplex units, Tan interlocked the apartments to create mezzanine levels that led to the more public living room and the more private bedrooms (fig. 4).[40]

---

[35] Singapore Heritage Society, "Too Young To Die," 18.
[36] New Nation, "8 Penthouses For Sale To Govt Officers," 4.
[37] For an interesting commentary on the bungalow type, see King, "The Bungalow."
[38] Yeh, Public housing in Singapore, 26.
[39] Chen, Pearlbank, 49.
[40] Chen, Pearlbank, 43. See also the Appendix, Oral Interview 2, 16.

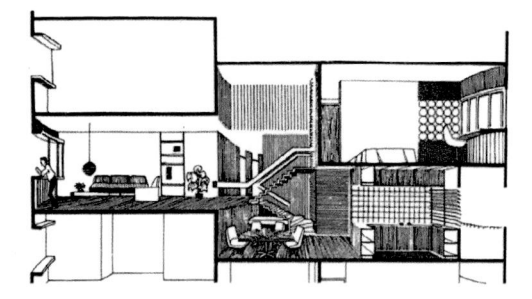

Figure 4.
Section Perspective of a Typical Unit in Pearl Bank./ Courtesy of Archurban Architects Planners.

Furthermore, instead of the dark and enclosed double-loaded corridor that would come to characterize the failure of the Unité d'Habitation, Tan maintained the logic of the single-loaded corridor to bring in light. The result would recall Alison and Peter Smithson's "streets in the sky," though it was probably more likely that it had been inspired by the first HDB designs in Singapore. As architect Wong Zihao argued, the split-level apartments created a "modified" type that could accommodate the required residential density while drawing on the prestige of landed property through the duplex design.[41]

Secondly, while the unit plans of Toa Payoh were designed for a single household, Pearl Bank afforded larger habitation sizes and a return to previous modes of domestic life. In early public housing units, the household—defined as a nuclear family unit that consisted of a heterosexual married couple and their children—was believed to be the ideal size for one apartment.[42] Most were comfortable only for a

41 Wong, "The Nation's 'Other' Housing Project," *Footprint: Delft School of Design Journal*, 78.

42 Yeh, *Public Housing in Singapore*, 27–39.

Figure 5.
Unit Plans of 5-Room Apartment in Pearl Bank./Courtesy of Archurban Architects Planners.

Say Hello, Wave Goodbye   259

43 Koh, "Singapore Stories," 117–118.
44 Singapore: Housing and Development Board, "First Decade in Public Housing," 26.
45 Loh, "Squatters into Citizens," 199.
46 Chua, "Political Legitimacy and Housing," 58.
47 Tajudeen, "Colonial-Vernacular Houses of Java, Malaya, and Singapore in the Nineteenth and Early Twentieth Centuries," ABE Journal and Chang, and Chang, "A Genealogy of Tropical Architecture," 39–46.
48 Shophouses tended to become subdivided for more rentable rooms. See the Baba House, a Peranakan Shophouse.

maximum of three adults.[43] In Toa Payoh, the ratio of sizes was: forty percent one-room, fifteen percent two-room, and forty-five percent three-room units.[44] The units would simply provide a large living room for residents to use for both the functions of dining and gathering. In fact, many residents of the early designs of the housing flats were shocked at how small the units were compared to their previous homes.[45] This represented a radical shift from previous ways of living, that included "large multi-families in the village."[46] Additionally, this removed the differentiation of functions between rooms which was commonplace in both indigenous Malay architecture and the adapted colonial bungalows in British Malaya (which includes today's Peninsular Malaysia and Singapore).[47] It was also a departure from the spatial organization of Singaporean shophouses which were terraced houses with diverse commercial and residential functions.[48]

In contrast, Pearl Bank's layout, with its mezzanine levels, allowed further differentiation of functions within the apartment (fig. 5). It used the split level to place the kitchen and dining room on the mezzanine level and the living room on the lower levels. Larger apartments would even have "conversation pits" and outdoor terraces. It thus provided an aspirational goal by providing a significantly greater amount of space while providing the functional differentiation and spatial generosity that the wealthier who resided in bungalows and shophouses had. The invitation of friends to the apartments would allow the display of material wealth, beyond the mere furnishing of the unit which was the primary way residents would display their taste and material possessions.[49]

Thirdly, Pearl Bank redefined communal experiences through the design of its circulation and inclusion of additional amenities compared to the bare minimum of Toa Payoh (fig. 6).[50] The placement of kitchens along the corridor corresponded to the indigenous Malay houses in British Malaya, where kitchens would open to the outside and encourage communal interactions.[51] For Tan, this was also reminiscent of the kitchens that connected to the back lanes in the shophouses of Singapore.[52] The single-loaded corridor was not linear, but curved. This would allow visual continuity across units and a connection to neighbors that would be impossible in the linear blocks of Toa Payoh.

In contrast to public housing, the responsibilities previously managed by the state were now

49 Salaff, "State and Family in Singapore," 127, 155, and 69.
50 Tan Cheng Siong claimed that he won the competition for Pearl Bank because of his emphasis on community. See "Pearl Bank Apartments," State of Buildings.
51 Chua, *That Imagined Space*.
52 Chen, *Pearlbank*, 56–57.

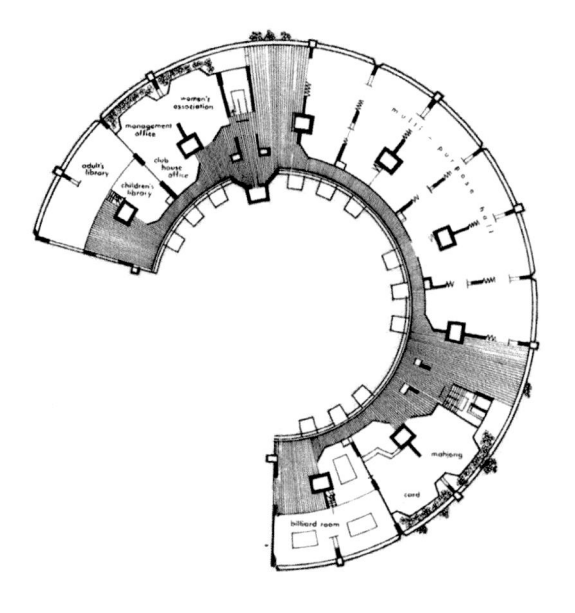

Figure 6.
Floor Plan showing Communal Deck on 27th Storey of Pearl Bank./Courtesy of Archurban Architects Planners.

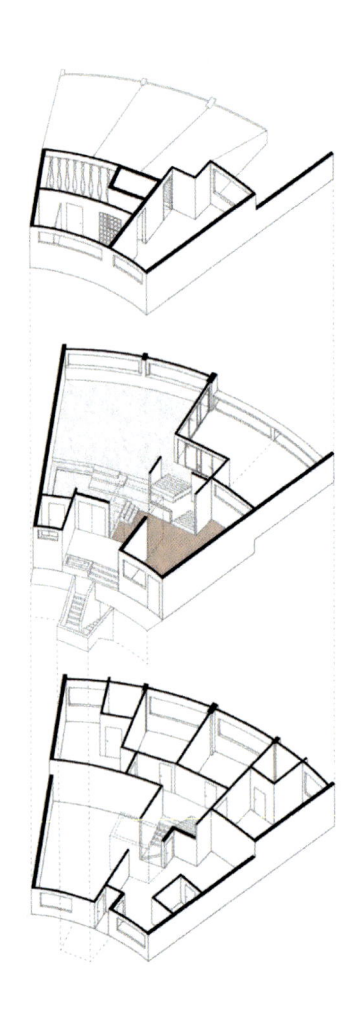

Figure 7.
Axonometric Drawing of Pearl Bank./ Courtesy of Sarah Lee Si En.

outsourced to individuals in the name of "aspirations" through the inclusion of privatized amenities and facilities for the residents.[53] This included shops on the ground floor; a creche, hall for toddlers with adjacent mother's club, gymnasium, and launderette on the eighth floor; a men's clubhouse, women's association, library, and a multi-purpose hall on the twenty-ninth floor; and a multi-story carpark with turfed open space on the roof with a kindergarten for forty children. Tan argued that these facilities would help educate the residents about how to live in a neighborhood independently without the government intervention expected in public housing.[54] The paternalistic tone that Tan took reinforces the intermediary role that he thought Pearl Bank would play. Residents from public housing who were used to state support in housing maintenance would "learn" how to collectively manage the building together in Pearl Bank—a step away from having to manage their homes independently in private landed properties. The collective-oriented design and inclusion of amenities seemingly presented a familiar way of living, but it had been reconfigured to complement the privatized logic of real estate development. Pearl Bank promised the possibility of returning to previous models of domestic life—if the family unit could afford it financially.

In conclusion, while Toa Payoh was justified by crisis to supply the minimum, Pearl Bank served as the next step for Singaporeans—the material manifestation of upward mobility. As Chua argued, high-income households' access to private housing and the

53 Chen, *Pearlbank*.
54 Chen, *Pearlbank*, See Appendix, Oral Interview 1, 8.

associated social prestige ensures the maintenance of their work ethic while providing a symbolic goal for lower income groups.[55] The intermediate form of Pearl Bank, the apartment sizes and functional differentiation, and the communal design provisions produced a steppingstone for the middle class while using the appeal of traditional modes of living. Pearl Bank may be a victim of the very intentions that made it possible.[56] Its disappearance could be attributed to the process of using housing as milestones that demonstrate material success. This has taken place despite a prolific public housing program by the state. As architectural historian Chang Jiat-Hwee has argued, the capitalist logic of development that requires the upgrade and renewal of real estate to allow for more capital accumulation means that buildings will continue to be demolished and redeveloped.[57] In Singapore's case, this may not come as a shock. Afterall, in 1973, the responsibilities of the URD were taken over by the Urban Redevelopment Authority.[58] This renaming of the department rings true to the focus that capitalist development and the Singaporean state have decided to pursue. If national survival is predicated on economic growth which is in turn dependent on real estate values, then the demolition and redevelopment of housing projects like Pearl Bank for greater capital gains and private investment is the most patriotic option forward. In continuing to provide the aspirational for residents towards the goal of perpetuating upward mobility, private housing in Singapore will be constructed, demolished, and redeveloped in the hopes of reinforcing a Tantalean desire for more. In 2019,

55 Chua, "Not Depoliticized but Ideologically Successful," 35.
56 Wong, "The Nation's 'Other' Housing Project," 85.
57 Chang, "Before and behind the Pioneers of Modern Architecture in Singapore," 62.
58 The Straits Times, "Now a New Ruling on Land Build-Up," 5.

Pearl Bank was collectively sold to the developer, Capitaland, and demolished for redevelopment (fig. 7).[59] Unsurprisingly, the majority shareholder of Capitaland is Temasek Holdings, the Singaporean state's sovereign wealth fund.[60] Today, the state remains closely associated with private housing development in Singapore.

59 Luo, "Pearl Bank Apartments in Outram Sold En Bloc to CapitaLand for S$728m.," *The Straits Times*.
60 Chang and Zhuang, "Everyday Modernism," *Architecture and Society in Singapore*, 74.

Figure 8.
Photograph of the Redevelopment of Pearl Bank Apartments as One Pearl Bank./ Courtesy of Jing Ren Tan.

References

Office Landscape

Canty, Donald. "Evaluation of an Open Office Landscape: Weyerhaeuser Co." *AIA Journal* 66, no. 8 (July 1977): 40–45.

Dunaway, Finis. *Natural Visions: The Power of Images in American Environmental Reform*. Chicago: University of Chicago Press, 2005.

Healey, Judith Koll. *Frederick Weyerhaeuser and the American West*. St. Paul, MN: Minnesota Historical Society Press, 2013.

Kaufmann-Buhler, Jennifer. "Progressive Partitions: The Promises and Problems of the American Open Plan Office." *Design and Culture* 8, no. 2 (May 3, 2016): 205–33. https://doi.org/10.1080/17547075.2016.1189308

McCabe, Nate. "Defining 'Habitat' Post-Weyerhaeuser: Critical Habitat Regulations Under The Endangered Species Act Must Promote Species Recovery." *American University Law Review* 71, no. 6 (2022): 2465–2501.

Montgomery, Roger. "A Building That Makes Its Own Landscape." *Architectural Forum* 136, no. 2 (March 1972): 20–27.

Mozingo, Louise A. *Pastoral Capitalism: A History of Suburban Corporate Landscapes*. Cambridge, Mass: The MIT Press, 2016.

Pelkonen, Eeva-Liisa, Kevin Roche, Kathleen John-Alder, Olga Pantelidou, and David Sadighian. *Kevin Roche: Architecture as Environment*. New Haven [Conn.]: Yale University Press : In association with Yale School of Architecture, 2011.

Schuh, Donald. "Managing Esthetic Values: Weyerhaeuser Company's Approach." *Journal of Forestry* 93, no. 2 (February 1, 1995): 20–25. https://doi.org/10.1093/jof/93.2.20

SOM. "What Ever Happened to the 'Original Green Building'?" *Medium* (blog), March 21, 2019. https://som.medium.com/what-ever-happened-to-the-original-green-building-191ceb2a4fec

Sullivan, Marin R. *Alloys: American Sculpture and Architecture at Midcentury*. Princeton: Princeton University Press, 2022.

The Cultural Landscape Foundation. "Peter Walker Says Weyerhaeuser Is Perhaps His 'Most Important' Project in His Six Decade Career," May 13, 2023. https://www.tclf.org/peter-walker-says-weyerhaeuser-perhaps-his-most-important-project-his-six-decade-career

Washington Senate Democrats. "Public-Private Partnership Charts the Path Forward to Preserve and Repurpose a South Puget Sound Icon, the Former Weyerhaeuser Headquarters Building," May 13, 2022.

Weyerhaeuser Company. "Weyerhaeuser Annual Report 1968." Corporate Annual Report. Seattle, WA: Weyerhaeuser Company, n.d. University of Washington Foster Business Library.

———. "Weyerhaeuser Annual Report 1971." Corporate Annual Report. Seattle, WA: Weyerhaeuser Company, n.d. University of Washington Foster Business Library.

———. "Timber Is a Crop." Accessed May 12, 2023. https://www.weyerhaeuser.com/company/history/#20

Weyerhaeuser Timber Co., dir. *Trees and Men*. Dowling and Brownell Production,1938, 16mm. https://www.filmpreservation.org/sponsored-films/screening-room/trees-and-men-1938

American Dream 2

Cameron, James, director. *Avatar: The Way of Water*. 20th Century Studios, 2022. 3 hr., 12 min.

Moore, Charles W. "Plug It in, Rameses, and See If It Lights up. Because We Aren't Going to Keep It Unless It Works." *Perspecta* 11 (1967): 33-43.

A Discontinuous Border

Agier, Michael. *Borderlands: Towards an Anthropology of the Cosmopolitan Condition*. Cambridge, Malden, MA: Polity Press, 2016.

Appadurai, Arjun. *Modernity at Large*. Minneapolis, Minn.: University of Minnesota Press, 1996.

Baruah, Sanjib. "Nationalizing Space: Cosmetic Federalism and the Politics of Development in Northeast India." *Development and Change* 34 (2003): 915-939.

———. *In The Name Of The Nation: India and Its Northeast*. Stanford, CA: Stanford University Press, 2020.

Bouissou, Julien. "Lafarge's India-Bangladesh Cement Project Remains Frozen," *The Guardian*, August 20, 2010. https://www.theguardian.com/world/2010/aug/13/india-bangladesh

Brown, Wendy. *Walled States, Waning Sovereignty*. Cambridge: MIT Press, 2017.

Easterling, Keller. *Extrastatecraft: The Power of Infrastructure Space* (London: Verso, 2014).

Global Cement. "EU and European ambassadors urge Bangladesh to lift restrictions on LafargeHolcim Bangladesh limestone sales." February 10, 2023, https://www.globalcement.com/news/item/15307-eu-and-european-ambassadors-urge-bangladesh-to-lift-restrictions-on-lafargeholcim-bangladesh-limestone-sales

Lafarge Holcim. "Equity Valuation Report on Lafarge Holcim Bangladesh Limited." March 29, 2018. https://www.cfainstitute.org/-/media/regional/arx/post-pdf/2018/03/29/equity-valuation-report-on-lafargeholcim-Bangladesh-limited.ashx

Ghosh, Sahana. *A Thousand Tiny Cuts: Mobility and Security across the Bangladesh-India Borderlands*. Oakland, California: University of California Press, 2023.

Hussain, Delwar. *Boundaries Undermined: The Ruins of Progress on the Bangladesh-India Border*. London: Hurst, 2013.

Kikon, Dolly. "The predicament of justice: fifty years of Armed Forces Special Powers Act in India." *Contemporary South Asia* 17, no.3 (2009) 271-282.

Krishna, Sankaran. "Cartographic Anxiety: Mapping the Body Politic in India." *Alternatives: Global, Local, Political* 19, no.4 (1994), 507-521.

Larkin, Brian. "The Poetics and Politics of Infrastructure." *Annual Review of Anthropology* 42 (2013) 327-343.

Lyngdoh, Rining. "HC Ban Hits Limestone Export," *The Telegraph*, August 8, 2015, https://www.telegraphindia.com/north-east/hc-ban-hits-limestone-export/cid/1392962

Nag, Sajal. "A Gigantic Panopticon: Counter Insurgency Operation and Modes of Discipline and Punishment in Northeast India." *Kolkata: Development, Logistics and Governance: Fourth Critical Studies Conference* (2011) 2-18.

Rajashree, Dasgupta. "With SC Set to Hear Petition, Killings at Bangladesh Border Back in Focus." *The Wire*, March 2020. https://thewire.in/rights/felani-khatun-killing-bangladesh-border-supreme-court

Derige, Mark, and Hustrulid, Andrew I. "Replacing the World's Longest Trans-Boundary Conveyor Belt." *Engineer Live*, May 10, 2021. https://www.engineerlive.com/content/replacing-world-s-longest-trans-border-conveyor-belt#:~:text=The%20conveyor%20was%20originally%20constructed,replace%20the%2034km%20of%20belting

Saikia, Arunabh. "As limestone piles up on Bangladesh border, anger against Congress brews in Meghalaya," *Scroll*, February 17, 2018, https://scroll.in/article/867669/as-limestone-piles-up-on-bangladesh-border-anger-against-congress-brews-in-meghalaya

The Times of India. "SC Okays Limestone Supply to Lafarge." November 24, 2007, https://timesofindia.indiatimes.com/india/sc-okays-limestone-supply-to-lafarge/articleshow/2566251.cms

Scott, James. *Seeing Like a State*. New Haven and London: Yale University Press, 1998.

Sheller, Mimi. *Mobility Justice: The Politics of Movement in the Age of Extremes*. London and New York: Verso, 2018.

Sur, Malini. *Jungle Passports: Fences, Mobility, and Citizenship at the Northeast India-Bangladesh Border*. Philadelphia: University of Pennsylvania Press, 2021.

"The Many Economic Guarantees and Promises of the Modi Government," *The Wire* (New Delhi), July 27, 2023. https://thewire.in/economy/the-many-economic-guarantees-and-promises-of-the-modi-government

Human Rights Watch. "Trigger Happy: Excessive Use of Force by Indian Troops at the Bangladesh Border." December 9, 2020, https://www.hrw.org/report/2010/12/09/trigger-happy/excessive-use-force-indian-troops-bangladesh-border

Tsing, Anna. *Friction: An Ethnography of Global Connection*. Princeton, NJ: Princeton University Press, 2005.

Weizman, Eyal. *Hollow Land: Israel's Architecture of Occupation*. London: Verso, 2007.

Four Acts

Amin, Kadji. *Disturbing Attachments: Genet, Modern Pederasty, and Queer History*. Theory Q. Durham: Duke University Press, 2017.

Haraway, Donna. "Situated Knowledges: The Science Question in Feminism and the Privilege of Partial Perspective." *Feminist Studies* 14, no. 3 (1988): 575-99. https://doi.org/10.2307/3178066

Terrafictions

Demoris, Rene. "Body and Soul: About the Practice of Painting in France (1660 -1770)." In *Painting beyond Itself: The Medium in the Post-Medium Condition.* Edited by Isabelle Graw and Ewa Lajer-Burcharth, 221-222. Berlin: Sternberg Press, 2016.Hohmann, Heidi and Joern Langhorst. "Landscape Architecture: A Terminal Case?" Landscape Architecture 95, no. 4 (2005): 26-45.

Krauss, Rosalind. "Photography's Discursive Spaces: Landscape/View." *Art Journal* 42, no. 4 (1982): 311-19.

Olwig, Kenneth R. "Recovering the Substantive Nature of Landscape." *Annals of the Association of American Geographers* 86, no. 4 (1996): 630-53.

Thinking through Painting: Reflexivity and Agency Beyond the Canvas. Edited by Isabelle Graw, Daniel Birnbaum, and Nikolaus Hirsch. Berlin: Sternberg Press, 2012.

Scanning Theory

Cirtwill, Paige. "After Industry: Akron, the Rubber Capital of the World." *Midstory*, October 20, 2021. https://www.midstory.org/after-industry-akron-the-rubber-capital-of-the-world/

Davis, Tim. "Photography and Landscape Studies." *Landscape Journal* 8, no. 1 (1989): 1-12. http://www.jstor.org/stable/43323996

Díaz-Vilariño, L., H. Tran, E. Frías, J. Balado, and K. Khoshelham. "3D Mapping of Indoor and Outdoor Environments Using Apple Smart Devices." T*he International Archives of the Photogrammetry, Remote Sensing and Spatial Information Sciences* XLIII-B4-2022 (June 1, 2022): 303-8. https://doi.org/10.5194/isprs-archives-xliii-b4-2022-303-2022

Eco, Umberto. *The Open Work*. Cambridge: Harvard University Press, 1989.

Encyclopedia of Arkansas. "Park-O-Meter." *Encyclopedia of Arkansas*, June 16, 2023. https://encyclopediaofarkansas.net/entries/park-o-meter-3116/

Failes, Ian. "'Mission: Impossible II' - a Virtual Production Game-Changer." befores & afters, May 27, 2020. https://beforesandafters.com/2020/05/27/mission-impossible-ii-a-virtual-production-game-changer/

Granshaw, Stuart I. "Editorial: Imaging Technology 1430-2015: Old Masters to Mass Photogrammetry." *The Photogrammetric Record* 30, no. 151 (September 2015): 255-60. https://doi.org/10.1111/phor.12112

Groth, Paul. "1. Frameworks for Cultural Landscape Study" In *Understanding Ordinary Landscapes*, 1-22. New Haven: Yale University Press, 2009. https://doi.org/10.12987/9780300185614-002

Marín-Buzón, Carmen, Antonio Pérez-Romero, José Luis López-Castro, Imed Ben Jerbania, and Francisco Manzano-Agugliaro. 2021. "Photogrammetry as a New Scientific Tool in Archaeology: Worldwide Research Trends" *Sustainability* 13, no. 9: 5319. https://doi.org/10.3390/su13095319

Moab. "Auto Touring - Arches National Park (U.S. National Park Service)." National Park Service, July 23, 2021. https://www.nps.gov/arch/planyourvisit/driving.html

Ohio Federal Writers' Project. *Quaker Oats Company Plant*. November 27, 1927. Still Image. *Mills and Millwork*. https://ohiomemory.org/digital/collection/p267401coll34/id/7857

Percy, Walker. "Loss of the Creature." *Forum* 2 (Fall 1958): 7.

Price, D. A. and Zhu Wang, "Explaining an Industry Cluster: The Case of US Car Makers From 1895-1969," *Economic Brief*, no. 12-10 (2012).

The Astronauts. "The Secrets of Witchfire Graphics: The Photogrammetry." The Astronauts, November 29, 2023. https://www.theastronauts.com/2023/11/secrets-of-witchfire-graphics-photogrammetry/

Ullman, Shimon. "The interpretation of structure from motion." *Proceedings of the Royal Society of London. Series B. Biological Sciences* 203 (1979): 405 - 426.

Urry, John, and Jonas Larsen. *The Tourist Gaze 3.0*. Thousand Oaks, Ca: Sage, 2011.

US Department of the Interior . "Park Reports." NPS Stats: National Park Service Visitor Use Statistics, 2017. https://irma.nps.gov/Stats/Reports/Park/ARCH

The Poiesis of Miesian Corners

Cohen, Jean-Louis, and Ludwig Mies van der Rohe. *Mies Van Der Rohe*. 2nd and updated ed. Basel: Birkhäuser, 2007.

Geist, Johann Friedrich, and Klaus Kürvers. *Das Berliner Mietshaus*. München: Prestel-Verlag, 1980.

Goldberger, Paul, Phyllis Lambert, and Sylvia Lavin. *Modern Views: Inspired by the Mies Van Der Rohe Farnsworth House and the Philip Johnson Glass House*. New York, NY, USA: Assouline Pub., 2010.

Krohn, Carsten. *Mies Van Der Rohe: The Built Work*. Basel: Birkhäuser, 2014.

Lambert, Phyllis, and Barry Bergdoll. *Building Seagram*. New Haven, Connecticut; London, England: Yale University Press, 2013.

Longerich, Peter. *Deutschland 1918-1933: Die Weimarer Republik; Handbuch Zur Geschichte*. Hannover: Fackelträger, 1995.

Mies van der Rohe, Ludwig. "An Address of Appreciation." In *Mies van der Rohe*. Edited by Jean-Louis Cohen. Paris: Hazan, 2007.

———. *Conversations with Mies Van Der Rohe*. Edited by Moisés Puente. 1st edition, English edition. New York: Princeton Architectural Press, 2008.

Mies van der Rohe, Ludwig, Phyllis Lambert, and Werner Oechslin. *Mies In America*. Montréal: Canadian Centre for Architecture, 2001.

Moyano, Steven. "Quality vs. History: Schinkel's Altes Museum and Prussian Arts Policy." *The Art Bulletin* 72, no. 4 (1990): 585–608.

Müller, Jörg. *Die Friedrich-Ebert-Siedlung in Berlin-Wedding: zur Bau- und Planungsgeschichte eines Wohngebiets der zwanziger Jahre*. Germany: Technische Universität, Institut für Stadt- und Regionalplanung, 1995.

Neumeyer, Fritz. *The Artless Word: Mies Van Der Rohe On the Building Art*. Cambridge, Mass.: MIT Press, 1991.

Ott, Randall. *German Facade Design: Traditions of Screening From 1500 to Modernism*. London: Routledge, 2016.

Rakatansky, Mark. "Tectonic Acts of Desire and Doubt, 1945–1980: What Kahn Wants to Be." *ANY: Architecture New York*, no. 14 (1996): 36-43. http://www.jstor.org/stable/41852140

Reiser, Jesse, and Nanako Umemoto. Atlas of Novel Tectonics. New York: Princeton Architectural Press, 2006.
Riley, Terence, Ludwig Mies van der Rohe, Barry Bergdoll, and Vittorio Magnago Lampugnani. *Mies In Berlin*. New York, NY: Museum of Modern Art, 2001.
Schor, Naomi. *Reading in detail: aesthetics and the feminine*. New York: Routledge, 2007.
Tegethoff, Wolf, Ludwig Mies van der Rohe, and William Dyckes. *Mies Van Der Rohe: The Villas and Country Houses*. New York: Museum of Modern Art, 1985.
Tigerman, Stanley. "Mies van Der Rohe: A Moral Modernist Model." *Perspecta* 22 (1986): 112-35. https://doi.org/10.2307/1567099
Wagner, Anselm. "Silent Spaces: Absent Signifiers in Modernist Architecture," in *Meaningful Absence across Arts and Media: The Significance of Missing Signifiers*, edited by Werner Wolf, Nassim Winnie Balestrini, and Walter Bernhart, 217-44. Leiden: Brill Rodopi, 2019.

Forget LEED

Bennett, Jane. *Vibrant Matter: A Political Ecology of Things*. Durham: Duke University Press, 2010.
Corkery, Michael. "As Dollar Stores Proliferate, Some Communities Say No." *New York Times*, March 1, 2023. https://www.nytimes.com/2023/03/01/business/dollar-stores-rejected.html
Dollar General. "Fast Facts." *Dollar General News Center*, October 12, 2023. https://newscenter.dollargeneral.com/company-facts/fast-facts/
———. "In Our Storied History." *Dollar General 75th Anniversary*, 2014, https://dollargeneral75.com/
"Dollar General Corporation v. Mississippi Band of Choctaw Indians." *Oyez*. Accessed September 10, 2023. https://www.oyez.org/cases/2015/13-1496
Gissen, David. *Subnature: Architecture's Other Environment*. New Jersey: Princeton Architectural Press, 2009.
Kauffman, Jordan. "To LEED or Not to Lead," *Log* 8 (2006): 13-20. http://www.jstor.org/stable/41765580
Meyersohn, Nathaniel. "Nearly 1 in 3 new stores opening in the US is a Dollar General." *CNN Business*, May 6, 2021. https://edition.cnn.com/2021/05/06/business/dollar-store-openings-retail
Morton, Timothy. *Hyperobjects: Philosophy and Ecology after the End of the World*. Minneapolis: University of Minnesota Press, 2013.
Reuter, Dominick. "Meet the typical Dollar General customer: An older rural worker with a high school education and an income of less than $40,000." *Business Insider*, August 16, 2021. https://www.businessinsider.com/typical-dollar-general-shopper-demographic-older-worker-earning-lower-income-2021-8.
U.S. Department of Commerce. "2022 U.S. Trade with China." *Bureau of Industry and Security*, 2022. https://www.bis.doc.gov/index.php/country-papers/3268-2022-statistical-analysis-of-u-s-trade-with-china/file
Whelan, Daniel, Director. *Bulkland*. Journeyman Pictures, 2017. 58 minutes.

Media on Media

Album et inventaire. Vol. 2 of *Les Immatériaux*. Paris: Centre Georges Pompidou, 1985.

Baudrillard, Jean. "The Beaubourg-Effect: Implosion and Deterrence," trans. Rosalind Krauss and Annette Michelson. *October* 20 (Spring 1982).

Crary, Jonathan. *Suspensions of Perception: Attention, Spectacle, and Modern Culture*. Cambridge: MIT Press, 1999.

Delis, Philippe. *Floor plan of Les Immatériaux*. 1985. Image.

Epreuves d'écriture. Vol. 1 of *Les Immatériaux*. Paris: Centre Georges Pompidou, 1985.

Goldfarb, Brian. "Introduction: An Ethos of Visual Pedagogy." In *Visual Pedagogy: Media Cultures in and beyond the Classroom*, 1-22. Durham: Duke University Press, 2002.

Heinich, Nathalie. "Les Immatériaux Revisited: Innovation in Innovations: Landmark Exhibitions Issue." *Tate Papers*, no. 12 (Fall 2020). Accessed January 28, 2024. https://www.tate.org.uk/research/tate-papers/12/les-immateriaux-revisited-innovation-in-innovations

Huk, Yui. "30 years after Les Immatériaux." *Yuk Hui*. Accessed January 3, 2024. https://digitalmilieu.net/symposium-30-years-after-les-immateriaux

Krauss, Rosalind. "The Cultural Logic of the Late Capitalist Museum." *October* 54 (Fall 1990): 3-17.

Kraynak, Janet. "Dependent Participation: Bruce Nauman's Environments." *Grey Room*, no. 10 (Winter 2003): 22-45. Accessed December 20, 2020. https://www.jstor.org/stable/1262635

"Les Immatériaux (1985): Overview of a postmodern manifestation in the Centre Pompidou." *Centre Pompidou*. Accessed January 3, 2024. https://www.centrepompidou.fr/en/collection/film-and-new-media/les-immateriaux-1985

"Les Immatériaux: A Conversation with Jean-François Lyotard. with Bernard Blistène." In *Flash Art*, no. 121 (March 1985).

Lyotard, Jean-François. "Les Immatériaux." In *Materiality*, edited by Petra Lange-Berndt, 201-06. Massachusetts: The MIT Press, 2015.

Lyotard, Jean-François. "Les Immatériaux." In *Thinking about Exhibitions*, edited by Reesa Greenberg, Bruce W. Ferguson, and Sandy Nairne, 114-126. London: Routledge, 1996.

Lyotard, Jean-François. *The Postmodern Condition: A Report on Knowledge*, translated by Geoff Bennington and Brian Massumi. Minneapolis: University of Minnesota Press, 1984.

Mondloch, Kate. "Body and Screen: The Architecture of Screen Spectatorship." In *Screens: Viewing Media Installation Art*, 20-39. University of Minnesota Press, 2010. Accessed December 20, 2020. https://www.jstor.org/stable/10.5749/j.ctttsj4b.6

———. "Installing Time, Spatialized Time, and Exploratory Duration." In *Screens: Viewing Media Installation Art*, 40-59. University of Minnesota Press, 2010. Accessed December 20, 2020. https://www.jstor.org/stable/10.5749/j.ctttsj4b.7

Obrist, Hans Ulrich. "Les Immatériaux." In *Ways of Curating*, 157-62. New York: Farrar, Straus and Giroux, 2014.

Planchet, Jean-Claude. *Installation view of partitions*. 1985. Photograph. Centre Pompidou, Paris.

———. *Plan of Les Immatériaux*. 1985. Photograph. Centre Pompidou, Paris.

———. 1985. Photograph. Centre Pompidou, Paris.
———. 1985. Photograph. Centre Pompidou, Paris.
Rajchman, John. "Les Immatériaux or How to Construct the History of Exhibitions: Landmark Exhibitions Issue." *Tate Papers*, no. 12 (Fall 2009). Accessed December 20, 2020. https://www.tate.org.uk/research/publications/tate-papers/12/les-immateriaux-or-how-to-construct-the-history-of-exhibitions
Restany, Pierre, "Immatériaux." *Domus* 662 (June 1985), 60-63.
Schneider, Cynthia, and Brian Wallis. "Introduction." In *Global Television*, 7-11. Cambridge: MIT Press, 1988.
"The Virtual Exhibition of Les Immatériaux." *Beyond Matter*. Accessed January 3, 2024. https://lesimmateriaux.beyondmatter.eu.
Touraine, Alain, trans. Leonard F.X. Mayhew. *The Post-Industrial Society: Tomorrow's Social History: Classes, Conflicts, and Culture in the Programmed Society*. New York: Random House, 1971.

Chinese *Xiaoqu*

"1987当事人当时事：土地第一拍' 推动宪法修改 [The 1987 Participants Recalling Events: 'First Land Auction' Driving Constitutional Amendments]." *深圳特区报*, December 1, 2010. https://www.chinanews.com.cn/estate/2010/12-01/2691763.shtml
Central Committee of the Communist Party of China. "关于进一步加强城市规划建设管理工作的若干意见 [Several Opinions on Further Strengthening Urban Planning and Construction Management Work]." 3.16, 2016.
Chen, Yi. "1951年上海市工作任务 [Order on 1951 Shanghai Development Guideline]." 1951.
"First Issue, 2004. Sector: Big Event." *Urban and Rural Planning*. Fudan University, 2004, 151. https://urplanning.fudan.edu.cn/_upload/article/files/26/fb/6bd43c184980ba31b3b4381c810f/89f39b6f-7064-43ae-8d88-d4f2f6fcdd5b.pdf
Hu, Yuwei. "Shanghai City Dwellers Develop New Bonds as They Barter Goods amid Lockdown." *Global Times*, 2022. https://www.globaltimes.cn/page/202204/1260328.shtml
Li, Wuying. "新中国大型居住社区的 "处女作"——上海曹杨新村的诞生及其规划设计轶事 [The First Large-scale Residential Community in New China - Birth and Planning Design Anecdotes of Shanghai Caoyang Xincun]." *建筑时报* [*Construction Times*], September 5, 2019. http://dzb.jzsbs.com/epaper/jzsb/pc/content/201909/05/content_4432.html
Liu, Bin, and Togniev. "城市住宅区的规划和建筑." *建筑学报* [*Architectural Journal*], 1958.
Lu, Duanfang. *Remaking Chinese Urban Form: Modernity, Scarcity and Space, 1949-2005*. London: Routledge, 2006.
Luo, Gang. "Space Producing and Space Change: New Residential Areas of Workers in Shanghai and the Experience of a Socialist City." *Journal of East China Normal University* 39, no. 6 (2007): 91-96.
Marx, Karl. "The Nationalisation of the Land." *The International Herald*, no. 11, June 15, 1872.
Shanghai Real Estate Exchange Center. "The fifth batch of concentrated listing for new properties in Shanghai in 2023." 2023. http://www.fangdi.com.cn/new_house/new_house.html

Wang, Dingzeng. "上海曹杨新村住宅区的规划设计 [Design and Planning of Shanghai Caoyang Xincun Neighborhood]." 1956.

Zeng, Zhihao. "當油麻地變成小區 [When YauMaTei Becomes a *XiaoQu*]." *Mingpao News*. January 22, 2021. https://news.mingpao.com/ins/文摘/article/20210122/s00022/1611240094243/當油麻地變成小區（文-曾志豪）

"中华人民共和国广东省经济特区条例 [People Republic of China Regulations of the Guangdong Province Economic Special Zone]." *YueChang* 11, sec. 1.1, 1980. http://www.gd.gov.cn/zwgk/gongbao/1982/1/content/post_3353883.html

"中华人民共和国城市居民委员会组织法 [Order on The Organization Law of Urban Residents' Committees of the People's Republic of China]." section 3.5, 1989. https://www.gjxfj.gov.cn/gjxfj/xxgk/fgwj/flfg/webinfo/2016/03/1460585590003713.htm

"深圳东湖丽苑: 我们的幸福家园 [Donghu Liyuan, Our Community of Happiness]." 2018.

"国务院关于深化城镇住房制度改革的决定 [State Council Decision on Deepening the Reform of Urban Housing System]." *GuoFa* 43, section. 1.2, 1994. https://www.gov.cn/zhuanti/2015-06/13/content_2878960.htm

"物业管理条例 [The City Residential New Development Community Management Regulations of People's Republic of China]." sections. 2.15, 2.20, 1990.

"走进 '村史馆', 去看新中国第一个工人新村的七十多年历史 [Entering the 'Village History Museum' to see the more than seventy years of history of New China's first workers' village]." *澎湃新闻*, September 26, 2023. https://m.thepaper.cn/kuaibao_detail.jsp?contid=24753957&from=kuaibao

Say Hello, Wave Goodbye

"8 Penthouses for Sale to Govt Officers." *New Nation* (Singapore), October 27 1979.

A Genealogy of Tropical Architecture: Colonial Networks, Nature and Technoscience. London ; New York: Routledge, 2016. https://doi.org/99987839137

Castells, Manuel, L. Goh, and R. Yin-Wang Kwok. *The Shek Kip Mei Syndrome : Economic Development and Public Housing in Hong Kong and Singapore*. Studies in Society and Space. London: Pion, 1990.

Chang, Jiat-Hwee. "Before and Behind the Pioneers of Modern Architecture in Singapore." *Docomomo Journal*, no. 57 (2017): 56-63. https://doi.org/10.52200/57.a.0448wlr4

Chang, Jiat-Hwee, and Justin Zhuang. *Everyday Modernism*. Singapore: National University of Singapore, 2022.

Chen, Gerry Yingquan. "Pearlbank: Reinventing the Domestic Realm in 1970s." M.Arch Diss., National University of Singapore, 2012.

Chua, Beng Huat. "Maintaining Housing Values under the Condition of Universal Home Ownership." *Housing Studies* 18, no. 5 (2003): 765-80. https://doi.org/10.1080/02673030304260

Chua, Beng-Huat. "Not Depoliticized but Ideologically Successful: The Public Housing Programme in Singapore." *International Journal of Urban and Regional Research* 15, no. 1 (1991): 24-41. https://doi.org/10.1111/j.1468-2427.1991.tb00681.x.

First Decade in Public Housing, 1960-69. Singapore: Housing and Development Board, 1970.

Goh, Chin Lian. "The Pioneer Club." *The Straits Times,* April 12 2014.

Goh, Robbie B. H. "Ideologies of 'Upgrading' in Singapore Public Housing: Post-Modern Style, Globalisation and Class Construction in the Built Environment." *Urban Studies* 38, no. 9 (2001): 1589-604. http://www.jstor.org/stable/43196729

Huat, Chua Beng. "Public Housing Residents as Clients of the State." *Housing Studies* 15, no. 1 (2000): 45-60. https://doi.org/10.1080/02673030082469

Johnson, Chalmers. *Miti and the Japanese Miracle : The Growth of Industrial Policy, 1925-1975*. Stanford, Calif.: Stanford University Press, 1982.

King, Anthony D. *The Bungalow: The Production of a Global Culture*. London: Routledge & Kegan Paul, 1984.

Koh, Ernest. *Singapore Stories*. New York: Cambria Press, 2010.

Kong, Lily. *Conserving the Past, Creating the Future: Urban Heritage in Singapore*. Singapore: Urban Redevelopment Authority, 2011.

Kong, Lily, and Brenda S. A. Yeoh. "Housing the People, Building a Nation." In *The Politics of Landscapes in Singapore*. New York: Syracuse University Press, 2003.

"Land Acquisition Act." edited by The Statutes of the Republic of Singapore. Singapore, 1966.

Lee, James. "Asset Building and Property Owning Democracy: Singapore Housing Policy as a Model of Social Investment and Social Justice Social Investments, Asset Building, and Social Development: The State of the Art: A Special Issue in Honor of James Midgley." [In eng]. *Journal of Sociology & Social Welfare* 45, no. 4 (2018): 105-128.

"Productivism, Developmentalism and the Shaping of Urban Order: Integrating Public Housing and Social Security in Singapore." *Urban Policy and Research* 26, no. 3 (2008/09/01 2008): 271-82. https://doi.org/10.1080/08111140802301732

Lee, Kah-Wee. "Regulating Design in Singapore: A Survey of the Government Land Sales (Gls) Programme." *Environment and Planning: Government and Policy* 28, no. 1 (2010/02/01 2010): 145-64. https://doi.org/10.1068/c08132

Lee, Sarah Si En. "Where the House Begins: Tracing the Interiorscape in a Subdivided Pearl Bank Apartment." M.Arch Diss., National University of Singapore, 2016.

Loh, Kah Seng. *Squatters into Citizens: The 1961 Bukit Ho Swee Fire and the Making of Modern Singapore*. Copenhagen, Denmark: NUS Press, 2013.

Luo, Stephanie. "Pearl Bank Apartments in Outram Sold En Bloc to Capitaland for S$728m." *The Straits Times*, February 13 2018. https://www.straitstimes.com/business/companies-markets/capitaland-acquires-pearl-bank-apartments-for-s728m-q4-profit-falls-38

"Now a New Ruling on Land Build-Up." *The Straits Times* (Singapore), December 3 1973. http://eresources.nlb.gov.sg/newspapers/Digitised/Article/straitstimes19731203-1.2.45.aspx

Ong, Wee Hock. *The Economics of Growth and Survival*. Singapore: National Trades Union Congress, 1978.

"Pearl Bank Apartments." *State of Buildings*, accessed March 4, 2023.

"Pearl's Hill." *National Library Board Infopedia*, 2018, https://eresources.nlb.gov.sg/infopedia/articles/SIP_116_2004-12-14.html

Political Legitimacy and Housing: Stakeholding in Singapore. London ; New York: Routledge, 1997.

Public Housing in Singapore : A Multidisciplinary Study. Singapore: Published by Singapore University Press for Housing and Development Board, 1975.

Quah, Jon S. T. "Why Singapore Works: Five Secrets of Singapore's Success." *Public Administration and Policy* 21, no. 1 (2018): 5-21. https://doi.org/10.1108/pap-06-2018-002

Salaff, Janet W. *State and Family in Singapore: Restructuring a Developing Society. Anthropology of Contemporary Issues*. Ithaca [u.a.]: Cornell Univ. Press, 1988.

"Singapore: A Country Study." *GPO for the Library of Congress*, 1989, accessed December 21, 2023, https://countrystudies.us/singapore/47.htm

"Singapore as Model: Planning Innovations, Knowledge Experts." In *Studies in Urban and Social Change Worlding Cities Modeling*, edited by Ananya; Ong Aihwa Roy, 27-54: Wiley-Blackwell, 2011.

Singapore Parliamentary Debates. March 20, 1981.

Society, Singapore Heritage. "Too Young to Die ". *Singapore Heritage Society*, 2018.

Soh, Eng Khim and Choe, Alan. "Alan Choe the Housing and Development Board's First Architect-Planner, and Founder of the Urban Redevelopment Authority." In *Speaking Truth to Power: Singapore's Pioneer Public Servants*, edited by Hoe Yeong Loke. Singapore: World Scientific Publishing Company, 2019.

Tajudeen, Imran bin. "Colonial-Vernacular Houses of Java, Malaya, and Singapore in the Nineteenth and Early Twentieth Centuries." *ABE Journal* 11 (2017).

"That Imagined Space: Nostalgia for the Kampung in Singapore." Singapore: National University of Singapore, Department of Sociology, 1994.

"Urban Conservation in Singapore: A Survey of State Policies and Popular Attitudes." *Urban Studies* 31, no. 2 (1994): 247-65. http://www.jstor.org/stable/43196091

Wang, Jun. "The Developmental State in the Global Hegemony of Neoliberalism: A New Strategy for Public Housing in Singapore." *Cities* 29, no. 6 (2012): 369-78. https://doi.org/10.1016/j.cities.2011.11.004

Wong, Tai-Chee, and Lian-Ho Adriel Yap. "From Universal Public Housing to Meeting Aspirations for Private Housing." In *Four Decades of Transformation : Land Use in Singapore, 1960-2000*. Singapore: Eastern Universities Press Singapore, 2004.

Wong, Zihao. "The Nation's 'Other' Housing Project: Pearlbank, Pandan Valley, and Singapore's Private High-Rise Housing Landscape." *Footprint: Delft School of Design Journal* 13, no. 24 (2019): 73-90. https://doi.org/10.7480/footprint.13.1.2136

Yeh, Stephen H. K. *Housing a Nation*. Singapore: Maruzen Asia for Housing & Development Board, 1985.

Yeung, Yue-man. *National Development Policy and Urban Transformation in Singapore: A Study of Public Housing and the Marketing System*. Research Paper. Chicago, Ill: University of Chicago, Department of Geography, 1973.

8'-2 ¾"

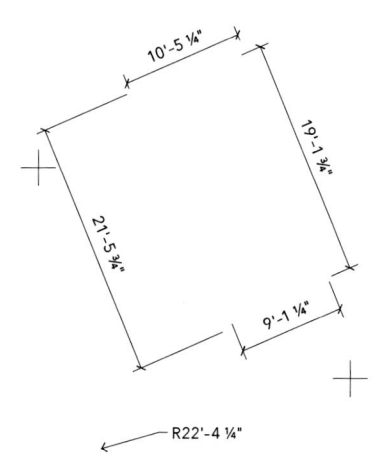

10'-5 ¼"

19'-1 ¾"

21'-5 ¾"

9'-1 ¼"

R22'-4 ¼"

Image Credits

Office Landscape

Figure 1. Stoller, Ezra. *Weyerhaeuser Corporate Headquarters Exterior*. 1971. Photograph.
Figure 2. Stoller, Ezra. *Weyerhaeuser Corporate Headquarters Interior*. 1971. Photograph.
Figure 3. Stoller, Ezra. *Rainforest by Helena Hernmarck*. 1971. Photograph.
Figure 4. Stoller, Ezra. *Weyerhaeuser Corporate Headquarters Exterior*. 1971. Photograph.

American Dream 2

All images from Adobe Stock. Ketchup: Lumos sp; Fingerprints: Vidady; Chocolate ice cream: Mara Zemgaliete; Coffee: Jukhu; Grease: Prikhodko; Lipstick: New Africa.

A Discontinuous Border

Figure 4. Google Maps. "The cross-border conveyer belt, cutting across the India-Bangladesh border. Shella/Bholaganj (India)-Chattak (Bangladesh) Border post." Accessed February 10, 2024.
All other images by author.

Contortions

All images by author.

Four Acts

Figure 1 and 2. Photo by Guillermo S. Arsuaga
Figure 3. Photo by Maxime Cavajani, December 10, 2021, Philadelphia, PA, U.S.A.

The Route to Beit Al-Eileh

All images by author.

Terrafictions

All images by author.

Scanning Theory

All images by author.

Taboo and Metaphor

All images by author.

The Poiesis of Miesian Corners

Figure 1. *Landhaus aus Backstein*, Foto 2: *Reproabzug, Entwurf Grundriss*, 1923. Akademie der Künste, Berlin, Mies-van-der-Rohe-Sammlung, Nr. 8.
Figure 2. *Landhaus aus Backstein*, Foto 1b: *Reproabzug, Exterior Perspektive Brick Country House*, 1923, Hall No. 1. Akademie der Künste, Berlin, Mies-van-der-Rohe-Sammlung, Nr. 8
Figure 4. Schinkel, Karl Friedrich. *Altes Museum Berlin: Blick auf das Treppenhaus,* 1852. Staatliche Museen zu Berlin, Kupferstichkabinett, https://commons.wikimedia.org/wiki/File:Altes_Museum_Treppe_Schinkel.jpg
Figure 5 & 6. Häuser Afrikanische Str., Berlin-Wedding, Außenansicht, 1968. Source: Akademie der Künste, Berlin, Reinhard-Friedrich-Archiv, Nr. Friedrich-Reinhard 473
Figure 15. Dearstyne, Howard. *Ludwig Mies van der Rohe and Lilly Reich on board an excursion boat on the Wannsee, near Berlin.* 1933. Photograph. The Museum of Modern Art, New York,
All other images by author.

Forget LEED

Figure 4. Platz, Abigail. *Dollar General Exhibition at University of Milwaukee-Wisconsin's Mobile Design Box Gallery.* 2022. Photograph.
All other images by authors.

Media on Media

Figures 1, 2, 5, and 6. Images by Jean-Claude Planchet, 1985. Courtesy of Centre Pompidou, Paris
Figure 3. Drawing by Philippe Delis
Figure 4, and 7. Image by the author.

Ten Reasons to Abstract Reflective Ceiling Plans

These ten RCPs were produced as a series of drawings during an Art Omi residency in Ghent, New York. All images by the author.

Chinese *Xiaoqu*

Figure 1. Bird's-eye View of Caoyang Xincun. Photo by Fayhoo, © 2016 Fayhoo. Used under a Creative Commons Attribution-Share Alike 3.0 Unported license. Original image available https://commons.wikimedia.org/wiki/File:Cao_Yang_Yi_Cun.JPG.
Figure 2. Site Plan of Caoyang Xincun by Wang Dingzeng, in 上海曹杨新村住宅区的规划设计 [Design and Planning of Shanghai Caoyang Xincun neighborhood] by Wang Dingzeng, 1956, 3.
Figure 3. Plan of a Soviet residential Microrayan, from Residential Construction in the Byelorussian SSR (1980).
Figure 4. Ration Tickets used in China. Photo by Red Guosam Zhu-Guang01, © 2018 Red Guosam ZhuGuang01. Used under a Creative Commons Attribution-Share Alike 4.0 International license. Original image available https://commons.wikimedia.org/wiki/File:SZ_深圳市_Shenzhen_福田區_Futian_當代藝術館_MOCAPE_Great_trend_in_Pear_River_大潮起珠江_Guangdong_Economic_open_reform_history_廣東改革開放40周年展覽_40th_years_Exhibition_in_November_2018_SSG_128.jpg.
Figure 5. Celebrated and praised, workers moving into Caoyang Xincun and walking through the gate of the community, 1952. Photo from 人民画报 [People's Pictorial], Issue 8, 1952.
Figure 6. Sign: Long Live Chairman Mao, in CaoyangXincun. Photo by Yang Cheng, in 澎湃新闻 [The Paper], 2009
Figure 7. Workers' children exercise in the primary school in Caoyang Xincun. Photo from 人民画报 [People's Pictorial], Issue 8, 1952.
Figure 8. Luo Jinxing, the manager of Shenzhen Real Estate Company (the one holding the number 11 sign), acquired the land use rights of a residential land auctioned by the city government. Photo by Chen Zhishan, Xinhua News Agency, 1987.
Figure 9. Bird's-eye View of Donghu Liyuan. Map image captured from Lianjia Maps on 2024/1/24. Available at: https://mr.ke.com/3dm-vp/#/590397?source=RESBLOCK.
Figure 10. Establishment of the Property Management Company of Donghu Liyuan. Photo by Sohu News, published on 2021/07/14, Available at:https://www.sohu.com/a/477344224_121100471

Figure 11. High Alert: two active members of the residents' committee on duty watching a strange man. Photo by Wu Qiang, from 吴强摄影集 [Wu Qiang's Photography Collection] by Wu Qiao, 1982
Figure 12. Photo by Author.
Figure 13. XiaoQu's Fencing Reinforced by Steel Plates during Shanghai Lockdown. Photo by Author
Figure 14. Shanghai Urumqi Middle Road protest rally. November 27, 2022. Photo by Philip Roin, 2022.

Reimagining Cultural Narratives

Say Hello, Wave Goodbye: The Concrete Aspirations of the Pearl Bank Apartments in Singapore
Figure 1. Photograph of the Façade of Toa Payoh Flats. Courtesy of Christian Chen, Unsplash.
Figure 2 Standard Unit Plans of Toa Payoh Flats. Courtesy of Author.
Figure 3 Photograph of the Façade of Pearl Bank Apartments. Courtesy of Gigi Ling, Unsplash.
Figure 4 Section Perspective of a Typical Unit in Pearl Bank. Courtesy of Archurban Architects Planners.
Figure 5 Unit Plans of 5-Room Apartment in Pearl Bank. Courtesy of Archurban Architects Planners.
Figure 6 Floor Plan showing Communal Deck on 27th Storey of Pearl Bank. Courtesy of Archurban Architects Planners.
Figure 7: Axonometric Drawing of Pearl Bank. Courtesy of Sarah Lee Si En.
Figure 8 Photograph of the Redevelopment of Pearl Bank Apartments as One Pearl Bank. Courtesy of Jing Ren Tan

Say Hello, Wave Goodbye

Figure 1 Photograph of the Façade of Toa Payoh Flats. Courtesy of Christian Chen, Unsplash.
Figure 2 Standard Unit Plans of Toa Payoh Flats. Courtesy of Author.
Figure 3 Photograph of the Façade of Pearl Bank Apartments. Courtesy of Gigi Ling, Unsplash.
Figure 4 Section Perspective of a Typical Unit in Pearl Bank. Courtesy of Archurban Architects Planners.
Figure 5 Unit Plans of 5-Room Apartment in Pearl Bank. Courtesy of Archurban Architects Planners.
Figure 6 Floor Plan showing Communal Deck on 27th Storey of Pearl Bank. Courtesy of Archurban Architects Planners.
Figure7: Axonometric Drawing of Pearl Bank. Courtesy of Sarah Lee Si En.
Figure 8 Photograph of the Redevelopment of Pearl Bank Apartments as One Pearl Bank. Courtesy of Jing Ren Tan

282

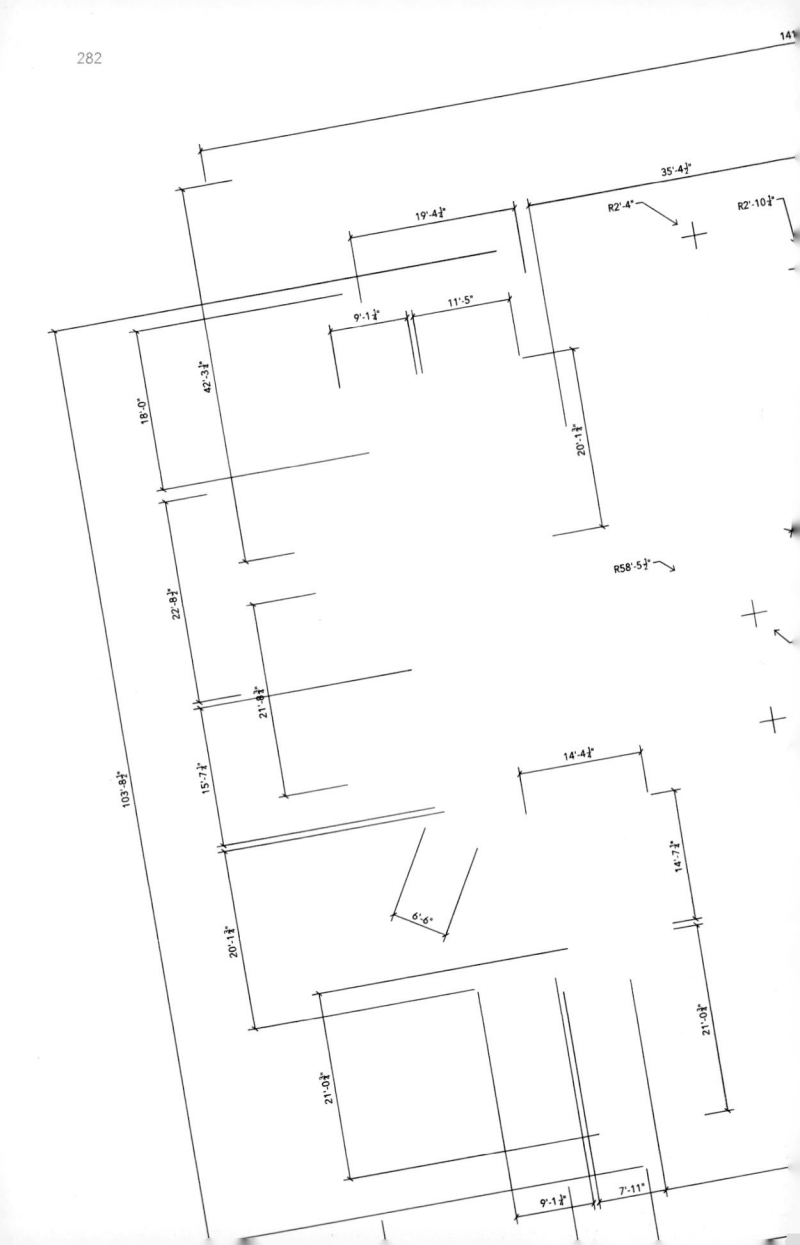

35'-4½"
R2'-4"
R2'-10¾"
19'-4½"
9'-1¾"
11'-5"
42'-3⅜"
18'-0"
20'-1⅞"
22'-8½"
R58'-5½"
21'-8¾"
15'-7¾"
14'-4¼"
14'-7⅞"
20'-1¾"
6'-6"
21'-0⅞"
103'-8½"
21'-0⅞"
9'-1⅛"
7'-11"

283

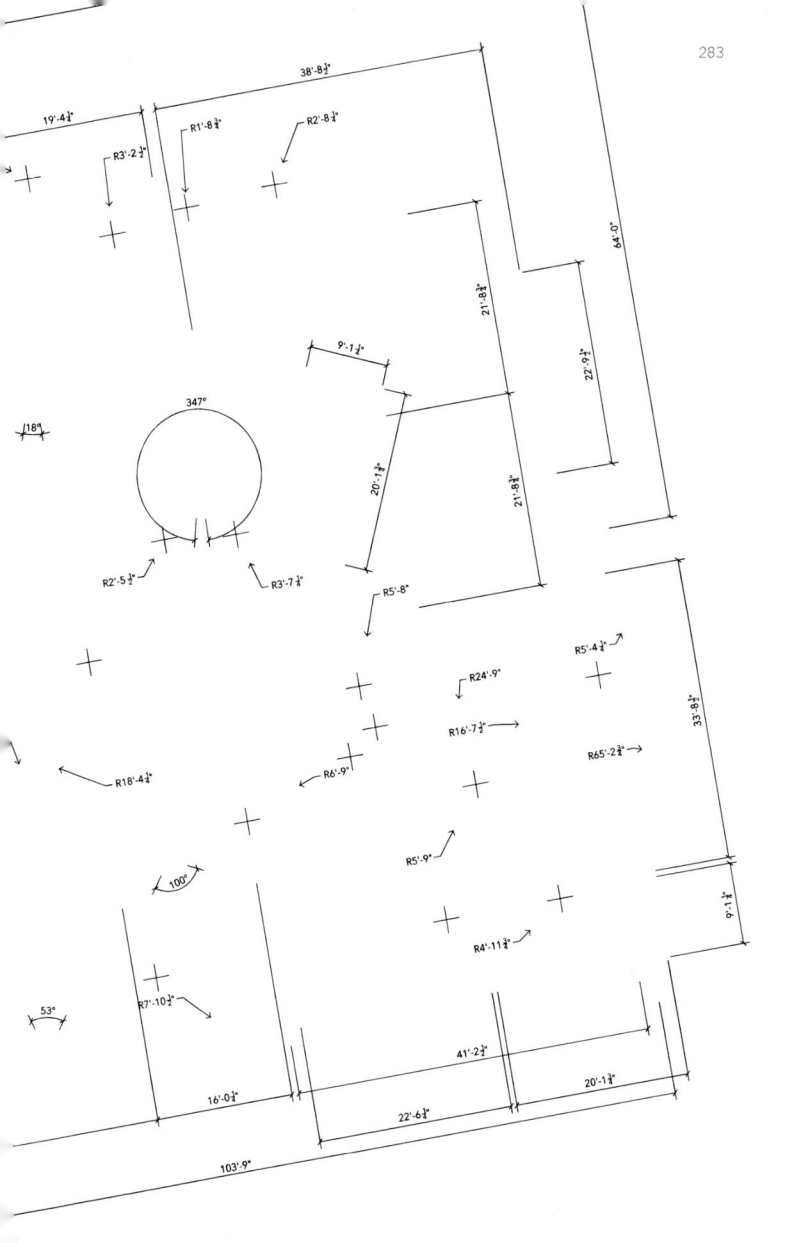

19'-4¾" 38'-8½"

R3'-2½" R1'-8¾" R2'-8¾"

64'-0"

21'-8¾"

9'-1½"

22'-9¾"

18" 347°

20'-1¾"

21'-8¾"

R2'-5½" R3'-7¼"

R5'-8"

R24'-9"

R5'-4¾"

R18'-4¾" R6'-9" R16'-7½" R65'-2¾"

33'-8½"

R5'-9"

100°

9'-1¾"

R4'-11¾"

53° R7'-10½"

16'-0¾" 41'-2½" 20'-1¾"

22'-6¼"

103'-9"

Contributors

Maysam Abdeljaber is a Palestinian-American MArch candidate at Princeton University. She holds a BS in Architectural Studies from the University of Wisconsin-Milwaukee. She is interested in utilizing alternative architectural practices that empower displaced communities, particularly refugees and immigrants, through place-making and community-centered design.

Sarah Aziz is an Assistant Professor of Architecture at the University of New Mexico and a PhD student at The Bartlett School of Architecture, UCL. Her background as a second-generation British Pakistani informs her research practice that maps patterns of migration across multiple scales and geographies, starting with her grandfather's walk from Delhi to Lahore during the Partition of British India. Currently, she is working with collaborators from across the Great Plains to tag, track, and build with tumbleweeds because they defy human-made borders and ask new questions of indigeneity and invasiveness. Her drawing work has been featured in *AD Magazine*, *PLAT Journal*, *Architect Magazine*, *Soiled*, and *CLOG*. Most recently, she was awarded a 2023 Architectural League Prize with Lindsey Krug, and in 2021, the pair received an ACSA Course Development Prize in Architecture, Climate Change, and Society to study the 19,300+ extra-ordinary Dollar General stores in America.

William Dolin is a designer from Los Angeles currently pursuing a MArch at Princeton University. He is interested in the historical entanglement of property and architecture. He has worked in the offices of SO-IL, Mork-Ulnes Architects, NEMESTUDIO, and Belzberg Architects, before which he received a B.A. in architecture from UC Berkeley.

S.E. Eisterer is an Assistant Professor at Princeton University. Her research focuses on spatial histories of dissidence, feminist, queer, and trans* theory, as well as the labor of social and ecological movements. Currently, she is working on two forthcoming book projects: the interdisciplinary history and translation project *Memories of the Resistance: Margarete Schütte-Lihotzky and the Architecture of Collective Dissidence, 1918-1989* and the edited volume *Living Room: Architecture, Gender, Theory*, which illuminates methods and theories in writing about feminist and LGBTQIA+ spaces in architecture.

Ariane Fong is a designer and researcher of exhibitions, architecture, and visual culture. She has received a MS in Critical, Curatorial, and Conceptual Practices from Columbia University, and a BA in Architecture from Princeton University.

Andy Kim is a designer based in NYC. Andy makes buildings and artifacts about and around the relationships, encounters and impressions of architecture, cities, and urban ecology. His work has been exhibited at A83 Gallery and AIA Javits Expo, New York. Andy received a post-professional MArch from Princeton University Graduate School of Architecture and BArch from Pratt Institute. Andy worked in the offices of MOS, Hume Coover Studio, Op-al and Grimshaw Architects.

Tekena Koko engages film, performance, and sculpture to probe the blurry edges of architecture. Parallel to running the architecture practice, Tekena Koko Office, he established Hotel, a transient art and design gallery in Los Angeles in 2021.

Lindsey Krug is based between Chicago and Milwaukee where she is an Assistant Professor of Architecture at the University of Wisconsin-Milwaukee. Through the lens of the architectural user as a body in space, Krug studies how design solidifies and reinforces taboos, hierarchies, and inequities into built form. Krug's research interests are organized around relationships between people and contemporary institutions born of American democracy and capitalism and their corresponding architectural manifestations and myths. Krug's on-going research looking at the relationship between legal and architectural definitions of privacy was awarded the 2023 Best Peer-Reviewed Research Project by the ACSA and the College of Distinguished Professors. With Sarah Aziz, Krug received a 2022 Course Development Prize in Architecture, Climate Change, and Society from the ACSA and the Columbia University Buell Center; and the 2023 Architectural League Prize from the Architectural League of New York.

Ryan Tyler Martinez (he/him) is a Los Angeles-based educator, curator, and painter. He is an Adjunct Assistant Professor at USC School of Architecture and is a Partner at Lauriault Martinez, Inc. Recently, he was awarded the 2022 Art Omi Residency and received a MacDowell fellowship in 2024.

Dhruv Mehta is an architect, furniture designer, and academic from India. He is currently a critic at the Rhode Island School of Design and an adjunct faculty at WIT SoAD. Over the last few years, Mehta's design work has explored themes of formalism, satire, non-linearity, and politics. Mehta graduated with an MArch II from Harvard GSD, where he researched contemporary construction and design globally and in South Asia. His practice in India works on residential projects and furniture design, which deal with ideas of labor and interiority within a complex context.

Jonathan Russell is an architect, writer and editor from Melbourne, Australia. A graduate from the Melbourne School of Design, he previously studied Urban Geography at Monash University and the University of California, Berkeley. Jonathan is a founding editor of *Inflection Journal* and leads the digital and research teams at the Robin Boyd Foundation. Jonathan writes on topics including infrastructure, urban theory and speculative architectural fiction.

Guillermo Sanchez-Arsuaga, an architect and PhD candidate at Princeton University School of Architecture, explores the junctions of architecture, power, and territorial management, particularly within the intricate geopolitical landscapes of the 1960s and 70s. In the 2022-2023 academic year, he was honored with the Mellon-Marron Research Consortium Fellowship, held at the Architecture and Design Department at the Museum of Modern Art in New York.

Steven Sculco is a designer based in New York. He received an MArch from Yale University in 2022.

Shivani Shedde is an architect and doctoral student in the History and Theory of Architecture at Princeton University. Her work addresses how multidisciplinary Third World actors instrumentalized architecture as a political imaginary to respond to the demands of decolonization; where architecture was reconfigured as a tool for emancipation attuned to methods of international solidarity rather than simple nation building. Her other research interests include the spatial imperatives of colonial mapping, visualization, and governance techniques; and the politics of extraction and its relationship with architectural materials.

Joshua Tan is a PhD student at the MIT School of Architecture and Planning (History, Theory, and Criticism). He was awarded the Edward P. Bass Fellowship (2022), read Architecture at Cambridge University (MPhil '23) and graduated from the Yale School of Architecture (MArch '22). His interests stand at the intersection of politics, housing, labor, and architectural representation. His research has been published in *I, Like Many Things*, *Dune Journal*, *Singapore Policy Journal*, *POOL Magazine*, *Yale Retrospecta*, and *Paprika!* with upcoming essays in *Agro-Ecological Urban Constellations in Pre-Columbian America* and *Dom Architectural Guides*. He has presented at conferences organized by the Alvar Aalto Foundation in Jyväskylä and the National Museum of Denmark in Copenhagen. His design competition entries have won awards in Buildner, The Big Thing, and Nonarchitecture. He was also the lead curator of the exhibitions Bamboo Pavilion and In-Sync, DeSync, Re-Sync that focused on vernacular construction and digital technologies.

Samarth Vachhrajani is currently a candidate in the Masters of Environmental Design (MED) program, at the Yale School of Architecture. His ongoing research deals with the spatial languages of mobility, sovereignty and citizenship in Northeast India. He thinks, reads and writes between the productive intersection of architecture with anthropology and geography. He has been trained as an architectural designer, and his work reflects on how violence is an essential problematic in architecture and spatial studies.

Pavan Vadgama is currently pursuing a post-professional MArch degree at Princeton University. He holds an MA from the Universität der Künste in Berlin, Germany, and a BA from the University of California, Berkeley. With professional work experience in Berlin, San Francisco, London, and Ahmedabad, he has engaged in a diverse range of projects of various scales. His primary focus has been on participatory design, collaborating with artists' collectives and agency groups that center on issues related to queerness, accessibility, and the environment.

Zee Ruizi Zeng (曾瑞紫) is a post-professional MArch candidate at Princeton University. She is interested in the emotional dimensions of spatial experiences, the nuanced perception of representation, and the significance of materiality within the realm of architecture.

ISBN 978-1-7341815-6-2
© Copyright 2024 Pidgin, all rights reserved.

All material is compiled from sources believed to be reliable but published without responsibility for errors or omissions. We apologize for any omissions and, if noted, will amend in future editions.

Contact
pidgin@princeton.edu

Pidgin Magazine
Princeton University School of Architecture
S-110 Architecture Building
Princeton, NJ 08544-5264

Editors
Jocelyn Beausire
Ibiayi Briggs
Hermine Demaël
Win Overholser
Kyara Robinson
Quoc Trung Nigel Van Ha
Chenchen Yan

Typography
Arnhem and Avenir Next

Printing
Printed in Exton, PA, by Brilliant Studio

Pidgin is a publication edited and designed by graduate students at the Princeton University School of Architecture. The views and opinions expressed herein are those of the authors and do not necessarily reflect the attitudes and opinions of the editors or of the school. Many thanks to the faculty and staff of the School of Architecture for all of their efforts and encouragement. *Pidgin* is made possible by the generous support of the Princeton University School of Architecture, as well as Elise Jaffe & Jeffrey Brown.